RAF SPECIAL DUTIES

RAJA L

RAF SPECIAL DUTIES

Unique Sorties of the Second World War

COLIN PATEMAN

FONTHILL

Hamilcar gliders lined up ready for deployment. On the extreme left, the glider's cockpit canopy rests in the open position while the tow rope connection onto the Hamilcar wing on the right is being examined. The thickness of the wing can be seen in this photograph as can the enormous size of the landing wheels.

On page 2: A No. 214 Squadron Wellington with its newly applied insignia for the Federated Malay States being admired by the pilot and a young member of the crew.

On page 8: Halifax aircraft towing Horsa gliders. Twelve combinations are crossing the French coast, with several of the glider pilots choosing to adopt the lower towing position. The tug pilot was needed to be aware of the glider's position at all times; if it drifted too low the Halifax was likely to be tipped upwards, and too high, it would be tipped nose down. Any extreme deviations induced excessive strain on the tow rope resulting in the rope fracturing or snapping.

Fonthill Media Limited
Fonthill Media LLC
www.fonthillmedia.com
office@fonthillmedia.com

First published in the United Kingdom and the United States of America 2015

British Library Cataloguing in Publication Data:
A catalogue record for this book is available from the British Library

ISBN 978-1-78155-304-6

Typeset in 10pt on 13pt Sabon
Printed and bound in England

CONTENTS

Acknowledgements

The research for this book has taken place over many years. Several of the contributors have sadly passed away and I respectfully acknowledge the original detail they recorded in their flying log books.

I wish to thank all concerned for the many letters and other forms of correspondence that have contributed to my research. In particular, Donald Whittle, Robert Orme, Bill Morris, Bob Body, Mrs Durell, Mike Gardiner, Derek Carter, Major Cross at the Museum of Army Flying, Ron Berry, Ken Speed, John Reid, Simon Muggleton and John Linnett.

Finally, I would like to thank my wife Sarah-Jane for her support, and acknowledge the loyalty of my retired police dog who has sat by my side during the writing of all my works. I fear that I will be denied that loyalty very soon, and sentiment has induced this final acknowledgement.

Photographs and images

The majority of photographs come from the personal collections of the individuals concerned, while others come from the author's collection. Wherever possible, I have sought to credit material with due diligence and integrity. Every care has been taken to trace copyright holders, however, I apologise if I have omitted anyone and will, if advised, make corrections to any future editions.

Preface

This book unearths the stories and operational records of RAF pilots and air crew who have, up until now, escaped publicity. These were ordinary men from an array of civilian backgrounds—a merchant seaman, a mechanic, an air-raid warden, a film cameraman, a Territorial Army officer, and young and spirited students—all of whom voluntarily took to the skies in various theatres of war to fight for their country. Taken from original wartime flying log books, each account details a form of Special Duties operational flying. The RAF adopted a technical definition for the term Special Duties, but in this book the term has been interpreted to apply to operations that, for reasons explained in each chapter, were in some way extraordinary.

Colin Pateman
November 2014

Introduction

Following Germany's withdrawal from the League of Nations and the International Disarmament Conference on 14 October 1933, Winston Churchill gave an outspoken warning to Parliament highlighting the threat posed by the growth of German military aviation. This was a perceptive and well-informed observation by the man who would later lead Great Britain in war against the belligerent German nation led by Adolf Hitler.

Throngs of volunteers, and later conscripts, elected to serve in the RAF and the Commonwealth air forces. Aware of its responsibility, the RAF was keen to accept them. The thousands of young recruits and the rapid development of aircraft and technology combined to create a formidable force capable of waging war in the modern era, and one which would continue to develop and evolve during the Second World War. The RAF and its Commonwealth counterparts jointly underwent a rapid expansion. The men of the regular pre-war air force were joined by those from the Royal Auxiliary Air Force (RAuxAF), which was formed in 1925 as an extension to the well-patronised military Territorial Associations from across the country. The RAuxAF was the vision of Lord Trenchard, who had been instrumental in establishing the RAF. Volunteers into the Auxiliary service were locally recruited in a similar fashion to the Territorial Army regiments. It proved to be a natural progression for the service, and many officers serving in the RAuxAF became vital to the development of the RAF.

The Royal Air Force Volunteer Reserve (RAFVR) was formed in 1936. Initially the RAFVR was composed of civilians recruited from the Reserve Flying Schools, with many recruits coming from universities. Appointed civilian contractors who also engaged instructors from the Reserve of Air Force Officers (RAFO) operated the Reserve Flying Schools. These were men who had previously completed a four-year short service commission as pilots in the RAF. Volunteers into the RAFVR, men between eighteen and twenty-five years old, undertook part-time training as pilots, observers, and wireless operators. The strategic vision was to create a reserve of trained air crew for use in the event of war. The Air Ministry made the RAFVR the principal means for air crew volunteers to enter the service. Following the declaration of war, eager volunteers signed up immediately in the hope of being accepted for air crew training, and after taking an oath of allegiance to the King, they were formally inducted. In wartime, the RAFVR was vital to the survival of the RAF.

There were three primary branches—commands—of the RAF, all of which were formed on 14 July 1936:

Fighter Command, HQ RAF Bentley Priory, Middlesex
Bomber Command, HQ RAF High Wycombe, Buckinghamshire
Coastal Command, HQ RAF Northwood, Middlesex

These commands were formed on both a geographical and functional basis. Each individual command had a senior ranking officer in charge of operational matters, and another officer responsible for the administrative and organisational matters. Both worked under the authority of the Air Officer Commanding that particular branch or command. Further operational control was delegated downwards to group level. Groups usually controlled a number of aerodromes or establishments, also known as stations, and would frequently have other subordinate units based there or in close proximity. These combined locations would have been responsible to an Officer Commanding.

During the Second World War the expansion of Bomber Command was such that there were insufficient senior officers with the relevant experience to command all the new stations. A system was therefore adopted that grouped three or four stations together under one commander. This system led to use of the term 'satellite stations', and the squadrons may well have been further subdivided into flights, although occasionally flights were formed to act independently, in exactly the same way that a squadron could be formed at any time. It became common at that time to designate flights as 'A', 'B', and 'C', with each commanded by an Officer in Charge. Often an entire flight, normally 'C', was dissolved to create a newly formed squadron. Many squadrons existed for only short periods, while others lasted longer, becoming deeply embedded in RAF history.

From this infrastructure, certain squadrons, groups, and flights were selected to perform 'Special Duties'. Some of those 'Special Duties' evolved only as a result of technological developments or to meet the specific needs of other services. I have chosen to expand the definition of Special Duties to include operational duties that took place alongside the primary responsibilities of pilots and air crews. These ancillary duties provided support to many military objectives and were often vital to the success of those operations, but in general they have not been well publicised. Many squadrons had operational duties imposed on them without the official 'SD' appearing after their units' identification number. In fact, the term SD was rarely officially used by the RAF.

An example of 'Special Duty' flying is illustrated on the cover: Flt Lt Lewendon is preparing to fly a captured Luftwaffe aircraft to study its operational performance for No. 1426 Enemy Aircraft Flight. Uniquely, he wore the German Flying Badge beneath his RAF wings. He flew to various airfields to display the enemy aircraft for recognition purposes, always in the company of an RAF escort to avoid being shot down. Officially recognised in service as the 'Enemy Aircraft Circus', No. 1426 Enemy Aircraft Flight was nicknamed 'The Rafwaffe' and surprisingly was never given any 'SD' reference. On 13 October 1944, Flt Lt Lewendon lost his life flying a captured Focke-Wulf FW190 fighter; he unsuccessfully tried to return the valuable aircraft to his airfield following an engine fire.

Squadrons across all of the commands were of various sizes and had individual functions. However, what may not be fully appreciated is that they were frequently subjected to moves between different theatres of war. In normal circumstances, squadrons retained their unique identification numbering. Commonwealth air crews from Canada, New Zealand, and Australia always sought to serve in the 400 to 499 allocation of squadron numbers, where they were likely to meet a high percentage of their fellow countrymen, while the Allied Polish, Dutch, French, Norwegian, Czechoslovakian, and Belgian contingents desired to operate within the 300 to 399 squadron allocation for the same reason. However, many of these nationalities were naturally absorbed into the plethora of squadrons that existed, and losses from across the commands demanded a constant stream of replacement crews and individuals to maintain efficiency.

Additional commands were formed to meet the developing requirements of the RAF to support the aerial war against Germany. These included working in close co-operation with the Army, which arose from the need to ensure that the anti-aircraft defences of Great Britain were calibrated and capable of being utilised properly. The ferrying of aircraft across the UK and abroad and the transportation of equipment over huge distances led to the establishment of the following commands:

Army Co-Operation Command, formed on 1 December 1940
Ferry Command, formed on 20 July 1941
Transport Command, formed on 25 March 1943
The 2nd Tactical Air Force, formed on 1 June 1943

The Tactical Air Force (TAF) was formed to support the Allied invasion of France and subsequent air operations in Western Europe. It was called the 2nd TAF because the previous Desert Air Force had been officially identified as the 1st TAF. The formation of a second TAF drew upon existing squadrons from the Fighter, Bomber, and Army Co-Operation Commands. The TAF was principally designed to provide close Army support duties with reconnaissance, fighter, and fighter-bomber units, operating from independent airfields or forward landing grounds situated close to the fighting fronts.

The gathering of military intelligence often created a need for Special Duties flying. Single-seater fighters on tactical reconnaissance sorties were frequently briefed to attack targets of opportunity; they account for many harassing attacks on enemy staff cars and other transportation targets. The tiny Taylorcraft Auster light aircraft, equipped with its small 130-hp engine, was used in Air Observation Post squadrons to perform artillery observations, scouting, and even casualty evacuation from small and difficult landing strips. The Auster was flown by army pilots (trained by the RAF) as were gliders in airborne assaults, which were towed into battle by Special Duties squadrons. Other examples of Special Duties flying include Mosquito aircraft flying sorties to destroy SS and Gestapo headquarters, Hudson aircraft on missions to drop agents into occupied Europe, and large four-engine aircraft, with a crew of eight, deployed on radio counter-measures, protecting the entire strength of Bomber Command over Germany. Additional units such as the Meteorological Squadrons flew daily to record temperature, humidity, and air pressure—essential intelligence that became a key component in mission planning.

This book explores the complete service details of several aviators—many officially recognised for distinguished flying during the Second World War—from their own flying log books, written and compiled by them during training, on operational service, and on Special Duties. Their individual accounts give a broad and fascinating perspective of Special Duties operations from across the RAF and Commonwealth air forces. It is to these men, some of whom paid the ultimate sacrifice, that this book is dedicated.

1

Jack Whittle DFC SOE Special Duties

On 27 April 1939, the Military Training Act introduced conscription for men aged twenty and twenty-one, beginning with six months of military training. On the outbreak of war, Parliament passed the National Service (Armed Forces) Act, which made all men between the ages of eighteen and forty-one eligible for conscription into the armed forces. The registration of men aged twenty to twenty-three began on 21 October, with single men being called up before married men. By the end of 1939, over 1½ million men had been recruited into the armed forces. The vast majority joined the Army, and the remainder were equally divided between the Royal Navy and the Royal Air Force. Registration progressed slowly towards the older age categories, not reaching those aged forty until June 1941.

Military service began with registration at the local branch of the Ministry of Labour and National Service. Two or three weeks later, the conscript would receive a notice to attend a medical examination to ensure that he was fit for military service. He would then attend an interview designed to match him to the service most suitable for his skills and experience. Within six weeks, an enlistment notice would be sent to the conscript telling him to report for training. Upon arrival, the new recruit was issued with his uniform and kit and given the regulation military haircut. Basic training lasted between eight and twelve weeks.

Jack Whittle of Redford House, Victoria Street, Loughborough, attended the Leicester medical examination facility on 11 December 1939. He was twenty years and 161 days old and 6 feet ⅛ of an inch tall. The conscription medical graded him 'One', which meant excellent. He was well educated, having attended the Stand Grammar School and Loughborough College, where he was still studying woodwork at the time of registration. His father was an engineer, having been a munitions worker during the First World War, and he had a brother, Donald, and two sisters, Dorothy and Irene. Jack elected to serve in the RAF and no doubt made it known that he wanted to train to become a pilot, as did many young men in similar circumstances. Only the most capable would achieve their ambition.

Jack attended the RAF Receiving Wing at Babbacombe in Devon, arriving on 12 September 1940, and progressed to the Initial Training Wing at nearby Oldway in Paignton on 27 September. The course at Paignton was effectively a ground school for potential student pilots, comprising of twelve to fourteen weeks on the theory of flight, engines, meteorology, navigation, and signals, which concluded with passing-out examinations and various psychological and aptitude tests. Jack was enjoying his life in the RAF and progressed to the Elementary Flying Training School (EFTS) at RAF Watchfield, Berkshire, in January 1941. It was there that he gained his first air experience, climbing aboard Tiger Moth R4833 on 9 January and taking to the sky for forty minutes. He flew solo just four weeks later and was totally convinced from that moment onwards that flying was what he wanted to do. On 7 March, Jack was assessed by the chief instructor, who marked his flying log book as 'average', but he had no faults and was allowed to continue with his pilot training. It was not unusual for some students to be removed from pilot training and transferred to navigator training at this early point.

Jack Whittle, standing second from left with his fellow student pilots. This image was most probably taken in January 1941 at RAF Watchfield. The early 1939-pattern flying boots are being worn; these had canvas uppers with a black leather shoe and leather or canvas strapping. Norman Moody, front row second from right, lost his life on 6 May 1941; Eric Turner, standing far left, lost his life on 21 September 1941 serving with 144 Squadron when, returning from an operation low on fuel, he helped his crew abandon the aircraft but was unable to save himself; Douglas Winstanley, standing third from right, was killed on the 4 October 1941; and George Eaton, standing fourth from right, lost his life on the 7 December 1941. (*Jack Whittle collection*)

In March 1941, Jack Whittle received a four-month posting to the Service Flying Training School (SFTS) at RAF Cranfield in Bedfordshire. There, he flew the twin-engine Oxford aircraft before converting to the Bristol Blenheim in June, when he was attached to the Operational Training Unit (OTU) at RAF Upwood. Jack was by now regarded as an 'above average' pilot and in September 1941 he was posted operational with Bomber Command No. 114 Squadron at RAF West Raynham in Norfolk.

Having arrived at RAF West Raynham, Jack was delighted to hear there was to be a royal visit. The King and Queen were due to make a morale-boosting tour of the aerodrome, accompanied by some high-ranking RAF personnel—a rather daunting prospect for the young sergeant pilot. Chosen personnel were to be presented to the King, but the majority were to parade before the complete entourage.

Most unusually, Jack was to fly his first operational sortie in daylight, attacking the power station at Mazingarbe in the Pas-de-Calais region of France. The Blenheims of No. 114 Squadron were escorted by Fighter Command aircraft as they were exceptionally vulnerable to attack by the Luftwaffe. The RAF had experienced terrible losses within its Blenheim squadrons, and the fighter pilots that protected them had the utmost respect for their bravery. During the three-hour operation, the escort was kept busy as the Luftwaffe made concerted efforts to shoot down the Blenheims, but back at the safety of

Standing immediately below the nose of the Bristol Blenheim with folded arms is Wing Commander Jenkins, Officer Commanding 114 Squadron. The Queen and King are central and far right is Air Vice Marshal Stevenson AOC, No. 2 Group.

RAF West Raynham, Jack was able to record a 'Green Ink' entry into his log book, denoting a successful daylight bombing operation. The following month, he and his crew returned once again to Mazingarbe in one of several daylight operational excursions into France and the Dutch coastal areas.

Jack's service in the RAF was to become very challenging. As well as an increase in low-level operations, which required precise targeting, No. 114 Squadron was ordered to participate in the first ever British Combined Operations raid, Operation Archery, an attack on the German-held Norwegian islands of Vaagso and Maaloy. On 23 December, Jack flew Blenheim T2224 to Lossiemouth in Scotland to be as close as possible to the intended target. The operation was planned for the 27th, and Jack and his crew, Sgts Denis Shanahan and Hoblyn (first name unknown), were required to attack the Luftwaffe airfield at Herdla, Norway. They were supporting the recently formed—but now renowned—British commandos on what was to become a significant raid against Hitler's forces in Norway. The squadron supplied thirteen aircraft, led by Wg Cdr Jenkins, the man who had signed Jack's log book several times after inspecting his recorded flying hours. Jenkins knew that Jack's flying abilities would be severely tested on this operation, which was to be carried out at exceptionally low levels. The timing of the raid on the Luftwaffe fighter airfield was imperative, and No. 114 Squadron excelled in their precision of both timing and accuracy of bombing. Having flown 300 miles at very low altitude, just above the crests of waves, the squadron arrived at the target area exactly on schedule. Tragically, two Blenheims collided in the air over the target area, killing both crews in what was otherwise a successful mission for No. 114 Squadron. Wg Cdr Jenkins received a Distinguished Service Order (DSO) and the navigation leader a Distinguished Flying Cross (DFC) for this feat of accuracy. This raid and the combined commando operation it supported are credited with diverting large numbers of German troops away from the Russian Front, and compelling Hitler to keep significant numbers of his forces in Norway to guard against a possible Allied invasion. In particular, he needed to protect the Reich's supplies of Swedish iron ore.

In the new year, Jack was tasked with night operations harassing Luftwaffe airfields, but he found them a challenge; several operations came to nothing due to cloud cover. His luck changed in early March 1942 when he found Schiphol aerodrome with its runway lights illuminated; the flare-path was bombed with good results, but it was little payback for the hours spent on those arduous operations. Jack's regular crew had consistently accumulated flying hours, but at the end of March only irregular duties came their way and once again they were sent to Lossiemouth. From there, Jack flew daylight weather reconnaissance sorties to the Shetland Islands and Norway, followed by several air-sea rescue sorties. During Jack's absence in Scotland, No. 114 Squadron's Blenheims Z7276, Z7307, and Z7700 all failed to return from operations over France and

Sergeant Jack Whittle, No. 114 Squadron. The pilot's wings worn on his thick and coarse material tunic are of the 'padded' type—these were normally purchased at the military tailors outfitters at far greater expense than the 'flat' type that were normally worn at that time.

Holland. The casualties included Wg Cdr Jenkins and his crew, all of whom had received medals for gallantry and had been about to complete their second full tour of duty. This grim news awaited Jack on his return to RAF West Raynham on 3 April, when he was also ordered to transfer to No. 18 Squadron. That unit had been all but wiped out while serving in Malta, and had returned to the UK to gain strength and equipment at West Raynham.

Despite the transfer, Jack's crew remained intact--something he was most grateful for—and it was not long before they were back on operations. Once again, Jack was to be engaged in a 'first': 'Operation Millennium', the first 1,000-bomber raid. Following delays due to adverse weather conditions, the attack on Cologne, in Germany's industrial Rhineland, finally took place on the morning of 30 May 1942. Several minor operations were planned to support the primary raid; once again the Blenheims were employed to bomb the Luftwaffe's night fighter aerodromes. St Trond aerodrome in Belgium was the target for Jack and four other crews from No. 18 Squadron, and he was delighted to observe very successful results after the bombing of the runway. The raid was added to the successes already recorded in his flying log book. St Trond was a very active aerodrome for the Luftwaffe, deploying He 111 and Ju 87 bombers initially, before later being used as a fighter base with Bf 109s operating from its single concrete runway. The purpose of these incursion raids was to weaken the Luftwaffe's ability to respond to Bomber Command's night offensives. Of the forty-nine Blenheims engaged in support of Operation Millennium, two aircraft failed to return. A grand total of forty-three aircraft and crews were lost that night, far exceeding anything previously experienced by Bomber Command.

Building on the apparently successful attacks on the night fighter aerodromes, No. 2 Group's Blenheim squadrons were tasked with performing similar incursions into Holland and France. Jack and his crew carried out additional operations against the airfields at St Trond, as well as Stade and Vechta in Germany, in June 1942. He also received notice that month of his commission as an officer and his new rank of Pilot Officer. His promotion was a cause for celebration in the Sergeants' Mess, but it also brought forward his inevitable separation from his crew, who had been by his side for some considerable time.

Jack's crew finally separated in July, when he was selected to train Blenheim crews at an Operational Training Unit. Before he could undertake instructional duties, he himself attended a short course at a Flight Instructor School. Subsequently, Jack served a lengthy twenty months of instructional duties at No. 13 OTU from July 1942 to February 1944. This was an exceptionally long period to be engaged in training pilots in Blenheims, and was doubly unfortunate for Jack as the entire period was spent flying in the early Mk I Blenheim. Many men served far shorter periods as instructors and were rewarded with some recognition, such as the Air Force Cross (AFC), which was entirely appropriate. Jack accumulated nearly 800 hours' flying time while instructing, and during those hours hundreds of pilots completed their courses with no accidents recorded. This was, in itself, exceptional. Jack had been promoted to the rank of Flying Officer on the completion of these duties and longed to fly operationally once again.

Jack Whittle's crew on the Blenheim had remained consistent for some considerable time and the three men were very close. The Observer/Navigator Shanahan had been promoted to Flight Sergeant while the Wireless Operator/Air Gunner Hoblyn still awaited his promotion. He is seen here wearing the battle dress tunic that was frequently worn under the leather Irvin flying jacket on operations.

Above: The Mk I Bristol Blenheim aircraft, the foremost aircraft displaying the 'K' serial number which was the type flown by Jack Whittle over hundreds of hours. These two 114 Squadron aircraft were photographed prior to the war, most probably during a test or delivery flight from the production line. Unusually, the emergency escape hatch on the top of the fuselage can be seen in the open position during this flight.

Right: Mk I Blenheim serial L1351. Jack Whittle flew this particular aircraft on several occasions during his service at No. 13 Operational Training Unit. On 3 July 1943 Jack was instructing a pilot and as their aircraft approached for a landing he was amazed to see L1351 standing almost upright having suffered a burst tyre on landing. The aircraft tipped over, ending up standing on its nose.

After what had seemed an eternity, Fg Off. Jack Whittle was posted on his second tour of duty to fly the Mosquito, another twin-engine intruder aircraft but superior in every respect to the Blenheim. Jack would have been one of the most experienced Blenheim pilots serving in the RAF at that time; on his arrival at RAF Hartford Bridge on 2 February 1944, he joined No. 107 Squadron. Although Jack had returned to serve in No. 2 Group, No. 107 Squadron was now part of the 2nd TAF, flying Mosquitos from RAF Lasham in Hampshire as part of No. 138 Wing, specialising in the precision bombing of high-value targets.

Quite remarkably, after a conversion flight with the Mk III Mosquito, Jack was teamed up with his old navigator/observer, Fg Off. Denis Shanahan, a fellow crewmember from his days with Nos. 114 & 18 Squadrons. This was far too much of a coincidence; no doubt strings were pulled and Jack was able to secure Denis as his navigator. It had been nineteen months since they had parted company, but they were reunited as crewmembers in the splendid Mosquito, known as the 'Wooden Wonder' for its fast speed and predominantly wooden frame. Jack would become engaged on Special Duties with No. 107 Squadron, deploying British Special Air Service (SAS) units behind enemy lines and hunting Gestapo HQs. Initially, however, the Whittle and Shanahan team were instructed to tackle V-1 flying bomb targets, which were notoriously difficult to locate and destroy. These operations, codenamed 'No Ball', were of high priority in early 1944. London and the southern counties would later suffer from the onslaught of V-1 flying bombs, known to the public as 'Doodlebugs', which fell indiscriminately, inflicting widespread destruction and casualties.

When flying the Mk VI Mosquito, it was common practice for the pilots of No. 107 Squadron to head at low level towards the Pas-de-Calais in France, where most rocket ramps were situated. Nearing the target, the Mosquitos pulled up to 3,500 feet and then dived to 1,500 feet, visually selecting the target and dropping four 500-lb bombs. Light anti-aircraft flak protected the V-1 rocket sites; numerous aircraft returned back to base with damage, and some were shot out of the sky.

On 18 March 1944, Jack and Denis flew on their first 'No Ball' operation to Preuseville in Normandy. The Mosquito lived up to its reputation for speed, and the attack was completed in just one hour and twenty-nine minutes. They were able to repeat that experience on 24 March and again on the 28th at the small and isolated site at Fréval. Returning low over the English Channel, Denis sighted two dinghies containing what appeared to be a ditched USAAF air crew. Denis reported their position and Jack repeatedly circled the dinghies, guarding over them until they were rescued.

On 22 April 1944, Jack and Denis flew their Mosquito to France for another daylight sortie, but it was not to be another 'No Ball'. They were to attack the railway repair sheds at Mantes-la-Jolie. This was an opportunity to adopt the 'dive attack' that Jack had mastered in the past few weeks. The operation was recorded in Jack's flying log book as 'very satisfactory', despite both heavy and light flak. A more precise delivery of their bomb load was required on 26 April, on another 'No Ball' to the remote French target at Heudière. On the last day of April, Jack was briefed for a night incursion to bomb the Luftwaffe aerodrome at Châteaudun, 70 miles south-west of Paris. In the operational briefing the importance of this mission was explained: Châteaudun was where the Luftwaffe's Me 262 jet fighters, which had just entered service, were thought to be based. It proved to be a simple operation; Jack noted in his log, 'No activity, bombs burst in dispersal area.'

No. 107 Squadron received detailed training in May 1944. Speculation of an impending invasion was difficult to contain as the Home Counties were awash with troops and materials. Jack could see the mounting preparations while flying on daylight sorties over Hampshire and Sussex. The pending invasion plans were to include Special Duties for his squadron, and clues were provided by the intense training that occurred that month. Jack was flying almost every day, performing low-level practice bombing drops and army co-operation bombing on smoke targets. These training sorties involved precise communication that enabled ground forces to call in an air strike, creating a highly capable force able to respond quickly to intelligence reports or physical sightings of desired targets. Jack had no idea that he would eventually be responding to the five-man SAS team codenamed 'Hugh', which had been parachuted into France from RAF Tempsford on 5 June by Plt Off. Tattersall and his crew from No. 161 Squadron. This special unit of men were under Special Operations Executive (SOE) command, but directly responsible to Special Forces HQ, and had been tasked to undertake Operation Bulbasket in France.

The same night that the SAS team had been dropped into France, Jack and his navigator had been briefed for their own special duty. No. 107 Squadron was required to carry out offensive patrols of roads and railways in western France. Seventeen Mosquitos operated between 2333 hours on the eve of D-Day, returning at 0515 hours. Attacks had been made on isolated vehicles, and bombs were dropped on bridges, rail junctions, and other communication-related targets of opportunity. Jack neatly recorded in red ink the following entry in his log book: 'Ops Road patrol for convoys in Cherbourg peninsula bombed hairpin bend in Defile Operation Overlord.'

Taking to the air again on 6 June to fly similar operations, Jack and Denis made up the only crew to undertake two individual sorties, both in Mosquito NS902. The log book reads: 'Ops Road patrol for convoys Vire-Fougeres. Bombed hairpin bend. Ops Road patrol Vire-Fougeres. Bombed road junction.'

Mosquito NS902 was a Mk VI fighter-bomber aircraft fitted with Rolls-Royce Merlin 25 engines. A relatively new aircraft, built at the Hatfield works

and delivered for service during the first few months of 1944, NS902 had been flown by Jack on many occasions. However, two days after his D-Day operations, NS902 failed to return from a sortie in France, although the two-man crew, Fg Off. Long and Sgt Robinson, managed to bail out safely.

On the evening of 10 June, Mosquito NT115 developed a fault that prevented Jack from dropping his bomb load on the target of St Sauveur railway station in Lille, France. He was still able to patrol the area south of Caen, looking for targets of opportunity for his cannons and machine guns, but electrical problems persisted and he soon returned to base, arriving at 0143 hours. At 0300 hours Jack took off once again to act as a reserve for road strikes in the Caen area. While waiting for a positive contact by other Mosquitos, the weather closed in, leaving him and Denis to search freely for individual targets. They used their cannons to good effect and dropped their bombs on a road junction they spotted through the cloud. At 0516 hours they finally landed at RAF Lasham and shut down their Merlin engines.

The SAS team operating under the SOE on Operation Bulbasket had been active in disrupting the movements of enemy troops and stores—particularly fuels—on the French rail network since D-Day. Capt. John Tonkin, 'B' Squadron, SAS, and 2Lt Richard Crisp, SAS, led the resistance unit which consisted of several French personnel. Tonkin was just twenty-three years of age, but he had impressive credentials; he had operated behind enemy lines in the Western Desert, been captured, escaped, and returned to the SAS. In France, the SAS cooperated with the French resistance in gathering important intelligence.

In early June 1944, the French network received news of several trains carrying petrol in well-camouflaged and protected railway sidings at Châtellerault, in the Poitou-Charentes region of France. At great danger to themselves, resistance operatives travelled the route as quickly as possible on pedal cycles to check the sidings visually. The information proved to be correct; the sidings were full of fuel bowsers and heavily guarded. This intelligence was radioed back to SAS HQ and immediately passed to the RAF. Time was going to be of the essence; Operation Bulbasket provided the opportunity to destroy a significant quantity of highly valued fuels required by the Wehrmacht. A strike was required by the fast and accurate Mosquitos of the 2nd TAF; on the evening of 11 June 1944, Nos 138 and 140 Wings would combine to attack Châtellerault.

Along with their squadron colleagues, Jack and Denis had received a stand-down from operations during the afternoon, having carried out some test

Opposite: Pre-invasion bombing by Mosquito aircraft upon the French railway network created disorganisation for the German Army. The restriction of troop and material movements was of significant importance to the overall planning of D-day. This Air Ministry photograph illustrates the damage caused by Mosquitos attacking the railway sheds; this particular target was at Hirson, near the Belgium boarder.

A Mosquito Fighter Bomber crew embarking on another intrusion sortie into France. The nose of the Mosquito carries a lethal combination with four .303 Browning machine guns, capable of very concentrated fire, and under the nose, four 20-mm cannons, capable of penetrating armoured vehicles and causing significant destruction to rolling stock and buildings. The pilot and navigator are seen on the step ladder about to climb into the cockpit. The crew's entrance hatch is hanging down; wearing flying gear and carrying navigational bags, it was a tight squeeze.

flights and compass alignments on their Mosquitos during the day. That swiftly changed when an emergency briefing was called, and the station personnel did a marvellous job of rounding up the air crews from the local attractions in nearby Alton. Such was the rush that the individual crews were briefed individually as they arrived back on station—a most unusual occurrence. Jack and Denis received their brief from Wg Cdr Pollard, who was going to lead the six Mosquitos of No. 107 Squadron. They were supporting the Mosquitos from Nos 464 and 487 Squadrons, which were scheduled to attack the target in the first instance. The involvement of the SAS in Operation Bulbasket remained highly secret; none of the crews were aware of it. Weather forecasts were not favourable, so as soon as the armourers had completed fitting the bombs into the Mosquitos, the aircraft departed Lasham. At 2110 hours, all six aircraft were safely in loose formation above the airfield. Jack and Denis were flying in

Fighter Bomber Mosquitos flying in formation on a sortie into occupied France. Their machine guns are visibly protruding.

a new airframe, Mosquito NT207, for the first time. The cockpit was ideal; they were sitting alongside each other, and the view from their seats was excellent.

The formation flew eastwards from Hampshire into Sussex, turning out over the Channel and making towards Dieppe. Jack made a detailed entry in his flying log book stating that the weather closed in after crossing the French coast, forcing the formation to fly above the cloud. The raid was a deep penetration into France and fortunately, after several miles, the cloud began to break up and allowed the Mosquitos to drop lower once more, at the same time enabling Denis to pick out pinpoints for navigation. Eventually the last remnants of light were lost from the long summer day, but as darkness fell, the horizon held a glow; Châtellerault was burning from the initial Mosquito attack. Wg Cdr Pollard controlled the second attack by instructing each crew to approach in line with the sidings and destroy the rolling stock that remained intact. Jack describes this in his log as a 'Shallow dive, dropping bombs and cannon firing.' Following the attack, each Mosquito returned independently. Jack landed at Lasham three hours and thirty minutes since taking off, after a long and intensely focused flight, but congratulations were in order; the raid had denied valuable fuel to the Wehrmacht, who were moving forward to reinforce the lines facing the Allied bridgehead at Normandy. From that day onwards, Mosquito NT207 was to be Jack Whittle's regular aircraft, in which he developed supreme confidence in flying.

It was not long before NT207 departed Lasham once more. The squadron's records indicate that six pairs of Mosquitos were sent to a railway terminal point at Le Mesnil-Mauger, north-west France, in the early hours of 12 June. Each pair of Mosquitos operated twenty minutes apart; once over the target area, one aircraft dropped flares to illuminate the railway while the accompanying aircraft attacked the target. These roles were then reversed and they departed allowing for the next pair to attack in exactly the same way. Jack was in the fourth pairing of aircraft. He identified his target, dropped his bombs, and raked the area with cannon fire. Later, in his log book, he recorded his satisfaction at taking part in this successful operation. After the raid, a stand-down of a few days was ordered for crews—ample reward for the intensity of flying during the first couple of weeks of June.

On 21 June 1944, Jack and Denis resumed flying. No. 107 Squadron was charged with harassing the nightly movements of the Wehrmacht on the railway network and roads. In order to achieve better results, flares were carried by each aircraft to drop and illuminate the ground when anything suspicious was sighted. Flying low in the darkness and seeking such targets was fraught with danger; power lines, church steeples, and tall trees could cause fatal consequences. Jack flew his Mosquito to seek targets on the Chartres to Versailles railway on 21 June, the Coutances, St Lô, and Granville areas on 22 June, and the roads and railways between Laval, Angers, and La Flèche on 23 June. Reserves of Mosquitos were available to follow up on any initial attacks, ensuring the destruction of a target once it had been spotted. Jack put this tactic into action when, on patrol over the Chartres to Versailles railway, he sighted a steam train pulling what appeared to be troop carriages; he dived over the target, dropping bombs and firing his cannons, and then called upon the reserve Mosquito flown by Flt Lt Turner, who followed up to finish the job. Jack's other targets were single vehicles which, once sighted, were dealt with effectively on his own.

The final operation in June took place on the night of the 27th. Jack was among the entire contingent of aircraft from No. 107 Squadron sent on close support duties with the Army. As usual, Jack was in Mosquito NT207 and Denis had expertly navigated them to the Falaise region where enemy troops were reportedly ensconced in wooded areas. Jack deployed flares in an effort

Opposite: A successful hit on a typical French railway target. The steam train has been completely destroyed and the tracks rendered useless, preventing German reinforcements and materials from reaching the Allied D-day bridgehead. This attack took place at Canisy in St Lo, Normandy, the patrol area for Jack Whittle on 22 June 1944.

to identify the target area, but they also illuminated the aircraft, inviting an onslaught of flak. Fortunately, all the Mosquitos of No. 107 Squadron returned safely back to base.

The squadron had amassed impressive statistics in June, carrying out 280 operational sorties at night and thirteen during the day. The combined time in the air over France had reached 758 hours and 20 minutes. These operations significantly contributed to Operation Overlord, establishing the foothold in occupied Europe that would eventually lead to the comprehensive defeat of German forces in Western Europe and the final destruction of the Third Reich.

July should have heralded good weather for the continuation of the Mosquitos' nightly assaults, but it was not to be. Rain and heavy cloud hung around for several days, and an attempted sortie by Jack to Angers demanded very restrictive flying. He returned home rather dejected in the early hours of 4 July. Later that same day, conditions improved and in the late evening Jack and Denis set off to patrol an area he describes as 'Belou-Sees-Nogent-Chateaudun-Orleans' in his log book. During that patrol, faint lights were seen in some woods; Jack unleashed his bomb load and rained cannon fire down on the lit area. From the fires and smoke they left behind, they judged their attack to have been a great success. Similar results were achieved on 7, 11, and 14 July, with Jack locating trains within his allotted patrol areas. Steam engines had blinds fitted to shield their fireboxes, but it was not always easy for the engine stokers to prevent some exposure as they worked on the footplates. The losses mounted for the Germans, who were forced to protect their valued engines by mounting light flak units on open flat carriages spaced every ten or twelve carriages apart. These defensive measures had the desired effect: casualties mounted for the Mosquito pilots, who now had flak batteries to add to the list of dangers in low-flying engagements on moving and stationary trains.

The resistance were also actively participating in the sabotage of rolling stock, and Capt. Tonkin and 2Lt Crisp continued to lead a large group. The units were supplied by the SOE squadrons, which dropped arms and ammunition as the units gained in strength. Unknown to Jack Whittle, as the SAS continued with their objectives on Operation Bulbasket, they would once again seek the assistance of the Mosquitos, this time focusing on the Poitiers to Bordeaux railway line. Until that time, Jack continued with his search and destroy sorties, which now included sectors along the River Seine where barges were located and destroyed by powerful cannon fire. The remaining July sorties saw a wide variety of targets destroyed, but the one on the 28th, a long-ranging intervention over Domfront, north-west France, was especially lively for Jack and Denis.

Ten vehicles in a convoy were bombed and wooded areas were strafed, but Jack's trusty Mosquito NT207 was hit by light anti-aircraft flak and suffered the loss of one of its Merlin engines, which had to be shut down. He feathered the engine, allowing the propeller to turn without power, which caused drag and reduced air speed. Jack limped home to land at Hartford Bridge, his old aerodrome in Hampshire. The following day, NT207 was repaired and able to return Jack and Denis to Lasham, where they were immediately sent on another incursion seeking targets on the River Seine around Mantes. This proved to be another profitable sortie, with an attack on a train and the destruction of some river barges—a combination that was rarely achieved.

The SAS unit had been reinforced with more SAS soldiers, but had suffered terribly when their camp was located by the enemy, quite possibly after a betrayal. Many men were captured, but a small unit escaped and remained active. The remaining Bulbasket team received information that SS troops had recently relocated into the Château du Fou, a few miles south of Châtellerault, where the railway sidings had been comprehensively destroyed a few weeks earlier. As the elite German troops were believed to be responsible for several atrocities, as well as the recent routing of the SAS camp, they were regarded as a significant target; the intelligence of their whereabouts was immediately transmitted to England.

No. 107 Squadron was selected to attack the Château du Fou. Wg Cdr Pollard, who had flown with Jack on many sorties, had departed from Lasham on 28 July; his replacement, Wg Cdr Scott, would lead his new squadron with all seventeen airworthy Mosquitos participating. In addition, a Mosquito from the RAF's Film Production Unit (FPU) would secure some dramatic footage of their daylight precision low-level raid. The briefing specified three waves of six aircraft, each led by an experienced officer. The operation was a deep penetration into France with little room for error, particularly as the Mosquitos would only just have enough fuel to make it back to their airfield in Hampshire. Jack led the second wave, with Wg Cdr Scott alongside him, departing at 1930 hours on 2 August.

The three waves of Mosquitos had specific objectives: the first two were to attack in quick succession at low level, initially with instantaneous bombs, followed by delayed action bombs to avoid blast damage, dropped within the chateau; and the third wave would attack with instantaneous bombs, dropped on shallow dives. At the height of the onslaught, the marauding Mosquitos would circle the target area and strafe it using their cannons and machine guns.

The importance of this raid had been emphasised, but information concerning the involvement of the SAS unit was again restricted. However, this was immaterial; the connection with the elite SS troops was more than enough motivation, as their reputation and direct connection with civilian and military atrocities was well known. No. 107 Squadron's operational records provide excellent detail on the events that unfolded after taking off from their airfield.

The aircraft crossed the English coast over the Selsey peninsula nine minutes after leaving Lasham, and flew low over the Channel towards France, crossing into enemy-held territory thirty-three minutes later. It would take another forty-five minutes before the Mosquitos reached their target, as they took

Flight Lieutenant Jack Whittle (left) with Flying Officer Denis Shanahan and their Mosquito NT207 'B'. The cannon portals can be seen clearly, as can the browning machine guns protruding from the nose. The Mosquito was known affectionately by many crews as the 'Mossie' as well as 'The Timber Terror', making reference to the fact the aircraft was predominantly made of wood.

Flying Officer Staple and his navigator, Flying Officer Wimmers—the crew who took Mosquito HJ771 'J' on the last wave of attack on Chateau du Fou. This aircraft was lucky to return from the operation after sustaining damage from light flak during one of their low-level attacks.

an indirect route in order to confuse German radar. The aircraft were now flying at some 4,000 feet and surprisingly little flak was being fired at them. Jack and Denis were fortunate to be accompanied by a number of capable crew members, among whom were two South African Air Force pilots—Capt. Brown alongside Jack in the second wave, and Capt. Thomas Hunt in the third wave. The first wave included Lt Cdr Skavhaugen, a Norwegian pilot, and his navigator, Fg Off. A. H. Bobbett. Jack knew the Norwegian pilot as 'Skav' and was aware that he harboured a burning desire to fly the Mosquito over the fjords of his home country to attack the enemy shipping. 'Skav' and Bobbett were to achieve that ambition with the famous No. 333 Squadron later in the war. No. 107 Squadron comprised men of many nationalities, and all were represented on the attack against the SS troops in the Château du Fou.

Denis was able to pick out pinpoints easily due to the good visibility, which was estimated to be between 15 and 20 miles. As they approached the target area a slight haze appeared, but it was insufficient to cause any problems with the sighting of the château and they arrived exactly an hour and forty-five minutes after leaving Lasham. The Château du Fou looked imposing, sitting on a slight ridge surrounded by areas of dense woodland. The substantial building had large conical roof turrets and was easily recognisable from the aerial photographs that had been passed around at the briefing.

Jack took his Mosquito on a low-level approach towards the front of the building, passing over the courtyards and pulling up as Denis released their eleven-second-delayed-action bombs, plunging them straight through the main entrance area. Jack climbed to escape from the blast and debris as smoke rose beneath them, causing the château almost to disappear from view. Men in uniform ran from the building to seek refuge in the nearby wooded areas, but as they did so the Mosquitos targeted them with their Browning machine guns. After the primary bomb loads had been dropped, sufficient time was available to strafe the adjacent woods. One particular area to the south of the château erupted with an explosion thought to have been caused by vehicles taking a direct hit. The sight of so many Mosquitos concentrating their destructive firepower on the confined target must have been hugely impressive. The camera unit also carried a bomb load, and once it had added its bombs into the consuming dust and smoke, it secured the desired filming of events.

The Mosquitos of No. 107 Squadron remained unmolested; they departed safely, having devastated their targets in and around the château. The return to Lasham was left up to the individual crews in the knowledge that little in the way of surplus fuel existed. Fg Off. Staple in aircraft 'J', as seen in the photograph, was unfortunate to sustain unexpected light flak on the way home. However, even though he was met with thick low cloud, he managed to land safely back at base, as did Jack and Denis at 2310 hours. Two aircraft reached Thorney Island airfield on the Sussex/Hampshire boundary, and aircraft

'D', NX822, captained by the South African Thomas Hunt, made a forced emergency landing. He had limped home on just one engine and, with no fuel left, crashed onto the runway, the 'wooden' aircraft literally disintegrating beneath him, but miraculously both crew members escaped uninjured. Capt. Hunt was later to receive the DFC for his remarkable exhibition of flying.

The Château du Fou was such a substantial building it was accepted that in all probability the force of Mosquitos would not have been sufficient to have destroyed it totally. What was not in doubt, however, was the fact that the attack was highly successful and that the infamous SS unit had suffered significant losses. The Mosquito units in Nos 138 and 140 Wings became recognised as 'Gestapo Hunters' within the 2nd TAF, and these Special Duties would rightly take their place in RAF history. The day after their exploits attacking the SS HQ, Jack and Denis returned to the skies of France to seek out the elusive night-time trade on the railways. They had no luck on this occasion, but they found an appropriate location on a railway line at Auneau to drop their bombs.

The pilots in No. 107 Squadron maintained a broad knowledge of Allied movements into France from D-Day, and on occasions worked in close support with the Army. Caen had been a hugely difficult objective to take from the enemy, being of immense strategic importance to both sides. It was a major road hub located on the River Orne and Caen Canal, and the 21st Panzer Division had put up a robust defence of the city for nearly two months. On 4 August 1944, No. 107 Squadron was called upon for a full-strength deployment behind the enemy line at Caen. All fifteen operational Mosquitos that took part in the patrol and attack reported the withdrawal of enemy forces from the city. The aircraft took off with twenty-minute separations, which enabled the battle zone to be patrolled consistently between 2314 hours on the 4th until 0530 hours the following day. Despite the battle zone being heavily protected by flak, most unexpectedly all the Mosquitos returned safely with nearly all of them having used up their ammunition. The battle for Caen had lasted eight weeks and was almost over, but it had been costly in lives and the city had been destroyed.

Flt Lts Jack Whittle and Denis Shanahan had been crewed together over an extended period, and their joint accumulation of operations flown registered them as having completed two full tours of duty. To have achieved that status in light bombers was in itself highly respected among their peers and commanders. Mosquito NT207 had been magnificent in sustaining their performance in No. 107 Squadron, and one final operation was rostered for them on the night of 5 August 1944. Each of the sixteen aircraft taking part in the operation had flares placed in their bomb bay and two 500-lb bombs attached to their wings; the well-armed squadron was to patrol the railways east of Paris and target rolling-stock, adopting staggered deployments to facilitate comprehensive aerial cover between 2239 and 0536 hours.

Jack and Denis were in the air between 0058 and 0359 hours, flying over the Lagny, Épernay, and Vitry areas. At La Ferté, they sighted a train; they dropped their flares and identified a fully laden troop train protected by a light flak unit, which immediately opened fire. Jack dived while Denis dropped the bomb load and Jack aimed cannon fire at the light flak unit, sighting strikes. In addition, search lights from Coulommiers were being deployed in an effort to assist the flak units defending the train. Fortunately, Mosquito NT207 lived up to expectations and escaped unscathed from the precarious situation. So ended the final operation with No. 107 Squadron for these two immensely proud and close friends.

Coincidentally, that same morning the surviving SAS operatives who had been engaged in Operation Bulbasket were recovered from behind the lines by the Special Duties Hudson aircraft of No. 161 Squadron, which landed on a temporary grass strip at Foussac Farm in Asnières-sur-Seine near Paris before returning them safely to RAF Tempsford. Unfortunately, 2Lt Richard Crisp was not with the group; he had been captured on 3 July and was later executed at Forêt de St Sauvant on 7 July. His grave was eventually found, in company with the twenty-nine other SAS soldiers who had parachuted into France to deploy under Operation Bulbasket. It has been speculated that the troops responsible for the execution of the SAS men may well have been resident in the Château du Fou, which had been so effectively attacked by No. 107 Squadron.

The bodies of the thirty-one murdered SAS soldiers were respectfully recovered from their self-dug shallow graves and reburied with full military honours at Rom Communal Cemetery. The body of Lt Stephens, who had been beaten to death prior to the executions, lies in the village cemetery in Verrières close to the location where the men were captured. The bodies of three SAS operatives who had been taken to hospital and murdered by lethal injection have never been found, but a memorial plaque was erected beside the SAS graves at Rom. The local population continues to tend and respect their graves with great pride.

In all probability, Jack and Denis never knew anything of the events that had surrounded their Special Duties operations in France. There was cause, however, to celebrate the double achievement of having completed two full operational tours of duty and that these inseparable friends had both been posted to serve in the Communication Flight within No. 2 Group. It was truly remarkable that they were to continue serving together. Wg Cdr Scott also submitted a joint recommendation for the award of a DFC to each man:

> As navigator and pilot these officers have completed a very large number of sorties, involving attacks on flying bomb sites, railways sidings and road and rail transport. They have displayed notable skill, courage and resolution.[1]

On 30 September 1944, Air Chief Marshal Leigh-Mallory, the commander-in-chief of the Allied Expeditionary Air Force, approved the awards by adding his signature to the recommendation document. Leigh-Mallory had been in command of the planning and execution of the air plan in support of the invasion of occupied Europe.

Just six weeks after recommending the DFCs to Jack and Denis, Leigh-Mallory became the new air commander for the South East Asia Command. He commenced the first leg of his journey to India, leaving RAF Northolt in Avro York MW126 on 14 November 1944, but tragedy struck when his aircraft was reported missing when flying over the French Alps. The crash site was eventually discovered on 4 June 1945. The most senior RAF officer to lose his life during the Second World War now lies in a civilian graveyard in the south of France.

Jack Whittle successfully applied for a permanent commission in the post-war RAF, qualifying to fly Meteor jets and later serving in Transport Command. In the 1960s, he was seconded to the Zambian Air Force, which entitled him to be awarded the Kenya Campaign Medal. The Queen was required to authorise the wearing of this medal, and Jack added it to the Cyprus and Borneo General Service Medals that he was also awarded during his post-war service. Eventually Jack retired from the RAF and returned to his passion for woodwork, engaging in antique restoration in South Africa and Great Britain, which he enjoyed until his death in 2003.

Flight Lieutenant Jack Whittle wearing the medal ribbon of the Distinguished Flying Cross and his campaign medals.

2

John Hardwick
Mediterranean Air Force

During the Second World War many men volunteered to join the Commonwealth air forces with the intention of becoming a pilot. The selection procedures were stringent and for the vast majority a commission as a pilot never materialised. Canadian John Hardwick, from Toronto, was to be among those fortunate men given the opportunity to start pilot training. He took to the air in his first solo flight on 11 June 1942, and progressed past his assessment check at fifty hours during the following month. It was a challenging course, but John possessed the passion and will to do his very best, and his classroom and study work was of the highest standard. Despite his efforts, he failed to pass a progression check in the air on 31 July and was removed from his pilot's course.

After suffering such disappointment and indignity, John attended the Air Gunnery School at Dalcross in Scotland, having elected to train as an air gunner. That decision was made in the knowledge that he would become operational in the shortest possible time, and he gained great satisfaction in being awarded his air gunner's brevet and his promotion to the rank of sergeant. During his final training, John formed up in a crew captained by Flt Sgt Neilly, and together they served in No. 6 Group RCAF, Bomber Command, at RAF Topcliffe. As a well-qualified rear gunner who had secured excellent assessments endorsing his skills in gunnery, John enjoyed the responsibility of defending his aircraft from within the Perspex turret perched at the tail of his bomber.

John had anticipated flying on raids to Germany as part of No. 6 Group, but surprisingly he and his crew were sent to fly in the Mediterranean theatre of operations. They briefly attended the Ferry Training Unit to conduct fuel consumption tests before taking their Halifax bomber on the long flight from RAF Lyneham in Wiltshire to Cairo. John was to fly with the Special Duties Flight 1575, undertaking SOE deployments to drop supplies to partisans and the resistance across much of southern Europe and the Balkans. He arrived at Bilda, their operational base in Algeria, in September 1943. However, it was not to be a pleasant experience; the conditions were poor, the unit was understaffed, the environment was harsh, and the incessant flies were a constant annoyance. John and his crew were immediately thrust into four Special Duties operations to Corsica in September, and seven long sorties into Yugoslavia in October.

John would enter his rear gunner's turret from within the fuselage of the aircraft, having climbed in through the crew access door towards the rear of the aircraft. After clipping his parachute to the hooks adjacent to his turret, he would get into his seat and close the turret's two doors behind him. It was a restrictive environment, with no room to wear or store his parachute, and he was frequently confined there for operations of over nine hours' duration. Held in by a simple lap belt, John was responsible for ensuring the safety of his aircraft and protecting his crew and himself from enemy fighters. He used the turret controls to scan the sky across each quarter, looking for the dark speck that could suddenly become a lethal threat to his life. Special Duties Flight 1575 changed its identity to No. 624 Squadron, and official records were to carry that

John Hardwick with his flight crew and one ground crew member in North Africa. They are wearing typical flying gear worn for that climate. Their Halifax 'N' identification letter can be seen on the landing gear shield immediately behind them. This aircraft has an unusually long aerial extending from the fuselage—in all probability this would have been for communicating with the SOE in air to ground-based communications.

identity after September 1943, although documented records of the squadron's activities remain very limited due to the secrecy of the work involved.

Rather unexpectedly, John witnessed the arrival of an additional crew member shortly after those changes. Oscar the pig had been born in Tunisia on 25 August 1943, and was liberated from a small village by the British Army in October that year. A negotiated transfer between the Army and the RAF took place, which saw Oscar join No. 624 Squadron as part of the crew headed by Flt Sgt Neilly. Why a pig should be called Oscar, nobody knows. However, animals within the RAF were occasionally adopted by individual crew members, or by collective crew agreement. In the case of Oscar, having endeared himself to Neilly and his crew, he was given the honour of crew mascot. More common were traditional dog mascots, many of which were black (considered to be a lucky colour), and a large number were unofficially taken up in aircraft. Oscar was no exception, but it is more than likely that he was the only flying pig mascot during the Second World War. Unfortunately, he was not the most popular crew member as he suffered rather badly from body odour, much to John's discomfort, since he was always downwind of Oscar in the rear gunner's position.

In November 1943, John flew night sorties delivering supplies and weapons to various resistance groups in Yugoslavia, Greece, Bulgaria, and Albania. His crew did not have a regular Halifax aircraft, but regardless of the particular machine, the cold night weather enveloped John in his Perspex cockpit and the ten-hour operations to Yugoslavia were highly unpleasant for him. Every operation was dangerous and John was very much isolated from the rest of his crew. If instructed by his pilot, he could abandon the aircraft by opening the turret doors, grabbing his parachute, clipping it onto his harness, and traversing the turret to the furthest position. Then by pulling the safety pin from his seat harness he could fall out backwards through the two doors that formed the back of the turret. In the event of him being injured, another member of the crew could release the door catch, and there was also a manually operated hydraulic valve that enabled the turret to be turned from within the fuselage. This facility was added after injured gunners had been trapped within their turret, with fatal consequences. Additionally, if the hydraulic supply to the turret failed, the gunner could turn the turret by means of a handle. All of these developments were designed to create a safer means of escape for rear gunners. One of the ever-present threats was the outbreak of fire from within the fuselage. Flames would be fanned by the rush of air towards the tail section, and often the rear gunner's parachute, stored in the fuselage, would be destroyed. This was a common cause of death for rear gunners in the Second World War.

John's last trip with Oscar on board was on 30 December 1943, flying in Halifax EB188, on a four-hour trip between Brindisi in Italy and Tocra in Libya. The New Year saw John's squadron tasked with night-time SOE delivery drops to Albania and northern Italy, in and around the Po Valley. Neilly had recently been promoted to the rank of Warrant Officer and was due to fly his last operation with his crew to the Po Valley, delivering supplies in the Flax Forest area on 16 January 1944.

Senior officers frequently welcomed the presence of mascots on various squadrons during the war, as they provided entertainment and boosted morale among the men. But Oscar the pig sealed his own fate when he was caught stealing from the Officers' Mess. As an almost fully grown pig, his insatiable appetite was the focus of constant attention. As a result of these events, an official notice was printed and passed around the squadron on 20 January 1944:

> Death of well-known member of a heavy bomber squadron
>
> It is with regret that the death of Oscar, the Flying Pig, is announced. He died at the hands of an assassin on Tuesday last, and details are as yet unknown, but from the scant news available, he went down fighting to the last, in the true traditions of the Royal Air Force, and the squadron of which he was a member.
>
> During the time that Oscar was with the R.A.F. he flew 1500 miles and had 10 flying hours to his credit. He joined the crew of Warrant Officer Neilly, and although at one time when on the way to dispersal, he protested strongly, and appeared to have a rooted objection to the idea of flying, he soon settled down once in the air. When flying, he occupied the position of assistant mid-upper Gunner with F/Sgt Galbraith, who took what might be described as a 'brotherly' interest in him and waited on him hand and foot. At mealtimes F/Sgt Galbraith was always to be seen carrying Oscar's meals to his living quarters, where our four footed friend would greet him with grunts of recognition and pleasure.
>
> In due course the powers that be decided that it was necessary for Oscar to be moved from Tunisia to Libya, and it was on this trip that he had his first experience of flying. Warrant Officer Neilly, knowing the excitable nature of Oscar, decided it would be best for all concerned if this additional member of the crew was encased in sacking, should the desire to dash up into the pilot's seat, or some equally important position in the aircraft, overcome him. It was unfortunate that he suffered rather badly from B.O. and consequently it cannot be truthfully said that he was a popular member of the crew.
>
> Our late friend did not seem unduly impressed by his new surroundings in Libya and often had the appearance of being 'brassed off'. However his stay was of short duration, and he once again took to the air, and flew from Libya to Italy. His escapades here seemed to indicate that he regained his

Opposite: Parachute supplies dropping from a 'Special Duties' Halifax aircraft to Marshal Tito's resistance forces in Yugoslavia.

> old zest for living as he made several efforts to 'desert' possibly with an idea of 'hitting the high spots' in the local town. On one occasion he was caught in the act of stealing food from the Mess. As a result of this criminal behaviour, disciplinary action had to be taken in accordance with the Air Force Regulations, and he was confined to pen until his untimely end.
>
> If any friends of Oscar, the Flying Pig, would like to pay him their last respects, he is to be found hanging in state, in the store room of the Sergeants' Mess. Although in rather a different form, his last physical appearance will be on the Mess tables in a few days' time, where it is felt his presence will be appreciated.
>
> 20th January 1944.[2]

The demise of Oscar had come at the hands of WO Neilly. The crew's air gunner/dispatcher, Jim Rosbottom, wrote in his memoirs:

> When it came to slaughtering the pig, Neilly missed with the second blow of his knife and severed the tendons in his own hand. The dinner itself turned into a riotous affair which ended in fighting and the mess tent being destroyed.

The unfortunate Neilly ended up in hospital as a result of his wound. His crew members became what was known as a 'headless crew' and filled vacancies within other aircraft; John acted as the dispatcher, pushing the supplies out of the Halifax flown by Flt Sgt Dowding in March.

Later, John and his colleagues re-formed as a full crew once more, captained by a new pilot, Fg Off. Driscoll. This pilot had experienced a serious crash-landing during his time at the Halifax Conversion Unit on 16 December 1943, when he and five other crew members had been slightly injured and his navigator killed in the crash. Driscoll had fully recovered and quickly endeared himself to his new crew. He proved to be a popular captain with No. 624 Squadron, and John was regarded as his regular rear gunner.

The squadron was not immune to flying accidents. Halifax BB386, flown by Flt Sgt Jackson, took off from Blida late in the evening on 4 March and, about five minutes into the flight, crashed 5 miles north-west of the airfield. The aircraft was completely burnt out and all the crew were killed. It was a stark reminder that accidents continued to take many lives while the squadron was operating from North Africa. The following day, Flt Sgt Craven crashed on take off, ending up no more than twenty yards off the runway. Fortunately, nobody was injured.

John's crew flew on eight long SOE delivery flights into southern France during April 1944, but the month was blighted by the loss of Halifax JN960 when it failed to return from a drop in France. The squadron's frequency of

No. 624 Squadron 'North Africa', 1944. Wing Commander Stanbury is indicated in the centre. The person sitting second left is wearing the Parachute Badge of the USA. The person sitting first right of Stanbury in the dark uniform shirt has the British Parachute Wings on the right shoulder while his pilot's wings have an unusual configuration. The range of uniforms and insignia illustrates the diverse duties undertaken in the 'Special Duties' of this squadron.

supply drops into France continued into the following month. John spent nearly forty hours in his rear gunner's turret while undertaking five operations. The month was disrupted by the temporary loss of Fg Off. Driscoll, who was admitted to hospital after he was bitten by one of the many stray dogs. He was not released from hospital until 17 May, rather sore but fit to fly. On the last day of the month, John witnessed six Halifaxes take off on operations without incident, but the seventh, flown by Plt Off. Johnston, swung off the runway. Johnston was unable to recover control and the undercarriage collapsed, breaking the back of the aircraft. The violence of the accident tore the port engine out of its mountings, but fortunately no one was injured.

The impending D-Day invasion of Normandy was being supported from southern France, and John flew his last operation on the eve of the invasion, taking off at 2328 hours on 5 June to deliver stores in the coded location of 'Accordeur'. The operation was successful and he landed back safely at 0650 hours, eager to learn more of the developments that were unfolding on the bridgeheads of Normandy.

Wg Cdr Stanbury DSO, DFC, the Officer Commanding No. 624 Squadron, subsequently dropped the first Operational Group (OG) of men into France on 8 June. The reference 'OG' relates to the American Office of Strategic Services (OSS) teams deployed from North Africa. They were specialist personnel performing very similar roles to the British SAS behind the enemy lines. This team was operating under the codename 'Emily' and consisted of fifteen men, all of whom were operating in military uniform. The close association with these specialist troops is shown by the individual in the squadron photograph from 1944 sitting close to Wg Cdr Stanbury and wearing the US metal parachute wing.

Stanbury applied his signature in John Hardwick's flying log book, endorsing the fact that he had completed a full tour of operations, having undertaken thirty-nine sorties in 300¼ hours. However, very few air crew personnel were additionally able to record having flown with such an unusual crew mascot as Oscar during the war!

John's departure as his tour expired was tinged with sorrow on hearing that his old crew, captained by Fg Off. Driscoll in Halifax JN896, had failed to return from a mission flown from Blida to supply the resistance on 13 August 1944. The only clue to their loss was a signal reporting an aircraft exploding in the air and diving into the sea at a location thought to have been between Palamós in Spain and Cape Efos in France. All of the crew were killed and, having no known graves, their lives are commemorated on the Malta Memorial at Valletta.

3

Michael Durell DFC SOE Special Duties, Resistance Rendezvous

Michael Durell, an 'inter-war' baby born on 16 February 1921, spent his childhood in Essex. He attended Sir Anthony Browne's Grammar School in Brentwood between 1933 and 1939, before gaining a place at the University of London. The declaration of war against Germany only temporarily interrupted Michael's life at university, when the institution and approximately 14,000 students were forced to relocate to various parts of the UK. The primary buildings were taken over by the Ministry of Information and the roof became an observation post for the Observer Corps, who plotted enemy aircraft movements for the RAF. Universities were fertile grounds for recruitment by the Air Ministry, particularly of pilots and navigators, and Michael became one of the many who volunteered for service as air crew. Aged twenty, he attended the Initial Recruiting Wing at Oxford on 28 May 1941.

Leading Aircraftman (LAC) Michael Durell's service number 1319493 was stamped on the twin identity discs that were handed to him, to be worn at all times. One was made of fire-retardant material—a sobering thought. Michael progressed through the initial training and various selection procedures, and on 15 January 1942 he was posted to Canada under the Commonwealth Air Training Plan, to be trained as an observer navigator at RCAF Chatham, New Brunswick.

On 2 February 1942, after a tiresome journey conducted with no assistance other than a rail warrant, Michael arrived at the Clyde docks where he was directed to an American troopship. Several warships were moored around the docks, and hundreds of troops were being directed to various ships in a scene of intense activity, with people and goods moving in all directions. Michael was allocated a bunk among the cramped conditions he found on the American vessel, but it was not until 4 February that his troopship departed. During the journey he became aware that the crew were making their displeasure known at what was perceived to be a lack of Navy protection for the convoy.

Michael Durell, photographed after his appointment to 'Air Crew under Training'. The white flash inserted in his side cap was worn during the entire training process and only removed upon the presentation of the brevet or wings on successful completion of the training. (*Michael Durell collection*)

On the eighth day of passage, a Catalina flying boat appeared and remained with them for some time, and later, at about 1600 hours, the convoy passed a homeward-bound convoy. On 12 February, the convoy arrived in Canada just before dusk; Michael was surprised to see the illuminated dock and street lights with no restrictions, in stark contrast to the blackout conditions back home in the UK.

Chatham had been selected for use as a Second World War airfield because it usually had clear skies and was therefore well suited for training purposes. RCAF Chatham became an operational field under the Eastern Air Commands, as well as the location of No. 3 Training Command. British Commonwealth Air Training Plan. No. 21 EFTS for pilots was located there from mid-1941 to mid-1942, as was No. 10 Air Observer School from mid-1941 to the end of the war, training both navigators and wireless operators. The Air Observer School was run by a pool of fully qualified civilian instructors headed by Mr R. H. Biddy. Michael gained his first flying experience on 15 March 1942, and was in the air for two and a half hours, flying over Prince Edward Island under the instruction of a Mr Stephens. Six days later, Michael was taken into the air with a Mr Willardson for a practical exercise, but the weather was not ideal. Michael made a diary entry: 'First aerial exercise quite bumpy horrible feeling.' His air sickness was conquered with several training sorties in the Avro Anson aircraft, and they later proved to be exhilarating experiences for him.

Michael's diary for 11 May 1942 reads:

> Went up on a photography flight this morning with Mr Hill, flew at 1,000ft came down to 500ft went out over coast along the estuary dive bombing the fishermen in their rowing boats took photographs of Chatham RC Church, Coggiville, Bartiborg Bridge, Sheldrake island and then Fox island. Circled Newcastle wonderful, best trip I have had so far. Pilot was looking for beach for swimming.

A move to No. 6 Bombing & Gunnery School at Mountain View in Ontario took place in early June. Michael was to undertake instruction in air gunnery and would mix with students who were going to be fully trained and operational air gunners, but he was required only to become proficient and capable in the trade as he was to be trained primarily as an observer.

Seven days after arriving at Mountain View, LAC Denis Showell was involved in a crash while flying a camera gun exercise. This was simply a firing exercise, with the student gunner exposing film and not firing bullets from his gun. The film would later be removed from the camera gun and developed, enabling the student to see the errors or accuracy of his firing. The target was normally another aircraft that was simulating an attack on the student's aircraft. Michael merely made a note that Denis's aircraft spun into the ground, killing the crew of three. Fatal accidents during training were always likely to happen; huge numbers of students were passing through these establishments on a continual basis.

As with all accidents in similar circumstances, the deceased were examined by the medical officer and the cause of death was established. In many instances the next of kin desired their loved ones to be buried in close proximity to where they fell. The funeral for Denis was held on 17 June and it involved the entire establishment at Belleville. Michael was part of the funeral escort; great efforts were made by the RCAF to honour Denis, and Michael was proud to have taken part in the ceremony.

The RCAF pilot of the crashed aircraft was Plt Off. Jack McGregor from Regina, Saskatchewan, who was buried in his home cemetery. The third casualty was LAC John Young from New York, who was later buried at the Mount Royal Cemetery, Quebec.

The next stage of training for Michael was the astro navigation course at RCAF Rivers in Manitoba. This operational venue was situated approximately 20 miles from Brandon, which was in itself little more than a hamlet. Rivers was a large airfield base with vast numbers of Avro Anson aircraft parked everywhere; they were effectively flying classrooms for navigation training exercises. With the influx of student observers from all over Canada, the school was a hive of activity. Many hours were spent learning to be proficient with

The image taken by Michael on his training sortie, 11 May 1942.

MOUNTAIN VIEW - ONT.

DESCRIPTION

Age 20

Height 6'2"

Weight 156

Eyes Blue

Hair Dark Brown

Complexion Medium

Visible marks, scars None visible

RCAF G84
40M—10-41 (1034)
H.Q. 885-E. 84

The identification card of Leading Aircraftsman Durell 1319493, issued at Mountain View on 24 June 1942.

the sextant and using it on practice flights. Students were also required to take a considerable number of star shots on the ground and plot them accurately. It was not easy to perform such tasks in the air. The astro navigation device was intended to supplement the other navigational aids and only used in an emergency; for that reason it was always thoroughly tested by the instructors, and a high level of competency was required from every student.

Michael departed Rivers happy to have survived what had been a highly intense training environment. He was fortunate that his university education had provided the very best foundation for him. Towards the end of the year he was serving at the No. 31 General Reconnaissance School at Charlottetown, Prince Edward Island. In the New Year of 1943, wearing sergeant's stripes and an observer's brevet on his uniform, Michael joined the participants at the operational training unit in Debert, Nova Scotia. This unit was operating the Lockheed Hudson, an American-built light bomber and coastal reconnaissance aircraft; training at Debert was focused on long Atlantic ferry flights. The Hudson was to become a significant aircraft in Michael's operational service, but at this time he had no idea what lay ahead.

In May 1943, Michael returned to the UK fully qualified and undertook a short refresher course at No. 1 OTU Thornaby on Teesside, where he teamed up with a pilot called Ron Morris. In September, Michael was given his first operational posting—to Gibraltar with Flt Sgt Morris to serve in No. 48 Squadron Coastal Command, flying Hudson aircraft on patrols over the approaches to the Mediterranean and escort duties for convoys to and from the Allied forces in North Africa. The squadron reported engagements with U-boats on an infrequent basis, but aerial combat was common with Germany's long-range Condor Fw 200 aircraft on patrols along the west coast of Portugal.

During his six-month posting, Michael made twenty-two anti-submarine patrols, five convoy escorts, and two air sea rescue sorties. Those duties amounted to 163 hours and 15 minutes in the air, but at no time did Michael sight a U-boat. On 11 December, he pasted a Reuters newspaper report into his flying log book:

> Twelve German fighters attacked and shot down into the sea a northward-bound four-engined American bomber off the south coast of Portugal today. The sole survivor, whose name is McCoy, was rescued by a fishing boat. Although the attack was of a concentrated nature, it is not believed here that there were any important personalities on board.

This had been just one of many incidents that took place during his operational posting, but fortunately Michael escaped unscathed in every respect.

In February 1944, No. 48 Squadron was withdrawn from Gibraltar. The majority of personnel were posted to RAF Down Ampney in Gloucestershire,

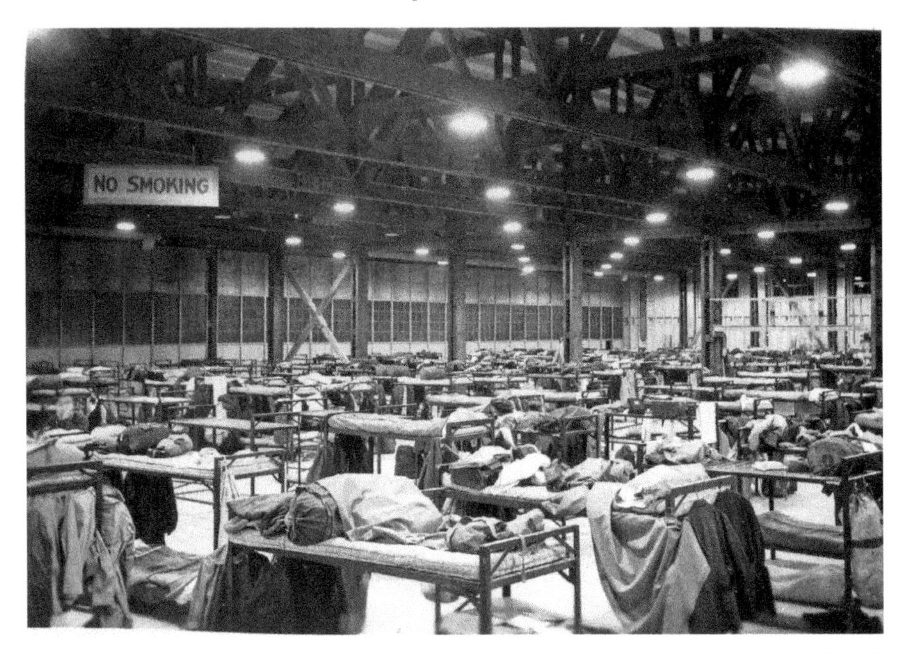

Accommodation at Rivers was in a massive aircraft hangar which the men shared with various wildlife including sparrows and beetles. Students could avoid the invasions of insects by choosing an upper bunk or avoid being bombed by sparrow mess by taking a lower bunk. Michael decided on a lower bunk as the bird population was significant.

The crew at No. 31 Operational Training Unit—the pilot, Sergeant Morris, the navigator, Sergeant Durell, and two wireless operators. Behind is a rather well-used Hudson aircraft with identification lettering rather carelessly applied, indicating changes between various units. A set of snow shoes can be seen in the window of the aircraft.

A No. 48 Squadron Hudson aircraft with the Coastal Command paint scheme. The unmistakable Rock of Gibraltar creates a remarkable backdrop to Michael's photograph.

where they converted to glider towing and parachute dropping duties. Many of these men were later to lose their lives over Arnhem, towing gliders and undertaking parachute drops and supply sorties. Michael and his pilot Ron Morris were to have a different fate. On 21 February, they boarded Dakota KG333 and departed Gibraltar for Portreath on the north coast of Cornwall. The journey, which required an indirect route via the south of Ireland and Wales, took over eleven hours to complete. The following day they flew the same Dakota down to Hendon, where they hoped to hear what was in store for them. It had become obvious that they had been separated from the rest of No. 48 Squadron, although they were not eligible to be classified as 'tour-expired'.

In March 1944, eight operationally experienced Hudson crews were specially selected to join No. 161 Squadron's Special Duties Hudson flight at RAF Tempsford, and Michael and his crew were among them. Before the Second World War, Tempsford was a little-known rural village in Bedfordshire, but in March 1942, from a nearby location known as Gibraltar Farm, the RAF began deploying aircraft on secret duties, delivering agents and saboteurs to occupied Europe. Single-engine Lysanders and twin-engine Hudsons took off from the airfield and landed in France under the very nose of the German forces. Tempsford operated at the highest level of secrecy with two primary squadrons, Nos 138 and 161. A sign on the access road to Gibraltar Farm read, 'This road is closed to the public', and the airfield drew little attention from anyone. Naturally, however, the locals knew an airfield existed in their vicinity: they saw and heard Lysanders, Halifaxes, Stirlings and Hudsons taking off and coming in to land at unusual times; the two local pubs, The Anchor and The Wheatsheaf, were often patronised by men in RAF uniforms; the village's Memorial Hall was frequently used for functions attended by RAF personnel; and the local manor house, Hazells Hall, served as relatively luxurious sleeping quarters for a small group of fortunate officers. The locals did not know anything about the operations that were carried out from this most secret of airfields.

During the three years that Tempsford operated, the Secret Duties squadrons stationed there transported over 1,000 agents, 10,000 packages, several thousand homing pigeons, and 29,000 containers into Western Europe. In addition, they provided direct radio communication links to the agents, a role that is less recognised due to its utmost secrecy at that time. Wg Cdr Pickard was responsible for introducing the Hudson into the squadrons based at Tempsford—it was capable of short landings and thus desirable for the secret-agent work that required covert landings in occupied Europe. The Hudson ideally required clearings or fields of 1,600 metres by 800 metres from which to take off and land—clearly wind direction and geography were crucial in these dangerous operations in the dark.

Michael and Ron joined No. 161 Squadron, one of the most secret squadrons within the RAF, which became known as the 'Moon Squadron' as it operated within full moon periods. Theirs was a trusted partnership and both navigator and pilot had great confidence in each other's abilities. This was a valued attribute, as the Special Duties aircraft and crews were very much lone entities; they had no fighter escort and needed to fly low under the most difficult conditions. Moonlit nights were favoured for Special Duties sorties, but it was exacting work that required the most accurate navigation. Locating the designated landing or dropping zone was often the hardest part of any flight, since reception committees naturally tended to select remote spots in forests or isolated valleys—in the absence of landmarks such as a river, road or railway, these were extremely hard to find. The only help received from the ground were the lights from a few hand-held torches, and these could easily be obscured by ground mist or low cloud. The torch holders flashed an agreed recognition signal and arranged themselves in a pattern to indicate the dropping or landing zones. Many instances exist where agents would be dropped blind, with no reception assistance on the ground, and these operations would be done with the utmost care. If at all possible, many pilots would take great risks in attempting to confirm the terrain before actually dropping their passengers.

Michael's navigation capabilities would be tested to the extreme on these operations. In early March 1944, his crew were trained on 'Gee', a new radio navigation system to be utilised on their secret sorties. The idea behind 'Gee' was fairly simple. A signal was transmitted from a ground station and the time it took to reach a receiver within the aircraft was measured; from this the aircraft's precise distance from the station could be calculated. If two or more stations were used, the location of the aircraft could be pinpointed. Michael had several long training exercises with 'Gee', which incorporated parachute dropping as well as an introduction to 'ascension' training, the direct radio contact with ground agents. During this training, Michael took a photograph of the power station at Little Barford, situated a short distance north of Tempsford, which he frequently used as a turning navigation point in daylight. The cooling tower and the adjacent power station were heavily camouflaged with paint in an effort to disguise them from German reconnaissance flights, but it later emerged that the tower was also used by the Luftwaffe as a navigational aid and was never likely to be targeted.

In addition to its other operations, No. 161 Squadron's Hudson Flight had the specific responsibility of undertaking 'ascension' flights, which again required a high level of navigational accuracy. The aircraft were flown to prearranged locations, normally isolated and remote, where the Hudsons were required to remain to enable agents on the ground to contact the aircraft directly by Ultra High Frequency (UHF) radio equipment. UHF equipment enabled two-way communication and was a safer method of contact for

Great Barford power station was frequently used as a marker and turning point by all the navigators. Although heavily camouflaged with paint, it was always easy to locate with the cooling tower being over 150 feet tall.

the most vulnerable agents, as they could be in open locations for which the equipment had been especially developed. 'Ascension' operations required expert navigational skills to maintain the aircraft's position within the capabilities of the UHF equipment. The use of UHF radio severely limited the ability of German counter-intelligence to locate and intercept radio operators. Even so, many agents were pinpointed by German radio detection equipment while still transmitting. If captured, these brave individuals faced intensive interrogation, torture, and in many cases, death.

Danger and tragedy were not restricted to those brave agents. On the night of 28 March 1944, Hudson FK767 flying from Tempsford crashed, diving into the ground near Arlesey, Bedfordshire. The three RAF crew on board were killed and the sole RCAF member, WO David Gillander, also lost his life. At the request of his family in Manitoba, David was later buried at the impressive military cemetery at Brookwood in Surrey.

The barns of what had been Gibraltar Farm, tucked away at one end of the air base at Tempsford, were used by the SOE for storage and as an agent reception and pre-flight preparation centre. Many agents were parachuted at low level into France and occupied Europe by the Hudson Flight of No. 161 Squadron. The agents, many of whom were female, were driven directly onto the airfield at Tempsford where the aircraft was ready to depart. The crew never knew who the agents were, what operation they were going to carry out, or indeed anything about them at all, and the agents never shared anything more than a polite exchange with the crew. Secrecy was respected in all quarters, and Michael knew that these brave individuals were placing their lives in the hands of others and that their survival chances were limited. It must have been poignant to see a young female completely isolated in a Hudson's fuselage, about to drop into the black sky at the direction of a crew she had only just met.

All agents were referred to as 'Joes', regardless of their sex. Women agents were frequently deployed as they did not initially attract the same attention in occupied Europe as a man of military age, who would normally have been conscripted for forced labour. Women were thus able to move around more easily and made ideal couriers and wireless operators, but dropping them in the correct location was always imperative.

Before he was given full responsibility as a navigator on an 'ascension' operation, Michael first had to pass a challenge set by the squadron's navigation leader to test his navigation skills on operation. The brief, given on the afternoon of 31 March 1944, was to take off from Tempsford and drop one agent and twenty-two containers of supplies to a drop zone in Denmark. Michael was to fly in one of the squadron's Halifax aircraft, piloted by Flt Sgt Tattersall. This was going to be a test of Michael's ability, and the crew's normal navigator would be overseeing his every move. The briefing was clear and the sortie was given the codename 'Tablejam 47', which identified the dropping zone to be in Denmark, and the exact locations where the agent and supplies would be dropped.

Michael Durell's flying log book provides detailed information of the operations on which he flew; together with the squadron's operations record book and the additional top secret details of work reports submitted after every sortie, these sources provide the opportunity to examine Michael's flying career with No. 161 Squadron in extensive detail. His first operation with No. 161 Squadron—the test—took six hours and was completely successful; from that point onwards he rejoined Ron Morris in their Hudson as part of the unit's Special Duties Hudson Flight.

On the night of 5 April 1944, Michael was briefed for an operation to France, identified as 'Stationer 59'. Three agents and three packages were to be carried and dropped to a reception party, which was to be identified by a flashing letter 'B'. This drop, to take place at La Châtre in central France, was estimated to take over six hours to complete. However, on their first run over the target area, none of the crew could see any flashing lights. It was a difficult area; the official report on this operation later stated that the target area was overflown slightly. The aircraft was required to return and navigate another approach, this time between a wooded area and a small village. On this second attempt, the dull but recognisable reception light was eventually seen. It must have been a moment of huge relief for Michael when the light was spotted and, at just 600 feet, the three agents dropped through the fuselage, followed by the three packages. Owing to the problems in locating the dropping zone, the aircraft had been flying over the dropping area for some fifty minutes. Returning across the English Channel, Ron was forced to land at Middle Wallop airfield in Hampshire, most probably being short of fuel. In compliance with orders from RAF Tempsford, the secret equipment was removed and an armed guard was placed on the aircraft; these measures were adopted at any airfield other than their home base, regardless of circumstances. Once able to proceed, the crew departed Middle Wallop at 1610 hours and arrived at Tempsford forty minutes later.

'Stationer 59' was a success. Unknown to Michael and his crew, the agents dropped were Capt. Marcel Leccia (codename 'Baudouin'), Lt Élisée Allard (codename 'Henrique'), and the Belgian radio operator Pierre Geelen. Within their packages was a large sum of money supplied by SOE 'F' (France) Section, which was to be taken to a safe house. SOE operations in France were directed by two London-based country sections: 'F' Section, under British control and strictly non-political; and 'RF' Section, which was linked to General de Gaulle's Free French headquarters. There were also two smaller sections: 'DF', which ran escape lines; and 'EU/P', which dealt with the Polish community in France. The SOE headquarters were in Baker Street, London, and other premises, generally within easy reach of Baker Street, were used for interviews and briefing agents. Country houses known as 'stations' were used for other activities, and agents frequently departed from these direct to the SOE airfields of Tempsford and Tangmere, a Fighter Command airfield in Sussex.

The three agents dropped by Michael and his crew landed safely and reached the safe house where the money was deposited. They were contacted by a double agent who later betrayed them to the Gestapo working in Paris. Leccia, Allard, and Geelen were captured and no doubt tortured at the infamous Fresnes jail in Paris, used by the Gestapo as a base for brutal interrogation and beatings of captured agents. The agony endured by these brave men and women was truly horrific, and many people lost their lives in the jail. In this instance, the three agents survived the brutality of Fresnes, but were subsequently executed at the horrific Buchenwald concentration camp.

On 7 December 1941, Hitler had issued the *Nacht und Nebel* (Night and Fog) Decree. Suspected underground or resistance agents would vanish without a trace; after interrogation the prisoners would be transported to Germany secretly, where they were placed in concentration camps and ultimately executed, with nobody knowing where they had gone.

Another two agents with eight packages were to be flown to France on 9 April, to a location identified only as 'Bob 165'. The Hudson reached the drop zone at 0152 hours, but no reception was sighted. The aircraft remained in the area until 0226 hours, but the 'Joes' were not dropped and the crew were again required to land at another Bomber Command airfield, having been in the air for over seven hours. Permission was given to land at RAF Waterbeach in Cambridgeshire where, once again, an armed guard was immediately placed on the aircraft. The short return to Tempsford took just fifteen minutes; the aircraft took off from Waterbeach at 0905 hours on 10 April.

The flow of agents departing from and arriving at the SOE barn facility was quite exceptional. That evening another sortie was required—operations were always concentrated during full moon periods—but this time they were briefed for two agents to be dropped in Holland. Michael may have wondered what had happened with the two agents he had returned to Tempsford with that morning, but it was of no consequence and most certainly nothing to question. Unknown to Michael, at that time they were all very much playing a part in the Allied plan for the invasion of France, which was then just two months away. The other Tempsford-based squadrons flying the much larger Stirling and Halifax aircraft were just as busy engaged in similar duties, supplying 'Joes' and materials for the SOE network.

For Michael in his small Hudson aircraft, that evening's flight to Holland—Operation Bradfield—required the dropping of two French Secret Intelligence Service (SIS) agents, also known as MI6 Secret or Special Intelligence Service agents. It was to be a blind drop, depending entirely on Michael's expert navigation—a 'dead reckoning' run at 500 feet from a flooded landmark pinpointing the confluence of the rivers Maas and Waal at Rossum. The normal procedure for an agent about to parachute from a Hudson was to sit with legs dangling through a hole in the floor of the fuselage and then, at a given hand signal, push off from the edge and down through the hole. The parachute would open automatically when the weight of the parachutist's body pulled a static line attached within the aircraft. The low heights adopted for dropping supplies and agents restricted the time they were in the air, and this increased the need for accuracy of the drop. To Michael's credit, during Operation Bradfield the agents were safely dropped in the target area.

Another SIS agent was taken to Holland on the night of 6 May, along with a container of several pigeons to be dropped at the same time. During the Second World War, the National Pigeon Service (NPS) supplied birds to the RAF for sending messages in emergency situations. The SOE also required considerable numbers of pigeons, but these were for dropping across occupied Europe, to be used by resistance operatives who sent information back to Britain in message pods attached to the birds' legs. During May 1944, in excess of 800 pigeons were dropped by aircraft flying from Tempsford. The NPS trained significant numbers of pigeons and assisted in developing the various means adopted to both carry and deliver the birds safely by parachute.

A sortie to Holland, codenamed 'St Valentines', took off from Tempsford just prior to midnight on 6 May. During the journey it was noticed that the pigeons had been wrongly marked with French rather than Dutch details; it was therefore decided to retain the birds and return them to Tempsford. The lone agent was dropped blind after an impressive 200-foot-high 'dead reckoning' navigational run—both the 'Joe' and the container were dropped safely. However, Michael's successful streak was bound to end sometime. On 9 May an operation over France could not be completed as there was no reception committee on the ground. From then on the number of operations reduced significantly with the changing phase of the moon.

Every operational sortie flown by No. 161 Squadron required the pilot to submit an ops report. The form was fairly large, with twelve areas to be completed, including details of the pilot, aircraft, personnel, and equipment to be dropped, instructions to the captain at the drop zone, the result at the drop zone, times, routes, enemy opposition, and the pilot's general comments. Each report was signed after inspection by the squadron's commanding officer, and these records now form the basis of much post-war research. In addition, each crew member was required to maintain his own flying log book. However, many log entries made when serving at such secret bases as Tempsford simply say, 'Operations as ordered'.

At 2245 hours on 28 May 1944, Hudson 'M', carrying two French agents and two packages, took off from RAF Tempsford with Michael as navigator. The operation was 'Overture II', with a drop area identified near Possigny

Date	Hour	Aircraft Type and No.	Pilot	Duty	Remarks (Including results of bombing, gunnery, exercises, etc.)	Flying Times Day	Flying Times Night
					Tim carried forward:—	475:55	103:25
3·4·44	1205	HUDSON M	F/S MORRIS	AIR TEST		00:20	
5·4·44	2145	HUDSON N	F/S MORRIS	OPS France	Landed at Middle Wallop. DCO (2)		06:15
6·4·44	1610	HUDSON N	F/S MORRIS	X Country	Middle Wallop – Base	00:40	
9·4·44	2250	HUDSON R	F/S MORRIS	OPS FRANCE	Landed at Waterbeach DNCO (3)		07:10
10·4·44	0905	HUDSON R	F/S MORRIS	X Country	Water Beach – Base	00:15	
10·4·44	2320	HUDSON R	F/S MORRIS	OPS HOLLAND	As detailed DCO (4)		03:30
27·4·44	1500	HUDSON S	F/S MORRIS	Local	flying	00:35	
30·4·44	1420	HUDSN N	S/L WILKINSON	Asc OPS	DCO	03:20	
			SUMMARY FOR	APRIL			
R.E. Wilkinson S/L			UNIT	161 Sqdn	TOTAL OPS APRIL	03:20	16:65
O.C. 'C' flight			DATE	2 MARCH 1944	TOTAL NON OPS APRIL	01:60	—
			SIGNED	M.A. Durell F/S.	TOTAL OPS 161 SQDN	14:25	22:05
[illegible] W/Cdr							
OC 161 Squadron							
2·5·44	1530	HUDSON M	F/S MORRIS	X Country	Waterbeach – Newmarket – Lincoln	02:15	
6·5·44	2355	HUDSON M	F/S MORRIS	OPS HOLLAND	As detailed DCO (5)		03:05
9·5·44	2145	HUDSON P	F/S MORRIS	OPS FRANCE	As detailed DNCO (6)		07:35
13·5·44	1130	HUDSON O	F/S MORRIS	X Country	Rugby – Westcott – Hartford Bridge	02:10	
12·5·44	1720	HUDSON L	F/S MORRIS	OPS Asc	DNCO	02:05	
15·5·44	1540	HUDSON P	S/L WILKINSON	Tugater	affil	00:40	
					TOTAL TIME....	488:15	131:00

Michael Durell's flying log book entries with No. 161 Squadron for April and May 1944. The pages illustrate the type of entries made at this secret airfield and hold the signatures of Flight Sergeant Durell, 'C' Flight Commander Squadron Leader Wilkinson, and the Hudson Flight commanding officer, Wg Cdr Boxer, later Air Vice Marshal Sir Alan Boxer.

in France. One of the agents was Bernard Bermond, and with him was his wireless operator Joseph Rocca-Serra. Both men were OSS agents attached to the Bureau Central de Renseignements et d'Action (BCRA), which had been created by the Free French during the early part of the war. The drop zone was identified by white flashing lights indicating the correct letter 'K', and the agents were safely deployed at 0127 hours.

The OSS Jedburgh teams were used on sabotage operations and also provided much-needed leadership for local resistance groups. Each team, consisting of men from the British SOE and the American OSS, together with men from the BCRA and the Dutch and Belgian armies, comprised a leader, an executive officer, and a non-commissioned radio operator. One of the officers would be British or American, and the other agent would be from the country to which the teams were being deployed.

The squadron's Hudsons suffered constant losses while on incursions into Europe with their 'Joes' and packages. The first operation in June 1944 saw No. 161 Squadron's Hudson V9155 fail to return from its sortie into Holland. The crew and one agent lost their lives in an area close to the Luftwaffe aerodrome at Gilze-Rijen. The Canadian pilot of this Hudson, Flt Lt W. M. Hale, was buried in Gilze, but after the war his body was recovered and reburied in the Canadian War Cemetery at Bergen-op-Zoom in Holland.

Little is known about when personnel at Tempsford were informed of the D-Day invasion, although the station had been engaged in significant duties delivering agents and many supplies, indicating a probable connection to the impending event. Meanwhile, on the night of 5 June, Michael was engaged on Operation Harlech. He progressed to Holland safely, but then his aircraft's intercom broke down. No. 161 Squadron had suffered several losses from night fighter attacks previously, and Ron Morris had no desire to remain over occupied territory with no means of communicating with any of his crew.

Back at Tempsford, newly promoted Plt Off. Tattersall, who had taken Michael on his test flight to France, took off in one of No. 161 Squadron's Halifaxes. Inside his aircraft were five men operating as a team, codenamed 'Hugh', under SOE command, but directly responsible to Special Forces HQ. A

Michael Durell's Hudson aircraft at RAF Tempsford with the squadron code lettering 'MA' clearly illustrated. The heavy camouflage on the fuselage and wings was standard with aircraft on No. 161 Squadron. Photographs taken at Tempsford are rarely seen due to the secrecy of the airfield.

British SAS team was to be dropped with orders to integrate with the Maquis in the Indre region of France under a special operation connected to the invasion known as Operation Bulbasket. Other aircraft at Tempsford that night were engaged in Operation Titanic, which was a direct contribution to the Allied invasion—they were dropping dummy paratrooper 'dolls' onto preselected target areas. Eleven aircraft dropped the dummy figures to create a decoy, taking the attention of the Germans away from the actual target areas. The 'dolls' created an illusion that was supported by fake gunfire and pyrotechnics, all of which was likely to induce radio or telephone communications to various German HQs, adding to the confusion about the true nature of events.

Another key component to the D-Day invasion was the rather problematic 'ascension' programme. The equipment had been designed and built by the Radio Communications Division of SOE, its development culminating in what was called the S-Phone. The agents had a backpack with shoulder straps that held the set with its directional aerial on the wearer's chest. A waist belt contained seven canvas pouches, five for batteries, the others for earphones, microphone, and aerial. The equipment had a variable range of efficiency, and most crews adopted their own preferred methods to make and retain contact with the agents using the device; however, the S-Phone proved to be more reliable in maintaining contact with the Tempsford Hudson flight.

The SIS and SOE had distributed the S-Phone equipment to several agents, and reception meetings at various locations were to become regular sorties allocated to Michael's crew. The first operation, on 9 June, resulted in no reception from the ground, and the same occurred on 1 July. Two nights later, Michael was briefed to drop two agents into France. Operation Destroyer was flown in Hudson 'P' on a direct route crossing Littlehampton on the south coast and over the strengthening Allied bridgeheads in Normandy. It was a blind drop for the two agents, who fell away safely from the aircraft, their parachutes opening correctly.

Another delivery of agents was required on the night of 5 July, this time to Holland. A total of fifteen agents were to be delivered across the lowlands that night—not an exceptional number of agents, as many operations required three or four of the squadron's Hudsons to deliver their 'Joes' simultaneously on one operation. Hudson FK790 was shot down by a night fighter over the Wadden sea mudflats that night, and the four agents and crew all lost their lives. However, Michael and his crew inside Hudson 'L' safely reached their dropping zone and successfully dropped three agents, one package and ten pigeons close to Elburg in central Holland. It was an excellent drop, with the aircraft only remaining over the dispatch area between 0142 hours and 0148 hours. Michael had no knowledge that these agents were Leonard Mulholland (codename 'Podex'), an SOE operative with 'N' Section who was later arrested by the Gestapo on 11 November 1944, and his wireless operator Arie van

A No. 161 Squadron Hudson with Michael Durell far left. The dispersal area provides a view of Gibraltar Farm Farmhouse in the background, and the special purpose huts can just be seen. In all probability these housed the stores that were packed into the various containers and dropped by Tempsford's aircraft. The Hudson aircraft aerials are clearly seen protruding on each side of the forward section of fuselage. The pilot Ron Morris is standing far right and Warrant Officers Street and Dunseith, wireless operator and air gunner, are standing in the middle respectively.

Duyn (codename 'Cribbage'), who dropped with him and was arrested while transmitting on 19 December. The third agent dropped that night was Bert de Goede (codename 'Rummy'). These three Dutch agents, all of whom had associations with the merchant marine, settled successfully in Rotterdam and were highly productive in their work for some sixteen weeks, which was worthy of recognition. It has been recorded that an SOE agent's life expectancy in the field (France) was only six weeks.

When Ron Morris was promoted to Pilot Officer, the nature of his close friendship with Michael was affected as officers and other ranks were separated, each having individual mess arrangements. For Michael and Ron, this situation merely induced more visits to the local pub in order to socialise together, but it would be another four months before Michael would be commissioned, joining Ron in the Officers' Mess. On 10 July, they took a Hudson to France, dropping two containers and one package at a reception point that was immediately identified with the correct letter signalled by torchlight. Within four minutes of reaching their objective, the goods had been dropped and they were on their back to Tempsford. The containers had been packed by the SOE section, and the crews transporting them had no idea what was inside. It was presumed that arms, ammunition, and demolition equipment would be the normal loads. Packages were smaller than containers, but again the contents were never known. Regardless of this, all deliveries were treated as being highly valuable to the agents and their resistance networks on the ground. It is worth mentioning that what might appear to have been simple package delivery operations still required enormous skill from the crews. If dropped from too high, the packages were liable to drift and land away from the dropping area, while if dropped too low, they could land heavily and split or rupture the containers, damaging or destroying the contents.

Several 'ascension' sorties were flown during July and August, but making contact with the agents was proving difficult. Michael was exceptional at navigation, but despite always being in the required location for an extended period, very few positive contacts were made. Those that were positive were transcribed by the wireless operator and the information was immediately handed to SOE personnel, who were always waiting at Tempsford. Also in August, four agents, two packages, and a load of pigeons were successfully blind dropped in Holland. Among those agents were Seerp Postma (codename

Ron Morris and Michael Durell in the cockpit of their Hudson—both are wearing the 'B' Type flying helmets. The Perspex canopy shows the emergency exit or crash points for breaking into the cockpit and the guide lines that allow blinds to be closed if required. The pilot and navigator frequently communicated like this while flying on 'Special Duty' SOE operations.

'Sculling') and his wireless operator Gerrit Reisiger (codename 'Turniquoits'), both of whom were SOE operatives. The short-wave transmitters or transceivers used by the radio operators were normally contained in a small suitcase; these units weighed about 30 lbs but required an aerial some 7 feet long to be arranged to send Morse transmissions. The agents worked in the Utrecht district and formed an efficient group until an unfortunate interception of a courier led to Postma's arrest on 22 November. He was later executed on 2 December, no doubt having suffered terribly at the hands of the Gestapo. Reisiger, another of those captured by the German intelligence radio direction-finding units, was detained on 27 December 1944. He was also executed, but not until March 1945, when the SS purged Neuengamme concentration camp near Hamburg of its sorrowful prisoners.

A lone operation by Michael and his crew took place on 10 September, once again to France, but this time they landed at Amiens. The city had recently been liberated and was exceptionally close to the Allied lines. The operation was named 'Titan', but little information is available to establish exactly what was involved. Michael's flying log book records the sortie as having been undertaken in daylight, simply noting 'Ops France landed Amiens'.

Amiens is a location now etched in RAF history; it was the scene of the impressive specialist operation by No. 140 Wing's Mosquito squadrons. The audacious aim of Operation Jericho on 18 February 1944 was to knock down the walls of Amiens prison to facilitate a mass breakout of resistance fighters and political prisoners. There were several hundred prisoners detained in the jail, many condemned to death, and the resistance had called for the RAF to bomb the walls to help them escape. It was an audacious and dangerous proposition, requiring pinpoint accuracy at very low level. The resistance accepted that lives would be lost, but nevertheless asked that it be carried out. Conflicting statistics exist, but the figures of 102 men killed, 74 wounded and 258 escaped illustrate the costliness of the operation. Among those prisoners who escaped were several important members of the resistance movement. Many would later be recaptured. This raid is also famous for claiming the life of Gp Capt. Pickard, the first RAF officer in the Second World War to be awarded the DSO and two bars.

From 14 September onwards, No. 161 Squadron's Hudsons were deployed on regular supply and special delivery flights into Brussels. Michael and his crew undertook fifteen sorties, concluding on 15 October. Prince Bernhard, who had been appointed by Queen Wilhelmina of the Netherlands to act as the liaison officer between the Dutch and British forces, had arranged for the Hudsons to fly 50 tons of small arms and explosives into Brussels in order to supply the resistance network that was still operating in Holland. The prince had trained as a pilot, gaining his 'wings' in 1941, and was given the honorary rank of Wing Commander in the RAF that year. Thereafter he often flew with his Sealyham terrier Martin, which logged more than 1,000 flying hours with his master before his death in 1954.

A real sense of achievement was felt by the crew when flying to several reoccupied airfields throughout France and Belgium, but No. 161 Squadron was still very much in demand for its Special Duties capabilities, delivering agents deeper into occupied Europe. On 20 November, Ron Morris was required for a special daylight 'ascension' operation in Holland. He and Michael were in their most regular Hudson, boldly marked 'M' on the fuselage, which was their favourite aircraft. The flight was nearly four hours long and they spent a great deal of time locating the agent in awful weather conditions. At one stage the aircraft was even struck by lightening; the crew were relieved to land unscathed at Tempsford shortly before 1800 hours. Lightning strikes caused chaos with compasses and, sometimes, fatal accidents. Michael and Ron had been very lucky.

On their next sortie, Operation Alder into Germany on 26 November, Michael performed an excellent job of pinpoint navigation in poor conditions. They were carrying an SIS agent intended to be dropped on a blind delivery. Having crossed successfully into the Rhine area, ground fog made navigation impossible, and they were forced to return and land at SOE's other airfield at Tangmere. Hudson T9463 had also been sent to Germany that night, but crashed on its return flight after dropping its agent. The aircraft came down near the border of Belgium and Luxembourg, adding to the ever-increasing losses of No. 161 Squadron. Michael had flown in that particular aircraft on more than a dozen occasions. Later that day, he took off from Tangmere and flew over the rolling South Downs of Sussex, landing at Tempsford forty minutes later.

Michael received notification of his promotion to Flying Officer on the last day of November 1944. As an officer it was Michael's responsibility to purchase his own uniform, and it was a pleasant task to arrange for a fitting, with Ron ensuring that he went to a tailor of repute. At last Michael could join his pilot and close friend in the Officers' Mess. Christmas was definitely worth looking forward to that year.

Michael's first operational flight as an officer was on the last night of 1944. Four of Tempsford's Hudson aircraft were tasked to fly deep penetration sorties into Germany, recorded as Operation Juniper. In Michael's aircraft sat two agents who were successfully dropped blind. Developments in communication aids may well explain the significantly high number of blind drops conducted by the SOE. Devices known as 'Eureka' radar beacons, which were regarded as highly secret, were capable of being deployed by agents behind enemy lines to mark clandestine drop zones. The SOE aircraft were fitted with the counterpart of 'Eureka', which was capable of locating the radar beacon. Getting the aircraft as close as possible to the drop zone was clearly imperative; in the darkness, the use of this device explains the

Prince Bernhard of the Netherlands in his battledress tunic, admiring his Sealyham terrier, which is wearing the special harness to which a small parachute could be attached. The dog accompanied the prince on all his sorties in his own aircraft. Prince Bernhard was instrumental in many operational matters concerning the deployment and operations of agents across the Netherlands.

Michael in the forward section of the Hudson cockpit where he operated as navigator. The views provided from the Perspex sections of the Hudson were excellent. The navigator's lamp fixed to the roof allowed him to adjust it into several positions and was capable of being dimmed or brightened as required.

consistently accurate and successful results for blind drops achieved by crews of No. 161 Squadron.

The year 1945 commenced with a period of exceptional snow and freezing conditions which restricted the use of Tempsford airfield. Despite this, No. 161 Squadron attempted seven 'ascensions' in Holland for intelligence gathering, but contact was established on only two occasions. These were to prove to be the last operations of this nature, not only for Michael's crew, but for the squadron as a whole.

In February, two consecutive nights saw Michael enter Germany once more. On 21 February, it proved possible to drop their SIS agent, but the following night the weather caused them to turn back despite having spent a lot of time over Germany seeking a break in the weather. In cases where the primary objective of dropping agents or parcels was aborted, crews were instructed to drop propaganda leaflets over locations identified at the briefing. In this instance, Michael dropped leaflets over four areas: Ochtrup, Bentheim, Nordhorn, and Emlichheim. Leaflets fluttered down in their thousands, scattering across large swathes of residential areas.

In March, weather conditions caused problems at Tempsford once again. Michael's crew attempted an operation into Germany once more on the

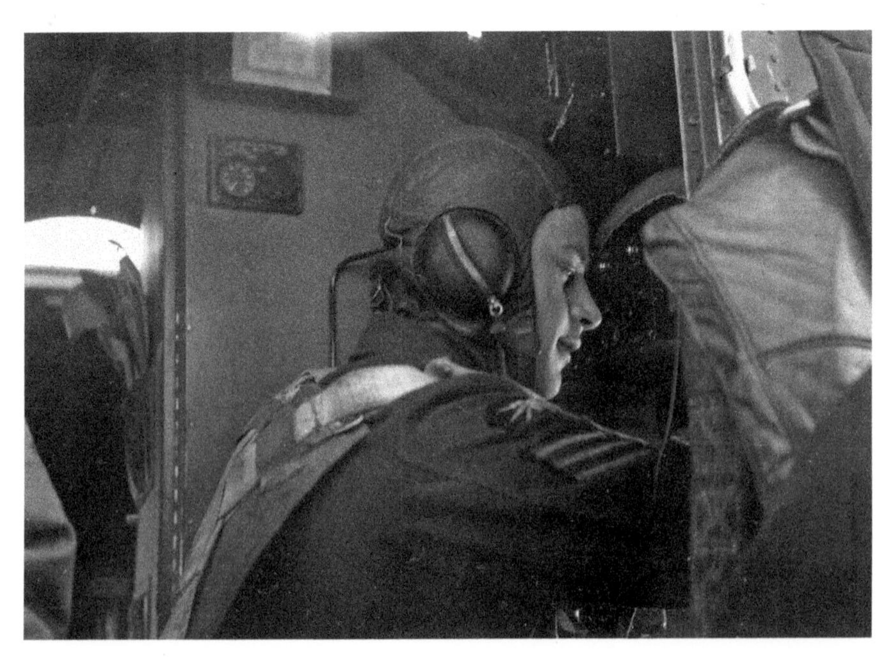

The crew's wireless operator Jack Street at work at his station. The wireless operator's work station was relatively close to the cockpit, as can be seen in this rare example of No. 161 Squadron at work. 'Eureka' radar would have been operated by wireless operators.

second day of the month, but again it was impossible to complete, not only for them but also for the other two Hudsons that attempted sorties that night. It was the same story the following evening, except with the addition of an unexpected Luftwaffe incursion over Mildenhall in Suffolk. As a Hudson flown by Fg Off. Ragan departed Tempsford and gained height, the night fighter attacked and caused serious damage, injuring some crew members. The experienced pilot displayed excellent skills in managing to return to Tempsford safely. However, for Michael's crew in Hudson 'P', they again had to make do with scattering leaflets.

No. 161 Squadron sent five Hudsons to Germany on the night of 20 March, and Michael and his crew finally completed Operation Acacia, which had been outstanding from the first failed operation that month. The crew returned safely, having deposited their agent. However, three other Hudsons failed to return to Tempsford that night. Hudson T9445 was lost near Samrée in Belgium together with the entire crew consisting of Flt Lt Allan Penhale, Fg Off. James Traill, Flt Lt Richard Ferris, and WO Robert Hutton. In accordance with the common wartime practice of burying air crew casualties close to their crash sites, these Canadian compatriots would later lie together when reburied at the war cemetery at Heverlee in Belgium. Another Hudson, AE595, was shot down east of the airfield at Rheine in Germany. The aircraft's pilot, Fg Off. Ragan, commanded a crew made up of RAF, RNZAF, and RCAF personnel, illustrating the diversity of Commonwealth forces engaged in flying from Tempsford.

Some parts of Holland remained in occupation during April 1945, and two SIS agents were dropped by Michael on the third day of that month. The following night, an eight-hour operation into deepest Germany saw another two OSS agents dropped from Michael's aircraft. The RAF's 2nd TAF squadrons were constantly attacking German vehicles withdrawing eastwards from Holland at this time.

Despite the end of the war being in sight, the SOE continued to send agents into Germany. Many of the orders given to these men and women remain unknown to this day. On 19 April, Michael transcribed into his flying log book 'Operations Germany Crossed Denmark'. This was a long sortie, leaving Tempsford at 2035 hours and returning at around 0500 hours. Four agents were dropped in two pairs over separate locations.

A bizarre incident was to take place in a Hudson 'L' that took off from Tempsford at 2105 hours on 21 April 1945. Ron and Michael had flown and navigated their aircraft with exceptional skill and ability on numerous sorties, carrying many agents and packages across occupied Europe. On this particular operation, 'Alder II', they were carrying two agents with two pedal cycles. Clearly, these agents had special orders and were expected to travel some distance after their parachute descent. The long flight was successful, crossing Denmark and then on into Germany. A member of the crew was

required to assist with the drop, as getting the bicycles out would be more difficult than handling a simple package. Unexpectedly, the two agents refused to be dropped. Michael had never before witnessed a refusal, and it became clear after two further runs over the drop zone that he would need to return the agents to Tempsford. Hudson 'L' landed safely at 0600 hours and the SOE contingent took control of the unusual events of that final operation.

This was a highly unusual occurrence, as all agents were thoroughly trained. Radio operators in particular undertook around nine months of intensive training—they were expected to be able to transmit twenty-two words per minute. All agents, regardless of their role, would have undertaken a minimum of five training parachute jumps and have been assessed as competent.

Two nights later, on 23 April, Michael Durell was briefed for what was to become his last operational flight during the Second World War. Four fully equipped agents were collected from the barns at Gibraltar Farm, to be carried across the English Channel and France and dropped into the night sky over Germany. The dropping area was heavy with cloud, but there was sufficient break-up for Michael to pinpoint it; within six minutes all four agents and two packages were safely suspended under their silk parachutes and descending into what was left of Nazi Germany. The final act of scattering propaganda leaflets took place over Germany, and Ron Morris safely landed Hudson 'L' back on the runway at Tempsford at 0440 hours on the morning of 24 April. The following day, news was broadcast that the Russian forces had fully encircled Berlin. Germany ultimately surrendered to the Allied forces on 8 May.

Michael Durell departed RAF Tempsford having recorded twenty-seven operational flights into the dangerous skies of Europe to deliver agents and equipment. These included seven duties to France, seven to Holland, and thirteen into Germany. In excess of fifty agents were parachuted with precision to their required dropping zones; several of those incredibly brave men and women were subsequently captured, tortured, and executed by the Gestapo. The full extent of the successful work achieved by these remarkable people will probably never be known in any detail, but what can be clearly understood is that the SOE contributed significantly towards the success of the Allied invasion of occupied Europe, and to the ultimate conquering of the Nazi regime during the Second World War.

Michael was to witness first-hand the barbarity of the Third Reich. After the surrender of Germany, the RAF immediately employed massive resources to repatriate Allied PoWs from the many prisoner-of-war camps. Collection centres were created to manage the task of repatriation at the earliest opportunity. Lüneburg Heath was close to Belsen concentration camp and

Opposite: Warrant Officers Street and Dunseith, the wireless operator and air gunner on Michael Durell's crew, alongside their Hudson at RAF Tempsford.

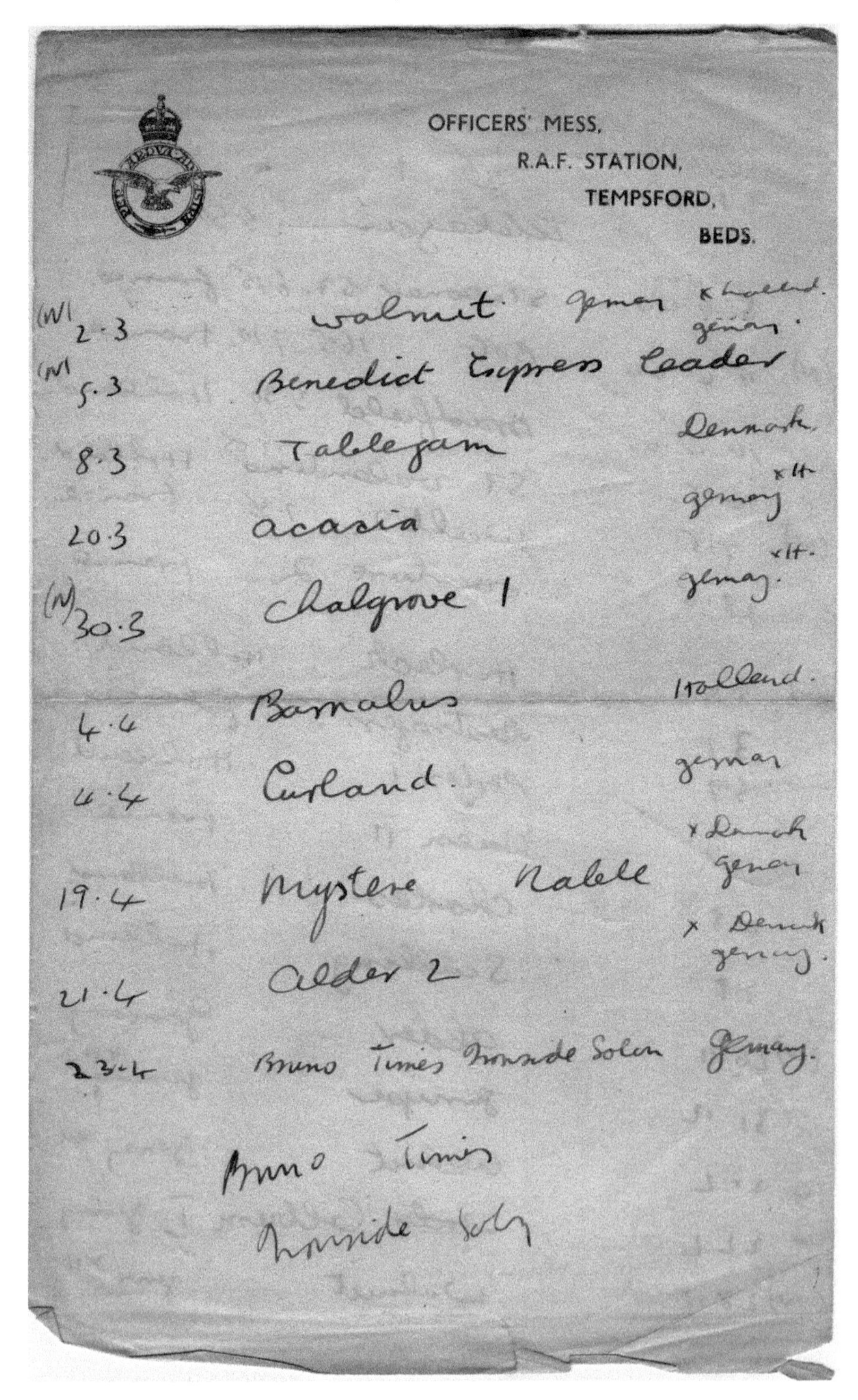

OFFICERS' MESS,
R.A.F. STATION,
TEMPSFORD,
BEDS.

(W) 2.3 walnut german x holland. german.
(W) 5.3 Benedict Cypress Leader
8.3 Tablegam Denmark
20.3 acacia germany x H
(W) 30.3 Chalgrove 1 germany x H.
4.4 Barnabus Holland.
4.4 Curland. german
19.4 Mystere Nabele x Denmark german
21.4 Alder 2 x Denmark germany.
23.4 Bruno Times Ironside Solon Germany.
Bruno Times
Ironside Solon

RAF Tempsford note paper with rough calculations of secret SOE dropping sorties made by Flying Officer Durell.

Field Marshal Montgomery receiving the official acceptance of 'Unconditional Surrender' by Germany. The signing, marking the end of the war in Europe, was filmed by Pathé News and recorded on BBC radio.

was also where Germany had unconditionally surrendered to Field Marshal Bernard Montgomery on 4 May 1945.

Michael and his crew flew to Lüneburg Heath on 9 May to collect and repatriate PoWs to RAF Ford in Sussex. Some of the Allied prisoners had been incarcerated since 1940, and many were emaciated and in poor health. The evidence of the poor treatment at Belsen was tangible, but the duty of collecting and transporting Allied soldiers, sailors, and airmen back to Britain was a joy to take part in. Two subsequent sorties to Lüneburg followed, and forty-one men were recovered by Michael and his crew in their relatively small and unassuming Hudson aircraft.

On 16 May 1945, Air Cdre Singer, the Air Officer Commanding, HQ No. 38 Group, read the recommendation of work relating to Fg Off. Michael Durell. It had been submitted by the wing commander of his squadron, and made reference to the fact that Michael had completed sixty-two operational

Michael Durell's Hudson with her cargo of Allied prisoners of war—some are wearing Army, Navy, and RAF uniforms, all in various conditions of dishevelment. These men had longed for the day of returning home; for Michael, this was the most pleasing duty he could have been given.

sorties and was a pioneer of new operational techniques adopted by No. 161 Squadron. The air commodore endorsed the report, recommending the award of the DFC. The war had been won and Michael's award was among many late or post-war recommendations that were documented within the formal procedures. On 20 June 1946 Michael left the RAF, but it was not until Tuesday 30 June 1953 that he attended Buckingham Palace to accept his well-deserved award. All DFC medals were issued with just the year of the award engraved on the reverse; Michael expressed his pride in his award by requesting that it be additionally engraved privately with his name and squadron.

After the war, Michael served his local community in Long Melford, Suffolk, where he owned the Oakleigh Stores until his untimely death in 1977, aged just fifty-five.

4

Alfred Webb DFC and Bar
Operation Colossus

Alfred Denys Webb was born on 15 January 1913 in Chester, where his father was the curate at St Peter's Church. Although Alfred had enjoyed the family life of his childhood, at the first opportunity he went to sea, seeking employment with the New Zealand Steam Ship Company and serving as a cadet aboard the freighter SS *Northumberland*. The Merchant Services provided the opportunity of seeing the world, and Alfred, an adventurer at heart, celebrated his eighteenth birthday while at sea, en route to New Zealand. On 3 February 1931, SS *Northumberland* was at anchor in Napier in Hawke's Bay, on the east coast of the North Island, where the crew were loading frozen meat on board. The weather had been warm and there had been no warning of anything untoward, when at 1047 hours a significant earthquake struck. An initial violent shock was closely followed by a second tremor that rocked the area for almost three minutes, creating a severe shockwave that sent a cloud of dust over the harbour. The wireless officer on board sent the first distress calls to London, as it was apparent that all the telegraph lines ashore had been destroyed and fires had broken out across the stricken area. The ship's captain sent the crew's first and third officers, along with the doctor and twenty-eight members of general hands, to help with the disaster. These men set up a food and water station at the school in Hastings Street. The earthquake had caused devastation to the town's buildings and many of the inhabitants had been killed by falling masonry. The total loss of life was eventually counted at 256 people.

Back home in the UK in 1936, Alfred was inspired by the active recruitment campaign run by the RAF; following the submission of a successful application he left the Merchant Service and enlisted into the air force. He adapted well to service life, having the advantage of previously experiencing the discipline of serving at sea, and his progression through initial RAF training presented little challenge for him. Alfred was additionally accepted for air crew training and attended No. 9 Bombing and Gunnery School at Penrhos in Caernarvonshire. It was here that he was introduced to the isolated world of rear gunnery, a trade that he was to excel at in later years. Alfred had witnessed Britain's deteriorating relations with Germany and the build-up of its military services, so when war was eventually declared on 3 September 1939, it came as no great surprise to him.

On 7 April 1940, Alfred was commissioned as a pilot officer air gunner. He was then posted to join No. 78 Squadron, Bomber Command, on 13 May 1940. Despite his officer status, Alfred was well respected by all ranks, being unofficially addressed as 'Webby', and he endeared himself to all those around him. He had a keen sense of humour and an ability to make up limericks and ditties that were enjoyed by all, particularly in the Officers' Mess. His squadron was equipped with Whitley bombers, and since the outbreak of war it had been tasked with the training of newly formed bomber crews prior to posting onto operational squadrons. Armstrong Whitworth Whitley aircraft began to enter RAF service in the early months of 1937, and by the outbreak of war they were the mainstay of numerous bomber squadrons. More than 1,800 of the type were to be built to meet the Air Ministry's specifications and orders. Capt. Archie Frazer-Nash has a strong association with the history of the Second World War, and is credited with designing the first power-operated gunner turret; his designs were constructed at the manufacturing base of Parnall Aircraft Limited at Tolworth in Surrey. Frazer-Nash turrets were installed in the Whitley aircraft, which subsequently achieved some of the major milestones of the early war years, including the first widespread leaflet raids over Germany in September 1939, the first bombing raid on Germany in May 1940, and the first British SAS airborne troop deployment over southern Italy in February 1941. Much of this we shall learn of later, as Alfred was engaged on that Special Duties operation.

Alfred had been slightly frustrated at not becoming operational, but eventually his squadron joined the front-line bomber force in July 1940. The rear turret Alfred occupied in the Whitley was the Frazer-Nash model, and he sat alone with the upright twin rudders on the aircraft's tailplane always in his peripheral vision as he guarded the aircraft against all fighter attacks from the rear with his Browning machine guns. The turning turret of the Whitley created the impression of being hung on the extremities of the fuselage, and its mobility allowed Alfred to monitor the sky effectively. However, in common with most gunners' turrets when operating at the very low temperatures experienced on night operations, the view was often restricted by mist and frost glazing over the Perspex panels. The removal of the front panel soon became widespread, which led to an official modification to the Frazer-Nash turret, whereby the front panel was mounted in side grooves, allowing it to be dropped down in order to give a clear frontal view. The technical field of view available to the rear gunner was a 94-degree traverse to each beam, an elevation of 60 degrees and a depression of 45 degrees.

The first opportunity for Alfred to enter 'operations' in his flying log book came on 21 July 1940, when he experienced the searchlights and flak over the

A Whitley aircraft, serial Z3640. The squadron code lettering EY has been blacked out, leaving the single identity letter Y visible. The Frazer Nash rear gunner's turret is surrounded by the unusual rudder and tail plane configuration.

substantial railway marshalling yards at Hamm in Germany. The bomb load was dropped accurately from 9,500 feet and exploded on the railway lines and installations below. During the following eight days he attacked Osnabrück, Sterkrade, and Wismar; in those initial operations in July, Alfred was encased behind his Perspex turret for twenty-eight hours and forty minutes. Operations continued into 1940, and Alfred flew a further seventeen before the end of the year. These included attacks on the German capital ships *Scharnhorst*, *Admiral Hipper*, and *Lützow* at Kiel, and the bombing of major German cities including Berlin. On one occasion, Alfred experienced a rather fraught forced landing on his return from Germany after responding to a sighting of a Luftwaffe night fighter.

The bombing of the Dortmund-Ems Canal on 29 October 1940 was to be one of Alfred's most important operations. The canal was vital to Germany's war effort since it formed part of an extensive industrial transportation system for heavy barges; aware that it was a likely target for the RAF, the Germans had brought in several hundred flak guns to defend the canal's infrastructure. Batteries of heavy flak units were deployed near the canal, and smaller flak units were located at locks and vulnerable safety gates. Alfred experienced the ferocious defences of the Dortmund-Ems Canal from the rear turret of his Whitley bomber; he appeared to be completely surrounded by exploding flak shells and expected at any moment to be shot out the air. Fortunately, his crew completed the operation successfully, but on examining their aircraft back at the airfield they found it had sustained flak damage in no fewer than six locations. Any one of these hits could have killed crewmembers or severed oil or fuel lines with catastrophic results.

It fell to Alfred as an officer air gunner to be appointed as the squadron's gunnery leader. This was a position of great responsibility as he was in charge of all air gunners on the station, but he was aware at that time that Bomber Command had additionally selected him to be among an elite group of forty-one air crew who were to be trained for very secret Special Duties. On 9 January 1941, Alfred joined the strength of those selected crews who were to fly specially modified Whitley bombers to practise dropping paratroopers. He was to be crewed with Sub-Lt Peter John Hoad, a naval pilot on attachment to the RAF from HMS *Daedalus*. Hoad had previously flown as a second pilot on several raids, but was now commanding his own crew.

The Army had previously selected volunteers from No. 2 Commando to undertake paratrooper drops, and to acknowledge their new role the first British parachute unit became the 11th SAS Battalion. The British SAS is of course now world famous, but this operation was to be their very first deployment. Thirty-eight men, comprising seven officers and thirty-one other ranks, were

Alfred Webb is standing far left, and next to him is Peter Hoad, immediately identifiable in his dark Royal Naval Air Service uniform. The other men in Irving flying jackets are presumably members of Alfred's crew.

designated as 'X' Troop, commanded by Maj. Pritchard, formerly of the Royal Welch Fusiliers. Attached to them were three Italian-speaking interpreters, Sqn Ldr Lucky MC, Rifleman Nastri of the Rifle Brigade, and a civilian, Fortunato Picchi. The objective of the operation, regarded as top secret, was to deprive the three significant Axis ports of Taranto, Brindisi, and Bari of their fresh water supply carried by the *Acquedotto Pugliese*. It was also known as the Tragino Aqueduct, and was built partly by a British company, George Kent & Sons, in 1914. Some plans and construction details of the aqueduct were used in the planning of this operation, but they were not comprehensive. The aqueduct was effectively a reinforced spanning concrete box on an elevated bridge; it was to be blown up by troops using explosives placed in critical locations.

Alfred and his crew were to fly just one training sortie in preparation for this special operation, dropping eight parachutists on 1 February 1941. They were allocated Whitley T4215, which was to be flown on the secret duty codenamed Operation Colossus. Numerous briefings were conducted to explain the complex operation. They were to fly from RAF Mildenhall to Malta, where they would be based for the operation. The attack was to take place at night—it would not be easy as the target area lay in a valley ringed with towering mountains, several thousand feet high. The troops were to be dropped at a maximum of 500 feet. In order to do that, the Whitley aircraft needed to fly into the valley with their flaps and undercarriage down to reduce the speed. The wheels would be down for only a short time, after which the paratroopers would jump, and then full power would be reinstated to lift the aircraft over the mountains. There was no margin for error, and the crews were well aware of the dangers involved in the operation. Meanwhile, the SAS men had concluded their preparations and had been transported to Mildenhall with all their equipment. Alfred and his crew had been on that station since 2 February and were eager to meet the men they were to transport on the first leg to Malta, and then subsequently to Italy. The SAS contingent allocated to their aircraft consisted of Capt. Gerry Daly, L/Cpl Tomlin and sappers Davidson, Parker, and Prior. In addition to the men, the crew were to carry six containers holding explosives and equipment. Alfred was aware that in the drop zone area he would also be acting as dispatcher, ensuring the troops jumped on the correct orders and that the supplies followed.

Additional equipment was stored in Whitley T4215, which took off from Mildenhall at 0815 hours on 7 February 1941 and made for Malta following the pre-flight briefing orders. This would be the first time that any Allied forces in uniform were dropped into enemy territory, and what lay ahead of them was very much unknown. The crew's navigators were to ensure that the precise route was followed: keeping to the west of Marseilles, Corsica, and Sardinia, continuing south towards the coast of Tunisia for a further 50 miles, then turning east to a position due south of Malta, and finally turning north to the island. This would prevent the enemy from knowing of the arrival

YO

of the Whitleys, which had been fitted with additional fuel tanks to ensure that it would be possible to fly this extended route. The flight of almost eight hours' duration was a serious test of endurance for Alfred, encased in his turret. All eight Whitleys landed safely, and after they were marshalled into their protected blast pens the crews were given a quick debriefing and sent to take up residence in the barracks at Sliema.

During the two following days the crews experienced life on Malta, which was dominated by enemy air raids and the rationing of almost every commodity. The Maltese people were enduring the almost continuous bombing of their island, and although the Whitley bombers were protected in their blast pens, concern was expressed over them sustaining serious damage. Refresher briefings on the target area were undertaken and it was stated that Operation Colossus was to commence early in the evening of 10 February. Alfred, his crew, and the SAS troops lifted off from Luqa airfield at 1815 hours. Unfortunately, this was a delayed departure as their aircraft had developed a fault, which meant that they were well behind the formation that had taken off on schedule. The eventual take off was a highly unusual experience for Alfred: the runway was shorter than those at airfields in the UK and his rearward view of the rocky outcrops of the island contrasted to the English fields, trees, and fences so familiar to him. Once in the air, Alfred began quartering the sky, well aware that Italian and German fighter aircraft frequently operated in the area. Meanwhile, at the front of the Whitley, his crew were engaged in intense map reading and navigation as they approached Italy. The preceding aircraft were flying in two loose formations led by the commanding officer, Flt Lt James 'Willie' Tait. However, one of them, flown by Plt Off. Wotherspoon, had developed engine trouble and been forced to land on the Italian coastline, where the crew were all taken prisoner and remained in captivity for the rest of the war. Wotherspoon and his crew had been briefed to drop a bomb load to divert attention from the aqueduct; it was extremely fortunate that his aircraft was not carrying any parachutists.

Alfred and his crew faced different problems. Flying completely on their own, they made landfall over Italy and mistakenly followed a river which took them to the Adriatic coast. They returned westwards to Scalea and finally reached what they thought was their objective at 2315 hours. The other aircraft engaged in the operation had departed the drop zone at around 2245 hours. The valley was fairly visible in the moonlight, and Alfred climbed from his rear turret to help the parachutists prepare to jump when the pilot gave the signal. The hatch in the floor of the Whitley was opened and Capt. Daly viewed the drop area; he was concerned that no activity could be seen,

Opposite: Three members of the SAS unit standing alongside a No. 78 Squadron Whitley. Central is 2nd Lieutenant Jowetty, formerly from the Highlands Light Infantry, and on his left the Italian Fortunato Picchi.

although all the landmarks appeared to be present. The containers were to drop automatically, so they landed in close proximity to the troops. These supplies were of great importance to the raid, as was Capt. Daly, who was the unit's Royal Engineers demolition expert.

Turning into the valley and dropping speed at a height of approximately 300 feet was a challenge for the pilot, but he achieved it admirably; the parachutists all departed safely. Unfortunately, due to a fault in the automatic release system, the containers failed to drop and remained in the aircraft. The crew were forced to return to Malta with them. Also, despite their efforts to drop the SAS troops in close proximity to the other contingent of men, they had in fact unknowingly dropped them into the wrong valley several miles from the aqueduct. The return flight to Malta was made difficult by low cloud, but eventually the aircraft made landfall, arriving about an hour later than the other participants. The crew finally completed their fraught operation, switching off their engines at 0200 hours.

The SAS troops were to discover that the aqueduct's pillar supports were made of strong reinforced concrete rather than the expected masonry. They concentrated the explosives on one full support and additionally on another small bridge that provided access to the aqueduct and would thwart the repair parties tending to the primary target. Having heard the loud explosion and thus knowing that the raid had achieved a successful result, Capt. Daly and his crew immediately began to make for the specified pick-up location on the coast, where an Allied submarine was scheduled to take them away. At daybreak the different groups went into hiding but were detected by various means and arrested. However, Capt. Daly's group, dropped by Alfred's crew, travelled for three nights, making good headway across the country. They covered over 30 miles, but were suffering from exhaustion and lack of food when they encountered a group of Italian troops. The interpreter Fortunato Picchi attempted to bluff them, claiming that they were German troops (they were wearing uniforms that could be mistaken as German) but they were discovered and detained.

Fortunato, who had emigrated to Britain in 1929, had been employed at the Savoy Hotel in London and was a devoted supporter of Arsenal Football Club. Having been interned by the British after war was declared against Italy, he was subsequently approached and offered training by the SOE, and was attached thereafter to the SAS operation. He was in possession of false papers, and the Italian troops handed him over to the Fascist Militia, Mussolini's national security force known as the Blackshirts, who tortured and interrogated him. Bravely, he withheld information, but was later executed by firing squad.

Operation Colossus made headlines in the Allied press and ensured that the enemy kept sufficient troops on the mainland to guard similar vulnerable locations against any future attacks. However, all of the parachutists had been taken prisoner—an outcome that had not been expected. The exploits of Royal Engineer L/Cpl Robert Watson, one of the men attached to the 11th SAS Battalion, are recorded in his Military Medal citation:

> Watson was captured on 13 February 1941 at Avelino after being dropped by parachute to carry out a special mission. As a result he was imprisoned at Naples, Sulmona and Aquila. Watson served as a member of the escape committee and sent valuable information to the War Office by secret means. Released on 11 September 1943, he found a shelter in the mountainous terrain at Coppito until his recapture on 6 December 1943. Six days later he escaped from the Germans and returned to Coppito. On 27 December 1943 he went with a companion to Aquila. At the beginning of May 1944 when attempting to reach the Allied lines Watson was caught. Imprisonment at Aquila and Laterina followed. Entrained for Germany on 23 June 1944, he and two others escaped through a hole they had made in the floor of the truck. Travelling north to Switzerland on foot, they crossed the border on 15 July 1944.[3]

The medal award was published on 31 January 1946.

The Whitley aircraft that returned to Malta after the operation were subjected to an immediate increase in bombing by both German and Italian aircraft. The attacks were intense, especially at night. After several days of hiding in the air-raid shelters, the crews had an opportunity to depart. One crew were dismayed to find that debris had been projected over the blast wall, punching a hole through their port wing measuring some 2 feet across, while other debris had struck the port rudder and tail fin, causing extensive damage. Substantial and well-constructed blast pens provided protection to the tethered aircraft on Malta, but the intensity of bombing had caused large rocks to be thrown into the air on unpredicted trajectories.

At 2200 hours on 18 February 1941, Alfred again climbed into his rear gunner's turret and, following clearance by airfield control, his Whitley took off from Malta at 2215 hours. Alfred anticipated the long ten-hour transit with some trepidation as he tried to prepare for the intense cold. That proved to be incidental, however, when the crew were faced with the serious possibility of having to ditch into the sea due to a shortage of fuel. Fortunately, however, they managed to make an emergency landing at Swanton Morley in Norfolk at 0915 hours. With no time to lower the undercarriage, Whitley T4215 slid along the runway exactly eleven hours after departing Malta. Thankfully, nobody was injured.

Some significant lessons were learned at the debriefing of Operation Colossus; the failures of the container drops and the means of dropping containers were examined with intense scrutiny to ensure such failures never occurred again.

Alfred returned to No. 78 Squadron. A few weeks later on 27 March 1941, his Royal Navy pilot, Sub-Lt Peter Hoad, failed to return in Whitley Z6470 from operations to Düsseldorf. He and the entire crew now lie together in the war cemetery at Jonkerbos in Holland. Alfred was promoted to the rank of Flying Officer on 7 April 1941 and was awarded the DFC on 30 June. The recommendation made reference to Operation Colossus and to his completion of twenty-six operational sorties, which entailed nearly 150 hours encased in his rear gunner's turret.

In his role as Group Gunnery Leader, Alfred was responsible for all matters affecting air gunners across the various squadrons of No. 4 Group. This required significant work in ensuring new information or training instructions were passed to the squadrons, and that the Group's gunners operated as efficiently as possible. He managed to undertake two operations, Bremen on 8 May and Hanover on 19 July, to keep himself in practice, but these were to be his last operational flights in the Whitley aircraft. Alfred's experience in gunnery leader duties led to his promotion to command 1484 (Bomber) Gunnery Flight at RAF Leconfield. This was No. 4 Group's Gunnery Flight training venue, and he commanded the unit from 10 December 1942 to 11 February 1944.

Alfred had been engaged in all aspects of gunnery developments since commanding the Gunnery Flight at Leconfield, but operational flights had been beyond his remit. He finally had another opportunity to fly operationally when he was posted to No. 77 Squadron on 12 February 1944. Alfred was to command 'B' Flight and fly in the Halifax bombers that equipped the squadron. The rear gunner's turret in the Halifax was the Boulton Paul Type 'E' turret, which proved to be one of the most successful turrets designed and produced during the Second World War. It was easily fitted into the Halifax fuselage, making its maintenance on station uncomplicated for the ground crews. Over 8,000 such turrets were produced and fitted to all of the RAF's Halifaxes. The Boulton Paul Company installed individual pumps operated by a 24-volt electrical supply feed to power the turret. It was capable of traversing at two speeds, selected by the gunner—generally 3 mph, but over short durations it could be switched to function at 5 mph. When compared to the Frazer-Nash turret, with which Alfred was more familiar, the Type 'E' looked rounder in its form, producing a more moulded profile to the aircraft, and was popular with the men who operated it. Any design modernisation regardless of model or type that created ease of use, comfort, or safety was always well received by air gunners.

In early 1944, the vast majority of rear gunners in Bomber Command were of NCO rank—sergeants and flight sergeants. When Alfred was on operations it would have been uncommon for the air crew to have a squadron leader as a rear gunner. Very few crews would ever fly with such an experienced man as Alfred. His second tour of operations included flying with various crews and entailed the bombing of coastal batteries prior to the D-Day landings, and the rocket sites at Forêt de Nieppe. Operating with the Pathfinder Force (PFF), Alfred was to witness the various illuminated markers deployed on both day and night operations. In his flying log book, Alfred recorded many green ink entries, showing the growing number of daylight sorties, which included supporting the Allied forces in Caen, where precise bombing was required just ahead of the Allied lines.

It was an intense second tour of operations, and with his enormous experience Alfred was chosen to try out the latest innovations in gunner technology. This included the rarely fitted mid-under gunner's position. Halifax MZ750 was fitted with this new gun position, located in the middle of the fuselage. Alfred sat directly above the two fully manoeuvrable Browning machine guns; the angle of depression was achieved by operating the control in a similar fashion to the pilot's joystick. He held the column that operated all the controls while looking into a periscope sighting device that ran down between his legs to the small turret beneath him. Constructed by Frazer-Nash, this gun position provided protection from Luftwaffe attacks from below. This gun required skilful operation as the only view available was the wide-angled periscope perspective, but the responsive controls provided full 360-degree manoeuvrability and made it an interesting device to operate. No doubt Alfred was engaged in the assessment of this new turret before it was fully adopted for use in Bomber Command. His second tour of duty concluded on 7 October 1944.

Alfred was recommended for his second DFC medal and the station commander, No. 77 Squadron, made the following remarks:

> Squadron Leader Webb has commanded his Flight with great distinction during his service with the Squadron. Although not a member of a crew, he has shown great eagerness to fly as air gunner and on several occasions has occupied the mid-under turret during trials with the modified gun installation. He has set a fine example not only to his own Flight but to the whole Squadron, and he is strongly recommended for the award of a Bar to his DFC.[4]

This exceptional air gunner wore the medal ribbon of the DFC with a silver rosette emblem, indicating that the award had been won on two occasions.

Statistically, rear gunners were exceptionally vulnerable as Luftwaffe night fighters consistently targeted these isolated men before moving in to destroy the Allied bombers. Statistics gathered by Bomber Command's Operational Research Section, relating to casualties incurred during April 1942 (available in document AIR 14/4525 in the National Archives) show that rear gunners operating in large bomber aircraft were without doubt the most vulnerable, with a death or serious injury rate of 47 per cent. It is important to note that those statistics related to returning aircraft with deceased rear gunners, and excluded the significant numbers of men within entire crews who had failed to return. At that time of the war those men were simply regarded as missing in action until established otherwise. Alfred's service and survival was therefore remarkable, bearing in mind that casualty statistics had no respect for age or experience, and that he served during the entire period of the Second World War.

5

Charles Shepherd Light Aircraft Spotter

The RAF often trained pilots from other services, including Royal Artillery pilots engaged in Air Observation Posts. In the First World War, pilots of the Royal Flying Corps, a branch of the British Army and the forerunner of the RAF, were used to correct the accuracy of artillery fire. Using wireless communication, they passed details to battery commanders of how far shells were landing from their targets. They used a simple system based on a clockface to report the accuracy of shellfire, with the target placed in the middle. A shell that fell beyond the target but on a straight line would be corrected with a call of twelve, and if it fell short on the same line the call would be six, and so on around the clockface. This system proved to function perfectly well throughout the whole of the First World War, aided by the fact that the war had been fought on a static and entrenched basis.

This system of correcting artillery fire remained unchanged during the inter-war period. The Air Council of the Air Ministry was against making alterations to the clock-code system as it was thought to fit the needs of the Army. In all probability, liaison between the RAF and the Army over this particular matter was seen as a low priority. During the inter-war period, there was intense rivalry between the two services, and one young man was to experience this turbulence personally. Charles Frederick Hobart Shepherd came from a military family and had recently passed out from the famous Oundle School, near Peterborough, having gained a 'Class A' certificate in the Oundle School Officer Training Corps. That qualification entitled him to apply for a commission in any of the Military Reserves across all of the services.

Charles Shepherd was eighteen years old, well-educated and in the privileged position of having direct access into any of the Territorial or Reserve forces. He chose to accept a commission in the Reserve of Air Force Officers (RAFO) and wore the uniform of a pilot officer with immediate effect. In December 1934, Charles was promoted to the rank of Flying Officer and it appears that he explored the possibilities of qualifying to fly. However, little evidence exists to

Charles Shepherd, far right, with members of the Oundle School Officers Training Corps shooting team 1931. (*Charles Shepherd collection*)

confirm whether he actually pursued this aim. In the meantime, the Air Ministry agreed to trials between the RAF Army Co-Operation Group and the School of Artillery in order to develop further the role of the artillery observer. These trials directed that the type of aircraft should also be reviewed. The results established that light aircraft over the battlefield could still observe fire by utilising the clock-code system, and that the Taylorcraft light aircraft, used for observing the artillery, had a good chance of dodging the fire of a modern fighter. The War Office established the Flying Observation Post and initiated plans to train gunners in the Royal Artillery and for the RAF to train officers to fly.

These developments were taking place while Charles was still serving as an RAFO. He witnessed the escalation of Germany's aggression and the efforts being taken to equip and recruit military forces in the UK. On 6 May 1939, Charles transferred from the RAFO into the Royal Artillery, accepting a commission in the Honourable Artillery Company, Territorial Army. This unexpected development may well be explained by the social standing of the Honourable Artillery Company; it was directly connected to the City of London, and Charles's father is thought to have had connections with it. Although war with Germany was declared on 3 September 1939, it was not until 14 June 1940 that Charles was mobilised as a commissioned officer in the Royal Artillery.

It was shortly after that time that the first Air Observation Post (AOP) was established. It engaged in air observations and artillery deployments alongside the Army Co-Operation Squadrons equipped with Lysander aircraft for reconnaissance duties in France. These slow and somewhat vulnerable aircraft suffered badly, and not only from the Germans. On 18 May 1940, Fg Off. Walker and his crewman Cpl Baillie from No. 16 Squadron were shot down by RAF Spitfires in their Lysander L4804. The Spitfire pilots had mistakenly identified the Lysander as a German Henschel Hs 126 light spotter aircraft. The AOP losses in France were significant and many lessons were learnt.

During these quick-moving, traumatic times, the commands of the School of Artillery, the Army Co-Operation Command, and the RAF established that a certain number of aircraft should specialise in artillery work. Furthermore, they should be trained by the School of Artillery so that they had the same tactical knowledge and understanding of gunnery as an artillery officer. Artillery officers were to be seconded to the RAF Army Co-Operation squadrons to be specifically trained for artillery work.

It has to be assumed that as a commissioned officer in the Royal Artillery, Charles's prior service in RAFO was known and that he became conversant with the significant developments of Royal Artillery AOP requirements. He was naturally qualified to fulfil the role and was posted to the Elementary Flying Training School at Peterborough to undertake a pilot's course under the instructions of the RAF. His rank was recorded as second lieutenant, Royal Artillery, and on 17 March 1942 he began his training in a Tiger Moth aircraft. Twelve days later, Charles flew solo for the first time. By May 1942 he had engaged in solo cross-country navigation exercises, being assessed as an 'above average' pilot navigator. He was posted to the De Havilland School of Flying at Hatfield to continue his training, and this was followed by a move to 1424 Flight at Larkhill, the specialist unit within No. 70 Group RAF, designated to train pilots to fly the small Auster AOP light aircraft.

No. 654 (AOP) Squadron was formed at RAF Old Sarum on 15 July 1942, under command of Maj. T. C. Willett, Royal Artillery, and was equipped with both Tiger Moth and Auster Mk III aircraft. Having gained his 'wings' at Larkhill and put his knowledge of Royal Artillery shooting into practice with numerous exercises, Charles was fully qualified and joined the squadron on 13 August 1942. The intensity of flying was to increase dramatically for Charles, who was now bearing the rank of a captain and wore the Army 'wings' of a pilot on his Royal Artillery tunic. The Taylorcraft Auster aircraft were flown to many military locations, engaging in various exercises and

Taylorcraft Auster light aircraft.

occasional live shoots. (The term 'shoot' relates to any deployment of British artillery, and this would be written in the flying log book of all AOP pilots.)

Charles's squadron was mobilised and sent to Algeria in North Africa; he embarked on the steamer *New Holland* at Gourock, Scotland, on 20 February 1943 and landed at Algiers on 6 March. Initially, the squadron was allocated to 9 Corps based at Jaffa, but it swiftly transferred under command of the Eighth Army. The long and arduous North Africa campaign was in its closing stages, and No. 654 Squadron was to be involved in the forthcoming Allied invasion of Sicily. Capt. Shepherd was in 'B' Flight and became operational on 3 April, at Le Kef in Tunisia. It was here that he chose to compile a new flying log book recording his operational duties. AOP pilots were issued with exactly the same flying log book as RAF pilots, and were required to compile them in exactly the same fashion.

One of the final and extensive battles in North Africa was taking place around Enfidaville in Tunisia, and Charles flew his Auster MZ117, which he

A family-commissioned watercolour painting of Captain Charles Shepherd in full uniform.

had christened *Eve*, in support of those final battles. Charles later commanded his squadron's 'A' Flight and became employed in sorties spotting enemy tanks. Allied artillery played a vital part in the victory over Germany's Afrika Korps; No. 654 Squadron's contribution during the battle of Enfidaville is shown by their engagement in over seventy artillery shoots.

On 22 April 1943, Charles flew *Eve* on a reconnaissance sortie to Blida with Maj. Cooper sitting alongside him. It was to lead to his first direct engagement with the enemy, when his aircraft was targeted by heavy machine-gun fire. The Auster light aircraft were frequently flown low, and machine-gun fire was more than capable of shooting them down. To add to the danger, AOP pilots did not carry parachutes as they would not have time to unfurl in an emergency. However, on 22 April Charles escaped unscathed, and LAC Sinnott, in charge of Charles's aircraft, was well equipped to repair light gunfire damage to the wings and fuselage. The following day, Charles flew Lt Col. Howell across the 11th Field's area of terrain at Enfidaville. The battle was eventually to lead to an Allied victory in early May 1943.

Despite No. 654 Squadron being an RAF unit, they were entirely commanded by Royal Artillery officers. Their support and provision of gun fire control for the infantry and armour units on the front lines saw them operate from advance landing strips, which were always within range of enemy artillery. On 12 May, Charles was tasked with locating a German Nebelwerfer unit launching high-explosive rockets that had great potential to deliver concentrated multiple charges onto relatively small target areas. These

The mechanic for MZ117 *Eve*, Leading Aircraftsman Sinnott, who also flew with Charles on the search for Captain Francis Lane at the close of the battle for Enfidaville.

rocket units were operated by specialist troops who had great flexibility of movement. Within twenty-five minutes of taking off, Charles, flying at low level, located them and immediately reported their position. Together, the Royal Artillery and the RAF deployed the appropriate force to attack and destroy the enemy unit.

Six days later, AOP pilot Capt. Francis Lane failed to return from a sortie over the desert. In company with LAC Sinnott, the leading aircraftsman responsible for keeping *Eve* airworthy, Charles flew extensive searches for the missing captain. Hope faded as the search continued above the desert terrain, but good news finally arrived: Capt. Lane had been picked up and was safe. In 1945, Capt. Lane was awarded a DFC for his gallant and distinguished service.

Operating immediately on the front line, Charles was engaged in sorties of short duration, usually only twenty-five minutes. As the Auster was capable of very short take offs and landings, it was absolutely ideal for the role it was performing. Once the pilot had returned to the advance landing ground, the aircraft would normally be camouflaged; in some instances, shallow pits were dug to allow the aircraft some protection. From 1943 to 1944, the Auster Mk III was deployed across the operational AOP squadrons, powered by the tiny 130-hp De Havilland Gipsy Major engine. Only 470 of these aircraft were built and they often achieved noteworthy results on Special Duties.

The Allied invasion of Sicily took place on 9 July 1943 and it became apparent that the tiny AOP Austers were not going to play any part in that

An Auster being removed from the protective pit which was designed to protect the aircraft from artillery shell damage and assist in camouflaging its position.

massive aerial and sea invasion. Preparations were under way to move the AOP squadron to Sicily once the bridgeheads had been secured; the aircraft were dismantled and carried in one of the giant LST (Landing Ship Tank) vessels. Charles landed at Syracuse on 5 August, the aircraft were unloaded and No. 654 Squadron became operational, initially supporting the 50th Division. On 11 August, the Axis forces started to evacuate the island and moved some 117,000 Italian and German troops onto mainland Italy. The squadron's Capt. Frederick Jackson was killed on 15 August, and like so many casualties from the fierce Italian conflict, his name joins the 4,000 Commonwealth servicemen whose graves are not known. Each man is commemorated on the Cassino Memorial situated south-east of Rome.

On 17 August 1943, Allied artillery began shelling Italian forces from Messina on Sicily. On the 26th, Charles took to the air to view a shoot made by the cruiser HMS *Uganda*. The vessel was part of the bombardment fleet for the invasion of Sicily and the subsequent invasion of Italy at Salerno. The

An Auster pilot extracts himself from the small cockpit; his notebook used in the flight to record the sightings and points of interest is seen on his lap. Wearing the leather jacket and flying boots, this aircraft was not the simplest cockpit to climb in and out.

following month, HMS *Uganda* suffered a direct hit from a German radio-controlled glide bomb, and the damage was so severe that it had to leave the Italian theatre of operations.

At the beginning of September, No. 654 Squadron packed up their aircraft and once more loaded them onto a giant LST in preparation for the invasion of mainland Italy. On 4 September, Charles wrote 'Portee L.S.T. 636 Salerno D-Day' in his flying log book. The invasion took place on the 9th, and some days later Charles took part in several reconnaissance sorties, flying to Naples, Pompeii, and Castel Volturno. The squadron was operating from the advance landing ground at Portico, which was unexpectedly heavily shelled by the enemy. Charles flew many operations, which were in effect 'panzer hunting' sorties, looking for German tanks that were difficult to locate in the Italian terrain.

The light Auster aircraft was an exceptionally stable platform in the sky, enabling its pilot to examine the ground below in detail and with ease. The

German equivalent of the Auster was the Fieseler Storch, an aircraft also referred to as the Stork. It had a 240-hp engine compared with the 130-hp engines in the various Auster types. The most famous operation involving a Stork was conducted in Italy on 12 September 1943, when German commandos landed on a tiny mountainside field to rescue the deposed Italian dictator Benito Mussolini.

Charles was flying his Auster from the advanced landing ground occupied by his squadron's 'C' Flight, supporting the battle at Monte Camino during November. German engineers had made very skilful use of the terrain and fortifications to hold back the Allied forces, having laid mines on the roads and obvious foot trails and in the natural cross-country approaches. They had also destroyed all bridges and culverts in order to disrupt the Allied advance. Machine-gun and mortar emplacements, many of them dug 4 or 5 feet into solid rock, covered nearly every vulnerable area. Not even intense artillery concentrations could smash these positions, and across the narrow valleys dozens of mutually supporting machine guns were sited to create a deadly pattern of crossfire.

Charles's sorties led to precise artillery bombardments or other offensive actions to counter these particular threats. These sorties were replicated at the battles conducted at Porcia, Trocchio, and Mount Cedro, all of which were to be entered into Charles's flying log book at the end of 1943 and in early 1944. The operations by No. 654 Squadron were supported by RAF Tactical Reconnaissance squadrons, which specialised in photographing enemy emplacements.

Between 9 September and 31 December 1943, No. 654 Squadron carried out approximately 500 operational sorties of a varied nature. Sadly, another AOP pilot, Capt. Peter Newman, was killed on 16 September 1943 and was later buried in the Salerno War Cemetery alongside the many casualties sustained in the Allied landings. By this time, Charles had accumulated some sixty hours in the air, performing dangerous low-level flying duties. Towards the end of February 1944, he was dispatched to Naples before later being transferred to Algiers.

Unbeknown to Charles, his hard and dangerous work in Italy had been noticed officially. On 24 August 1944, *The London Gazette* announced that the King was pleased to approve an award for Charles, in recognition of gallant and distinguished service while operating in Italy. He had been 'Mentioned in Dispatches' and was sent the 'MID' certificate along with the small bronze oak leaf emblem, together with instructions on how it was to be worn.

In April 1945, Charles began flying in Germany with No. 662 AOP Squadron. He was, however, still attached to No. 43 OTU as an instructor. It is quite probable that Charles was posted to Germany to provide only temporary support to the squadron, which was engaged with the Army's

30 Corps in the final push into central Germany. The advance went from Enschede to Salzbergen, Lingen, Quakenbrück, Vechta, Wildeshausen, Delmenhorst, Bremen, and finally Bremerhaven. Germany was now collapsing and there were many refugees and prisoners everywhere, although there was also sporadic but determined resistance by the German forces along the route. Charles found himself flying in support of several divisions as the Allies delivered the final death knell.

Charles was working with 30 Corps, pushing through the Reichswald Forest to the airfields at Nordhorn and then Vechtel, where he flew in support of the battle for Menslage near Osnabrück. On 11 April, Charles noted the withdrawal of infantry troops, who were seen crossing the river. The next day he searched for a reported head of German tanks and landed at the vacated Quakenbrück airfield, where the Luftwaffe had recently withdrawn. Tank hunting would normally entail operating at around 6,000 feet with an RAF observer using binoculars. Once a tank had halted, it was engaged by a single gun, frequently knocking down a building that the tank was hiding behind. The German tank commanders were well aware of the targeting process by the artillery, and the zoning in, or bracketing, of shells was always likely to induce their movement from cover. Often they would move just as the artillery bracket had been verified, and the process would have to be repeated.

On 17 April 1945, Charles flew his last operational sortie supporting 51 Division at Winkelsett, just south of Bremen. Some of the last vital strongholds in Germany were being staunchly defended, but the services of the Auster light aircraft were no longer required. Charles departed the fighting front and was transported to Brussels and then back to the UK. Hitler's suicide, thirteen days after Charles left Bremen, initiated the final sequence of events which led to the end of the war.

The credibility of the AOP squadrons had been well and truly established. They had flown in every theatre of war and had made a significant contribution to the efficiency and effectiveness of artillery. Their outstanding attribute was their ability to put a skilled artillery observer into the air at short notice, who was fully aware of the tactical situation and the needs of the troops on the ground, and able to direct the fire of every gun within range. By the end of hostilities, Air Observation pilots had been awarded more than 100 DFCs. Their courage and sacrifice is poignantly displayed on the Roll of Honour, where sixty-seven are listed killed in action.

6

Rex Dunkerley AFC Artisan Pilot, Tactical Reconnaissance

Born on 1 May 1910, Rex Dunkerley was a native South African who grew up in the Mowbray district of Cape Town. He later found employment at J. A. Railways in nearby Salt River. Having taken a keen interest in flying when he was growing up in South Africa, Rex developed the ambition to become an 'artisan pilot', a civilian pilot of a recognised level of competence.

The first involvement of 'citizen-aviators' in a military sphere in South Africa can be traced back to 1913. Cecil Compton Paterson was appointed as the first instructor at the Military Aviation School, which had been established to train potential aviators for the South African Aviation Corps. The Transvaal Air Training Squadron (TATS) was also established to train aviators for the regular air force, but this was a slow process and by 1923 only seventeen officers and 218 other ranks were serving. A Special Reserve of Flying Officers (SRFO) was established to speed up the process with flying refresher courses, and in 1926 the SRFO additionally undertook cadet training. The previous year, the South African Air Force (SAAF) had begun training cadets to supplement the SRFO pilots. Ten student pilots were awarded their 'wings' in 1927 and were absorbed into TATS. Two courses followed in 1930, producing a further thirty-eight cadets, and a scheme to train fifty artisans was initiated at the same time. In addition, part-time courses for undergraduate pilots and later for artisans were developed, with training scheduled outside normal working hours. The scheme closely resembled the RAF's Auxiliary Training Scheme in the UK, and Rex signed himself up for a course.

In Europe the rumblings of an impending war could be heard, and along with European nations, South Africa began to assess its military resources. In 1936, the Thousand Pilot Scheme was conceived in South Africa, designed to create 1,000 reserve pilots by 1942, as well as 1,700 artisans. Initial training was entrusted to civil flying clubs and the SAAF, utilising Avro Tutors, Westland Wapitis, and Hawker Hartbees aircraft. In addition, 200 Harts were to be supplied by the British Government at a nominal price, and these

Rex Dunkerley alongside the 'Bucker Bu131D' Jungmann aircraft, displaying the civilian registration ZS AOR. This aircraft was later allocated to the South African Air Force (SAAF) in March 1940 and given the SAAF registration number 1445. Rather ironically, the Jungmann aircraft was a German design for the Luftwaffe and used by them in basic training during the Second World War. (*Rex Dunkerley collection*)

aircraft started arriving in South Africa in 1938. In July of that year, TATS was reorganised into thirteen Flights and located at strategic locations across the country. At this time it was also renamed the Union Air Training Group.

In 1939, Lt Rex Dunkerley formally enrolled into the SAAF as a qualified pilot. At that time, instructors were being actively sought and the SAAF were training pilots at Benoni; it was a natural assumption that with over 300 hours' flying experience, Rex would be accepted into the Union Air Training Group. Having been promoted to the rank of captain, he was posted to the Air School in Vereeniging. There he progressed as a flying instructor with significant accomplishment, and his flying log book was endorsed with praise for his ability. As a result, his duty was extended far longer than would normally be expected. Between 1 August 1940 and 1 February 1943, Rex had commanded two Flights and accumulated 1,025 flying hours instructing trainee pilots. This exceptional service was recognised with a recommendation for an Air Field Cross (AFC) for his significant contribution to pilot training. The SAAF awarded the AFC to just eighty-eight recipients throughout the Second World War. Its silk red and white medal ribbon was rarely seen on the uniform of a South African pilot; by contrast, the RAF awarded 1,676 AFCs over the same period.

In 1943 Rex was thirty-three years old and the father of a very young child, but he was regarded as an elder statesman by the novice pilots he had been training, who were aged between nineteen and twenty-two. His experience in the air in relation to his accumulation of hours spoke volumes. However,

Rex Dunkerley in the cockpit of a Westland Wapiti, *c.* 1938. The observer or air gunner's gun mounting can be seen in the empty cockpit. Fixed alongside the pilot's cockpit were two machine guns, the rear portion of which can just be seen in this image.

Captain Rex Kenilworth Dunkerley, sitting far right. Among the seated officers are two RAF pilots and another one is standing in the centre of the first row. The aircraft behind is almost certainly one of the British-supplied Hawker Harts.

he was inexperienced in operational flying against the enemy, having had no opportunity to receive any such training. But after more than three years with the Union Air Training Group, Rex was finally released from his duties as an instructor and sent to train as an operational pilot.

Rex arrived in Cairo on 3 July 1943, hoping to be trained in flying fast single-seat fighters. He commenced training to fly the Spitfire, and within twelve weeks, Rex had the exhilarating experience of converting onto the Supermarine Spitfire Mk VB. He passed through the OTU and was fortuitously posted to a South African unit, No. 40 SAAF Army Co-Operation Squadron. The transition from instructing student pilots in relatively slow and easy-to-fly machines to the ultimate high-performance capabilities of the Spitfire was, for Rex, a dream come true.

No. 40 SAAF Squadron was equipped with Supermarine Spitfires and deployed in a tactical reconnaissance role. This Spitfire variant had clipped wingtips to enhance its low-altitude performance and roll-speed—highly desirable for its specialist duties, which included using an oblique camera installed behind the pilot's cockpit. Rex would be flying his Spitfire on frequent and dangerous low-level sorties, gathering intelligence and identifying targets for the fighter-bombers. These duties required pilots to operate in pairs, with one weaving and protecting from a greater height; it was exhilarating but very dangerous and challenging work.

Tactical reconnaissance embraces all types of visual reconnaissance, with or without photographic confirmation, and generally covers an area from the enemy's front lines to a depth of 50 to 60 miles. The prime objective of No. 40 SAAF Squadron was to use their aircraft and pilots to secure information that was of the utmost importance for the Allied forces. The South African pilots flying these reconnaissance and tactical sorties were the front-line seekers of intelligence, frequently flying very low to photograph direct line-of-sight targets seen fleetingly by the pilots. The Spitfires were always exposed to the hazards of light anti-aircraft fire, and several aircraft were lost to this ever-present danger.

Artillery reconnaissance was an additional role for No. 40 SAAF Squadron, and was particularly relevant to the campaign in North Africa and Italy. The nature of the conflict suited heavy artillery barrages on specific targets, which were frequently identified by tactical reconnaissance. The squadron's pilots were also deployed over enemy lines to monitor the accuracy of the barrages and ensure that targets were being hit.

During the fighting in North Africa and the invasions of Italy, ground forces became increasingly reliant on air support and the intelligence they were able to provide. No. 40 SAAF Squadron was frequently responsible for both artillery and naval gunfire co-ordination—a dangerous responsibility.

On 6 March 1944, after the renewal of Allied efforts to take Monte Cassino, Lt Aronson's Spitfire was hit by enemy light flak and came down in

A pair No. 40 Squadron SAAF Spitfires with Tactical Reconnaissance pilots flying in close company, as they would in the vast majority of their operational deployments.

flames. Flying low, these pilots knew that the chances of using their parachutes were always slim, but the horror of being encased in a burning aircraft was a worse fear. The fire and debris strewn about on a high speed impact into the ground literally obliterated any remains. As is common with many pilots who were killed in this way, Lt Aronson has no known grave and his life is commemorated on the Malta Memorial.

No. 40 SAAF Squadron continued to operate from Trigno until 16 March, when they moved to the landing ground at Lago, followed swiftly by another move to Marcianise, a town in the province of Caserta in southern Italy. These frequent relocations meant that Rex and his colleagues had to live in tents, regularly moving between advance landing grounds as Allied forces pushed further into Fascist territory. On 18 March, when Lt Col. Nel, the squadron's commanding officer, went low to strafe a staff car in the Anzio area, he noticed over 500 camouflaged vehicles hidden among trees in a nearby valley. The US 27th Fighter Group responded to the intelligence but unfortunately bombed the wrong valley. The following day, a Spitfire seeking the same elusive target was hit by light flak during a low pass. The pilot, Capt. van der Poel, was fortunate to make it back to the landing ground.

Lago di Patria, near Naples, was a location that had been frequently covered by the pilots of No. 40 SAAF Squadron. It was a place of strategic importance, and reconnaissance sorties had accumulated evidence of significant defences there. Rex would have contributed to reconnaissance reports such as the one below, which was part of a larger Enemy Defences report for the Lago di Patria area:

> Combined roadblock and anti-tank gun emplacement near Lago di Patria
> This double barrier was well set strategically, dominating the coastal road at its most vulnerable point. Its location is south of the Volturno, near the mouth of the narrow channel which connects the Lago with the sea. Its most unusual feature is the large anti-tank gun emplacement attached to the roadblock. This consists of a concrete platform approached by a ramp; a semi-cylindrical block of concrete projects from this platform reached by a set of L-shaped steps. Additional room for ammunition is provided by a low separate chamber appended to the main structure. From this position or vantage point, an anti-tank gun would have a full sweep of the opposite road and the sand dunes behind it.[5]

Lago di Patria was well defended, but the Allied advance could not be stopped; Rex and his fellow pilots commenced flying from a landing ground within the area once it had been secured. Two shoots with the 955th US Field Artillery in early March were very successful, having targeted enemy guns west of Cassino. On 26 March, two of the squadron's Spitfires were unexpectedly attacked by four Luftwaffe Bf 109 fighters. Marauding Luftwaffe fighters were always a threat as the enemy fully appreciated the vital role played by the Spitfires in controlling the heavy Field Artillery guns. The Luftwaffe successfully shot one Spitfire, flown by Lt Brande, out of the sky, while the other escaped to safety against all odds.

The squadron undertook constant deployments. One request for photographic reconnaissance of a location close to a well-hidden enemy airfield required an escort of eight Spitfires from the RAF's No. 92 Squadron. The River Rapido that ran through Cassino to the Gari was photographed for the Eighth Army in preparation for the pending Allied advance into that area. By 26 April, up to eight sorties per day were being undertaken, increasing the risks for the pilots—on the 29th, Lt Webb only just managed to evade six prowling Luftwaffe Fw 190s. April ended with No. 40 SAAF Squadron having flown 139 sorties, and as two aircraft were deployed on each, this represents a significant effort by the squadron. Rex had certainly played his part, with nearly sixty operational sorties to his name by this time.

On 11 May, in a planned Allied offensive, 2,000 guns opened fire on selected targets between Cassino and the Tyrrhenian Sea, while across those target sectors, No. 40 SAAF Squadron flew artillery reconnaissance sorties from dawn to dusk. Despite significant enemy radio jamming, Rex was able to direct fire onto three large enemy gun pits. The next day, the squadron maintained almost uninterrupted surveillance over the front line during the hours of daylight. Bitter

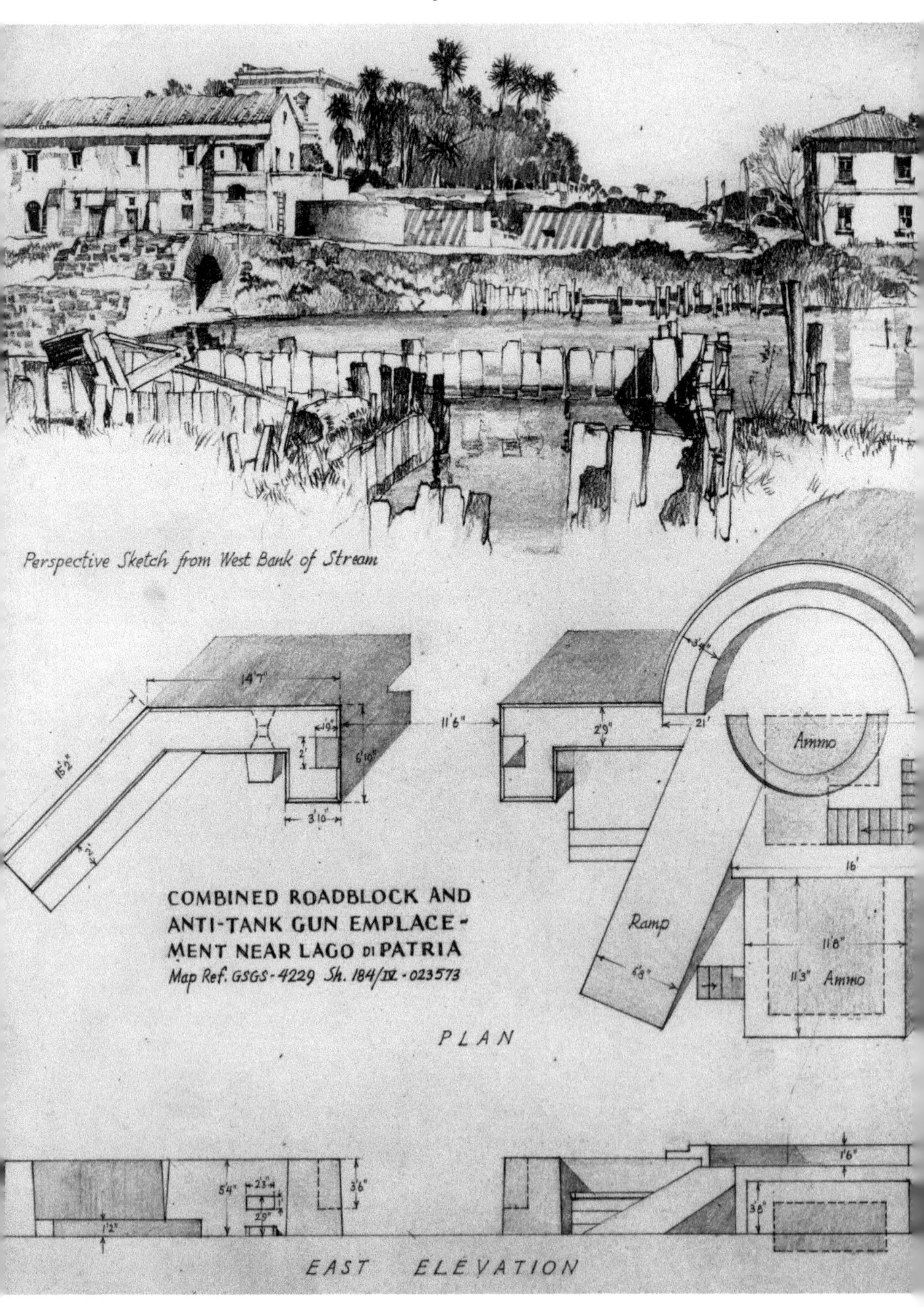
Perspective Sketch from West Bank of Stream
COMBINED ROADBLOCK AND
ANTI-TANK GUN EMPLACE-
MENT NEAR LAGO DI PATRIA
Map Ref. GSGS-4229 Sh. 184/IV-023573
Ammo
Ramp
Ammo
PLAN
EAST ELEVATION

fighting was taking place at Cassino; over the following days, Rex was engaged in flying his Spitfire to locate railways, bridges, and viaducts that were to be destroyed in a concerted effort to cut the enemy off from their supplies.

No. 40 SAAF Squadron had flown a significant total of 226 sorties in May. On the last day of the month, the Spitfire piloted by Lt O'Keefe, Rex's close friend, was struck by light flak. The pilot was unable to keep control and plummeted to the ground where he died on impact. O'Keefe's covering pilot who had been providing aerial protection related the incident to Rex back at base. On another low-level sortie by one of the squadron's Spitfires, the pilot saw a German tank holding up an Allied advance and made several low-level dummy attacks, simulating an attempt to bomb the tank. The exhibition of daring sweeps and strafing was enough to enable the Allied troops to overrun the area and destroy the enemy tank.

Battlefield air support with air-to-ground sorties continued to develop as the Allies moved beyond Rome and encountered the German defensive Gustav Line. Rex Dunkerley and his fellow pilots had frequently experienced problems of enemy interference with the radio channel links between the aircraft and ground stations. The final development of air support was the British institution of the 'Rover' system, so called because the forward air support post could switch from one ground brigade headquarters to another without interrupting communications or air support operations. The Rover unit consisted of an RAF controller and an army air liaison officer, with VHF radio for aircraft communications. Although the Rover units customarily operated with a view of targets, they could also operate blind on the basis of information reported to them. Their function was to apply air power to targets, often very close to the front line.

Impressed by the British efforts at the Salerno landings, the US forces adapted their own communication links to include many features of the British system, leading to differentiations like the British 'Rover David', the US 'Rover Joe', and the British 'Rover Frank', which specifically related to air strikes against minor German artillery targets. In support of the US Fifth Army, No. 40 SAAF Squadron's operations covered the Cassino to Rome road and the Anzio beachhead. The squadron maintained its reputation for efficiency and gallantry, as shown by a letter dispatched from the 5th Canadian Armoured Division Headquarters:

> Our thanks for oblique sortie S.B.31. This sortie has been of tremendous value to our patrols. Please convey our appreciation to the pilot who took these pictures as obviously he took great risks in flying so low to procure such splendid photographs.

Opposite: A scale drawing of a combined roadblock and anti-tank gun emplacement with a sketch of the area.

The 'Rover' air support position operated by a pilot with direct communication to close support or Army Co-operation Tactical Reconnaissance pilots. This type of control became very effective as the pilot on the ground was able to assess the requirements of the task from the perspective of the pilot in the aircraft.

Rome fell to the Allied forces in June and the Germans began their withdrawal to defend their Gothic Line, which crossed the country between Pesaro and Pisa. This withdrawal gave an opportunity for No. 40 SAAF Squadron to undertake an offensive role, harassing the German withdrawal by selecting targets as they were sighted, and engaging on low strafing runs on convoys. For Rex and his fellow pilots, such operations were always eagerly anticipated.

Operation Hasty involved a group of sixty men from the 6th (Royal Welch) Parachute Battalion—including signallers—and a detachment of the 127th (Parachute) Field Ambulance being dropped behind the German lines to harass the enemy on its withdrawal route to the east of Rome, from Sora to Avezzano. During the evening of 1 June 1944, three Dakota aircraft took off carrying the small force commanded by Capt. Fitzroy-Smith. They were followed by eight more Dakotas carrying dummy troops that would also be dropped behind enemy lines to give the enemy the impression of a far larger Allied force. The men were successfully dropped near Torricella, and had soon

Captain Dunkerley AFC, front row third from the right, in front of a Spitfire. Note the squadron mascot dog far right in that row. The pilots are wearing various outfits—not an unusual occurrence in that theatre of operations.

all regrouped. Radio contact was established shortly afterwards, and Capt. Fitzroy-Smith advised that the supply drop should proceed as previously planned. After establishing a base, he divided his force into three groups: one under his command, one under Lt Ashby, and one under 2Lt Evans. For the remainder of the week these groups harried the Germans wherever and whenever they could, and with a certain degree of success. In doing so, however, they incurred casualties, which included the capture of their signallers. Moreover, contact with the 2nd New Zealand Division was lost when the single remaining radio became inoperable, and the force's carrier pigeons failed to reach their destination.

On 3 June, No. 40 SAAF Squadron was given the task of trying to re-establish contact with the British paratroopers south of Avezzano. During their low passes in the area, the Spitfires were subjected to intense light flak, and there were no confirmed sightings of the Allied group. A number of additional artillery reconnaissance sorties were undertaken during the day, resulting in the destruction of several enemy gun pits. However, the location of the paratroopers was the primary concern. During the day, containers with emergency supplies had been dropped on what was hoped to be their location. Rex spotted the containers and monitored their position for over an hour at various heights, but nobody appeared to claim them; with his fuel running low, he was forced to return to the landing ground at Venafro.

The information gathered by Rex was given to Brig. Pritchard. The next day a pilot on tactical reconnaissance noted that the supply containers had been removed, but intense light anti-aircraft fire over Gioia had forced him to crash-land near Alvito. The squadron's operational aircraft flew a further six sorties that day, and almost without exception enemy troops were identified in the area reportedly held by the paratroopers. The aircraft had to put up with light and heavy flak from below.

Captain Rex Dunkerley AFC relaxing at one of the operational landing grounds. Adjacent to him is the warning siren used to alert the airfield staff of any enemy aircraft approaching. Rex is wearing his normal flying uniform, no doubt awaiting a briefing for one of several sorties which he was likely to fly that day. Rex was by now extremely experienced, having recorded over 100 hours' operational flying in his Spitfire.

On 5 June, No. 40 SAAF Squadron, including Rex Dunkerley, were tasked with another special mission to locate the paratroopers. This required them to fly exceptionally low, almost certainly exposing their aircraft to light flak and small arms fire. From over the target area two light but detectable areas of smoke were seen in some wooded areas; several low passes were made, but nothing further was seen.

Despite cloud cover that made low flying highly dangerous, a second effort was made to locate the Parachute Battalion near Capistrello; three fires were seen smoking and white ground signals were sighted at Civita d'Antino, where a parachute was also seen on a grass patch north of the town. Frustratingly, no confirmed contact was achieved, but enemy movements were unquestionably taking place in and around their presumed locations.

On the evening of the following day, the squadron's final mission got airborne at 1930 hours. Rex's orders were to reconnoitre the Terni–Rieti areas. Heavy cloud was again encountered, and with the failing light Rex instructed his wingman to abandon the sortie. The weather deteriorated significantly and they were forced to seek refuge at the landing ground at Nettuno, south of Rome. Rex landed safely with his Spitfire's landing gear firmly planted, but immediately afterwards, a USAAF Thunderbolt came in to land and crashed into his aircraft. The impact was severe and the scene was one of carnage. Rex was rescued from the wreckage and removed to hospital in a serious condition, having sustained horrific scalp injuries and concussion.

The following day it was decided to withdraw the Allied paratroopers, but there was no way of directly communicating with them. Leaflets bearing the cryptic message 'PROCEED AWDRY FORTHWITH' were dropped over the area; the paratroopers were well aware that Capt. John Awdry was in the 6th (Royal Welch) Parachute Battalion and was acting as a liaison officer with the 2nd New Zealand Division. The leaflets were interpreted correctly, and the paratroopers made their way back to Allied lines in their small groups. Almost two-thirds of the force had been lost during armed engagements with the enemy. However, the operation achieved a certain amount of success in that it caused the Germans to deploy significant forces to counter it, in the belief that a much larger number of Allied troops had been dropped behind their lines.

On 11 June 1944, No. 40 SAAF Squadron's commander Lt Col. Nel received notification that Capt. Rex Dunkerley AFC had died from the injuries he had sustained at Nettuno. He was later buried at the Beach Head War Cemetery, Anzio, an area that he had flown over many times during his operational flying in Italy. Originally the Anzio beach medical clearing station, the cemetery now contains 2,316 Commonwealth graves from the Second World War, 295 of which remain unidentified to this day.

Recognising Rex Dunkerley's dedication, Lt Col. Nel recommended the posthumous award of being Mentioned in Despatches. The tragic news of his

Above left: The original temporary grave marker erected for Rex Dunkerly.

Above right: Thelma Dunkerley standing at her husband's grave, commemorated by the Commonwealth War Grave Commission headstone. Engraved on the stone is Thelma's personal dedication and she wears the medals awarded to husband on her blouse. Thelma and Rex's child was just eight weeks old when Rex signed his attestation papers, volunteering to serve his country.

death was passed to his wife Thelma in South Africa, and she was eventually given the opportunity by the Commonwealth War Graves Commission to request a personal inscription on her husband's gravestone. 'Love and Remembrance Live for Ever' was inscribed at the base of the headstone, at a personal cost of 2*s* per letter. Thelma Dunkerley would eventually see her husband's grave several years after his death, proudly wearing his medals as she stood at his graveside.

A Mention in Despatches was the only form of award, apart from the VC, that could be bestowed posthumously. The MID bronze oak leaf was awarded together with a small dedication certificate signed by the Secretary of State for the Air. A total of 37,508 MIDs were awarded to members of the RAF during the Second World War. In addition, 2,200 went to the Royal Canadian Air Force; 1,797 to the Royal Australian Air Force; 548 to the Royal New Zealand Air Force; 719 to the South African Air Force; and 63 to the Royal Indian Air Force.

7

Thomas Butler 'Window' Jamming

When Thomas Butler volunteered for air crew service in the RAF, he had no idea that he was destined to fly in the famous American B-17 Flying Fortress and become attached to the 'Window' force in the RAF's Special Duties No. 100 Group.

Thomas had wanted to fly since the declaration of war in 1939, but it was not until 1944 that he was old enough to join the RAF. He knew that the swiftest way to qualify and become operational was to immediately volunteer to serve as an air gunner. Having passed all of the medical and fitness procedures, Thomas found himself posted to No. 4 Air Gunnery School at Morpeth in Northumberland. In 1944, the training of air gunners was a slick process, and Thomas soon gained the skills required to protect bomber aircraft with air gunnery from several turret positions—something that he was to excel at. Between July and September that year, AC Butler flew several varied training sorties and recorded a total of nearly twenty-three hours of flying time in his personal flying log book. His examination result of 83.9 per cent indicated that he had become a competent air gunner. The next progression in his training saw him serving at No. 1699 RAF (Bomber Support) Conversion Unit in November 1944.

No. 1699 (BS) CU was based at RAF Oulton, near Aylsham in Norfolk. The unit, equipped with American B-17 Flying Fortress and B-24 Liberator aircraft, was training selected air crews for operational service within Nos 214 and 223 Squadrons, both of which operated from the same airfield and engaged in the secret world of aviation electronic counter-measures. Thomas had little knowledge of this clandestine work, and undoubtedly his posting was unexpected. His expectations had been to join a mainstream Lancaster squadron operating within Bomber Command; the reasoning behind the decision to post Thomas into this Special Duties squadron will probably never be known. However, it was a decision that would lead to rare opportunities for him. Very few RAF personnel operated in the Flying Fortress.

Thomas was positioned in the mid-waist section of the Flying Fortress, a very different prospect to the Lancaster Perspex turret that he had been expecting. Alongside him was fellow waist air gunner Sgt Lewis, and the two men were to forge a lifelong friendship. The worst problem about being a B-17 waist gunner was frostbite; the mid-fuselage windows on the B-17 were completely open to 200-mph slipstreams at 50 degrees below zero. Exposure to this extremely cold air for even a few seconds could cause frostbite, and the gunners wore several layers of heavy clothing and an electrically heated suit to defend themselves against it. These conditions also caused ice to form in the gunners' oxygen masks, which had to be cleared frequently to avoid blockages that in turn could render them unconscious. The handling of the heavy gun in the slipstream was far removed from the more controlled environment of the enclosed turrets, in which Thomas had previously trained. Additionally, the gun fitted in the waist position was a .50 calibre, much larger than the .303 fitted within the standard RAF turrets. The .50-calibre machine guns were aimed with a basic ball and ring sight, which meant that if the gunner was not looking through the sight at exactly the right angle, his aim would be off the target.

No. 100 Group had been created by the RAF in November 1943, and was the last home-based group to be raised within the RAF during the Second World War. Responsible for the deployment of all offensive and defensive electronic and radio counter-measures, the Group utilised a wide variety of aircraft for its bomber support duties, including the American B-17 and B-24, which both carried secret jamming equipment and deployed the metal foil strips known as 'Window'. Other units within No. 100 Group operated Halifaxes and Stirlings, and were tasked with creating false radar echoes on German offensive radar detection equipment; for this they used the same metallic strips as the B-17 and B-24, as well as electronic measures to create non-existent squadrons on Luftwaffe radar. Initially based at West Raynham in Norfolk, the Group moved its headquarters to Bylaugh Hall in January 1944, and had airfields at North Creake, Little Snoring, Sculthorpe, Oulton, Foulsham, Great Massingham, Swanton Morley, and Swannington. It was commanded by Air Vice-Marshal Edward Addison, an exceptionally well-versed specialist in signals and electronics, who described No. 100 Group as follows:

> Bomber Command had called for a unit equipped to undermine the enemy's use of electronic devices, and a novel and highly specialised unit employing skilled scientific and service personnel was required and realised. For the first and only time during the war, an operational group that was a mixture of bomber and fighter squadrons came into being, the utmost priority having been given to the forming of this strange conglomeration.[6]

The RAF operated the American B-17 within No. 100 Group because of its ability to fly several hundred feet above the main bomber streams, where it could throw out its protective electronic screen to help conceal the primary bomber force flying below. The B-17 crew normally consisted of ten men, including the pilot, navigator, engineer, wireless operator, and bomb aimer who acted as support for all crew positions. The four air gunners were located in the mid-upper rear and waist positions, but the famous underbelly ball turrets were removed. When equipped with the special broadcasting equipment, the crew included a German speaker who operated the jamming or transmitting equipment and broadcasted false instructions to Luftwaffe night fighter pilots. The pilots assumed they were receiving directions issued to them by their own control rooms.

The special 'Window' force within No. 100 Group was specifically tasked with deploying tin-foil strips from the air—these were an integral part of the scientific measures used against the Luftwaffe. By late 1943, the RAF and USAAF were dropping hundreds of tons of 'Window' a month. The thin strips were 12 inches long and were manually thrown out of aircraft by crew members in packets containing 2,000 strips each. The Germans would never defeat 'Window' completely, but they were able to develop other counter-measures that helped them locate and attack Allied bombers. In fact, RAF night bomber losses continued at a high rate, which leads to the uncomfortable question of just how bad they would have been if Winston Churchill had not sanctioned the deployment of 'Window' and continued with the development of counter-measures.

Squadrons of Allied counter-measures aircraft had screened the airborne D-Day assault force. They carried two types of radar jammers—'Mandrel' and 'Airborne Grocer'—and additionally dropped 'Rope', essentially the same as 'Window' but consisting of foil strips over 5 feet long. 'Window' and 'Rope' were collectively known as 'chaff', a term frequently used in official RAF documentation.

On 23 November 1944, Thomas Butler flew his first operation while still undertaking training at No. 100 Group's 'in-house' conversion unit. His crew were engaged on a Special Duties sortie to support Bomber Command in the area of Cologne. It was a successful raid, completed in their favourite Flying Fortress 'O', 'Orange'. Thomas was able to make his first red-ink entry in his flying log book, recording four hours and twenty minutes in the air. (Air crews operating within Bomber Command adopted the practice of writing in red ink when completing night operations and green ink for daylight operations.) The crew returned to their training duties having experienced for themselves the dangers of flying over Germany.

At the end of November, Thomas and his crew were posted for operational duty with their home-based unit, No. 214 Squadron. Thomas's tour of duty commenced in earnest on 4 December; it was to be an eventful first raid for the crew over the industrial area of the Ruhr Valley. The briefings undertaken at Oulton were extremely precise: the crew were required to drop 'Window' according to very specific orders. The crew's pilot was Flt Lt Telfer, in command of Flying Fortress 'Q', HB772. The operation was a success, although the aircraft returned to Oulton with just three working engines and crash-landed on the airfield. As a result of that incident, Thomas and his entire crew were directed to return to the Conversion Flight, where they were instructed to re-form with a new pilot, Flt Lt Don Austin. He was an experienced pilot, having recently completed a tour of duty with No. 101 Squadron and rewarded with a DFC in February 1944. The newly formed crew very quickly returned to full operational status and continued with their Special Duties with No. 214 Squadron. Flying Fortress 'Q' was repaired and the crew would once again fly in her on operational duty.

Radio counter-measures combined with specific 'Window' deployment were able to produce completely fake bomber streams to confuse the enemy's radar operators. Ten aircraft deploying 'Window' could create the impression of 100 aircraft in a main bomber stream heading towards a false target in Germany. Special 'Window' operatives needed precise timing and a high level of navigational skill; they dropped several packets per minute, whereas normal crews also using 'Window' during operations dropped just one bundle every two minutes. Manually passing the packets out of the special chutes fitted in the floor at the waist gunner's position for extensive periods could prove to be an

Crew photograph: Flt Lt Austin DFC, pilot, Flt Sgt Geoffrey, navigator, Sgt Knox, engineer, Flt Sgt Bostock, bomb aimer, WO Pate, rear gunner, Sgt Lewis, waist gunner, Fg Off. Levine, special operator, Flt Sgt Richardson, wireless operator/air gunner, Sgt Piper, air gunner, and Sgt Butler, waist gunner.

exhausting task; Thomas was connected to the oxygen supply and was wearing the extensive clothing required to combat the freezing temperatures. Scientists had attempted to devise automatic dispensers, but they were proving difficult to develop to the required levels of accuracy. In contrast, the special dispatch chutes adjacent to the waist gunners' positions were found to be very effective; they remained in use for the special 'Window' forces aircraft until the end of the war. The foil strips were wrapped in brown paper bundles about 1 foot long by 3 inches across. Each individual bundle had a string attached, and Thomas would push the bundles down the chute holding onto the looped string. As it reached the slipstream, the string ripped the wrapping and the contents was scattered.

In February 1945, Thomas completed a further seven 'Window' patrols. One raid to München-Gladbach on the night of the 22nd was conducted over a lengthy six hours, during which his Flying Fortress 'U' was attacked by a belligerent Luftwaffe fighter. The two waist gunners, Sgts Butler and Lewis, standing no more than a couple of feet apart, operated their guns in earnest during a sustained attack that saw the fighter eventually defeated. In his flying log book entry, Thomas neatly wrote, 'Combat Fighter Driven Off'. The Special Duties squadrons deploying radio counter-measures to the skies over Germany completed no fewer than forty-eight individual sorties on that particular night.

On 2 March 1945, Thomas and his crew operated a 'Window' patrol for the raid to Delmenhorst, near Bremen. Flying Fortress 'Q' was operational for the first time since its crash-landing three months before. The operation went without incident until Flt Lt Austin landed at Oulton, and one of the tyres unexpectedly burst on touchdown. Flying Fortress 'Q' had once again suffered some damage, but fortunately the crew sustained no injuries. The aircraft was repaired and flown just five days later by the same crew, but it seemed that 'Q' had become a rather jinxed aircraft. One engine failed completely, forcing the pilot to return just one hour into the operation. Worryingly for Thomas, his log book recorded the next sortie as his unlucky thirteenth. Once again, his crew had been allocated the recently repaired 'Q'. The superstitious airmen would have much rather taken another aircraft on that particular night, but the six-hour-twenty-five-minute raid to Hanau, east of Frankfurt-on-Main, took place without incident. Regarding this flight, No. 214 Squadron's operations records state: 'This aircraft carried out a Jostle patrol, jamming being carried out.' 'Jostle' was the codename for electronic counter-measures equipment carried in the aircraft's bomb bay. The 'Jostle' hardware was impressive for its day, and the transmitter, built into a high-pressure cylinder, weighed over 600 lbs. The pressurisation of the device was needed to prevent electrical arcing at high altitudes. It was used primarily against HF and VHF transmissions, employing narrow band jamming against specific enemy emitters on VHF and broad band jamming on HF.

Thomas had by now accumulated well over 100 hours of night flying. In April 1945, he completed a further two successful 'Window' operations and five 'Jostle'

Sergeant Butler, leaning on his gun in the waist gunner's opening with his fellow waist gunner Sergeant Lewis alongside him. The 'Window' chute can be seen below right and the trailing aerial point below left. Of particular interest are the shields designed to prevent any field of gunfire from being discharged into the wings or tail of the Flying Fortress, and the small wind deflection shield fitted to the fuselage to reduce the wind across the gunner's position. These two men would be photographed together in a similar pose, still serving together as Air Cadet Corps instructors, nearly forty years later.

sorties, visiting Stade, Lübeck, Plauen, and Kiel in Germany, as well as Pilsen and Komotau in Czechoslovakia and Tønsberg in Norway. A raid on 10 April to the extensive railway network at Plauen saw the crew flying for nearly nine hours. All of the pre-flight operational briefings stipulated the exact distribution of 'Window' required; the rate could fluctuate between an initial forty bundles a minute to sixty bundles a minute. That type of distribution required Thomas to sit on the floor of the aircraft, surrounded by the brown paper packages. He would be assisted by another member of the crew, but one waist gunner's position was manned at all times. The 'Window' packs were marked according to their type as the reflective metal tin-foil strips were cut and packed to differing lengths; once again, the dropping orders specified the type to deploy.

By now, Thomas's total operational sorties had risen to twenty, but his pilot, Flt Lt Austin, in his second tour of duty, had accumulated a sufficient number of raids to be regarded as tour-expired. He was rested from operations and would later be rewarded with a bar to his DFC for his services with No. 214 Squadron. One of the squadron's now famous pilots, Flt Lt Johnny Wynne, had recently made a remarkable return from an operation over Germany in which his aircraft had been badly hit by enemy flak and had caught fire. The situation was considered to be hopeless, and all the crew bailed out as ordered by the pilot, who thought that they were well over Allied territory and that the crew would therefore be landing in safety. A serious fire was burning in one engine, perilously close

Time carried forward :— 47·50 72·

Date	Hour	Aircraft Type and No.	Pilot	Duty	Remarks (including results of bombing, gunnery, exercises, etc.)	Flying Times Day	Night
3/45	19·00	FORTRESS. 'Q'	F/LT. AUSTIN.	WAIST GUNNER	OPS. 9TH WINDOW PATROL. DELMENSHORST. (TYRE BURST ON TOUCH-DOWN.)		4·2
/45	17·25	FORTRESS. 'U'	F/LT. AUSTIN.	WAIST GUNNER.	OPS. 10TH CHEMNITZ. TARGET.		8·4
/45	18·10	FORTRESS. 'U'	F/LT. AUSTIN.	WAIST GUNNER.	OPS. 11TH WINDOW PATROL. FEHMARN.		7·0
/45	17·45	FORTRESS. 'Q'	F/LT. AUSTIN.	WAIST GUNNER.	EARLY RETURN. № 2 ENGINE FAILURE.		2·0
/45	17·40	FORTRESS. 'T'	F/LT. AUSTIN.	WAIST GUNNER.	№ 2 ENGINE FAILURE IN CIRCUIT.		0·2
3/45	18·10	FORTRESS. 'U'	F/LT. AUSTIN.	WAIST GUNNER.	OPS. 12TH WÜRZBURG. TARGET.		7·3
3/45	01·20	FORTRESS. 'Q'	F/LT. AUSTIN.	WAIST GUNNER.	OPS. 13TH HANAU. TARGET.		6·2
3/45	00·05	FORTRESS. 'V'	F/LT. AUSTIN.	WAIST GUNNER.	OPS. 14TH WINDOW PATROL. HALLE. (SECONDARY TARGET)		8·4

Flying log book entries recorded for March 1945. Note the events of the burst tyre and engine failures during this period of duty.

to the wing fuel tank, and Flt Lt Wynne was anticipating his own escape when the aircraft unexpectedly started responding to the controls and the fire appeared to be extinguishing itself. His parachute had accidentally been deployed in the aircraft as he extracted himself from his cockpit seat in anticipation of baling out, so he was forced to attempt to fly the aircraft back to England. The engine fire did finally go out, and remarkably, against all odds, he managed to navigate back to Britain where he made an emergency landing at RAF Bassingbourn.

Within a few weeks of that amazing escape, Johnny Wynne adopted Thomas Butler's crew and began flying with them on 20 April 1945. He had personally written to the families of his crew members who had parachuted from his stricken Flying Fortress, confident that they had landed in Allied territory and would soon all return safely. Unfortunately, that was not the case. They had in fact landed in Germany, and his hopes rested with receiving news from the Red Cross of their imprisonment and status as PoWs. However, unbeknown to Flt Lt Wynne, several of his crew had suffered a terrible fate. Five of them had been executed by members of the Hitler Youth and other civilians under the instruction or incitement of local Nazi leaders. Post-war investigations located the majority of those responsible, and a trial took place in 1946. Twenty-two defendants appeared, of whom five were acquitted, three sentenced to death, and one given a life sentence. The remaining offenders received prison sentences ranging from two to fifteen years. One of the three surviving crew members, Fg Off. Dudley Heal DFM, a member of Guy Gibson's famous No. 617 'Dambusters' Squadron, had been lawfully detained by the Wehrmacht after landing on a factory roof. He became a PoW for two months until the end of the war, and was repatriated on 17 May 1945. It was only in 1993 that Dudley found out to his horror that five of his former crew from No. 214 Squadron had been murdered. His former crewmate, Fg Off. Tom Tate, the crew's special operator, had escaped murder but had witnessed it, and was later to provide evidence of the crimes committed.

The bodies of the five murdered airmen now lie in the war cemetery at Durnbach. The cemetery was chosen for these men shortly after hostilities had ceased. The great majority of those buried there are airmen shot down over Bavaria, Württemberg, and Austria. It is also the last resting place of the men who were killed while escaping from prisoner-of-war camps in the same areas, and of those who died towards the end of the war on forced marches ordered by Hitler from the camps threatened by the Russian advance from the east.

At the cessation of hostilities, Thomas Butler had completed twenty-two Special Duties operations over occupied Europe. On average, the operational

'The Boys May 1945'—Johnny Wynne's newly adopted crew seen alongside Flying Fortress KJ117 'E' Easy. The nose art 'Take it Easy' apparently depicted St Peter and the Devil gambling with dice—no doubt derived from the term 'dicing with death'. The large radar housing is clearly seen sitting below the nose section. Standing left to right are Fg Off. Stevens, WO Bostock, Flt Lt Wynne, WO Godfrey, and Flt Sgt Richardson. Front row left to right are Fg Off. Moore, Flt Sgt Butler, Plt Off. Knox, Flt Sgt Lewis, and Flt Sgt Piper.

hours recorded in his flying log book equated to a duration of five hours and forty minutes per operation. During Operation Exercise, between June and September 1945, No. 214 Squadron had flown a number of important sorties designed to test and examine the effectiveness of the Allied radio counter-measures. Many of the German electronic counter-measures were now accessible to the Allies, and Operation Exercise was able to demonstrate how both sides had progressed in this new, complex, and technical field.

In September 1945, Thomas and his crew were posted to the Radio Warfare Establishment at RAF Foulsham. The final flight recorded in Thomas's flying log was made on 12 January 1946. At 1020 hours he took off in Flying Fortress 'E', KJ117, with Flt Lt Wynne and completed a fifty-five-minute air test. Thomas retired from the RAF on 16 March 1946, a lifelong friend of Johnny Wynne. His flying log book recorded a grand total of 315 hours and 50 minutes' flying.

During the post-war years, Thomas Butler developed a passion for flying gliders while serving with No. 624 Gliding School, Volunteer Reserve Unit, at Chivenor in Devon. He later became a fully qualified flying instructor on gliders, recording a total of 3,127 glider flights between 1964 and 1980. With the rank of Flight Lieutenant, he commanded No. 624 Gliding School between 1974 and 1980. His fellow waist gunner from No. 214 Squadron, Sgt Lewis, also served in a similar capacity in the Air Cadets. The two friends were once more photographed together on 25 August 1983, but on this occasion in the fuselage of a helicopter. Both men proudly wore their air gunners' 'wings' and medal ribbons. For his services to the Air Cadets, Thomas was additionally awarded the Cadet Forces Medal.

No. 214 Squadron 'Air Gunners' Flt Sgt Butler and Flt Sgt Lewis, *c.* 1983.

8

Harold Jepson DFC (USA) Electronic Jamming

Harold Jepson's military service changed completely when he transferred from the 93rd Regiment Royal Artillery into the RAF. In early 1941 he attended the RAF Receiving Wing at Stratford-upon-Avon with aspirations of becoming a pilot, and commenced what was to be a highly eventful career in the RAF.

On 25 June 1941, at the Airwork Reserve Training School in Perth, Scotland, Harold took his first solo flight in a Tiger Moth after less than ten hours' instruction. It was soon obvious that he had an aptitude for flying, but still, his training was not without incident. His first experience of what can go wrong in an aircraft occurred on 8 October, while flying under instruction in an Airspeed Oxford at No. 15 Flying Training School. Harold's aircraft R6159 'pranged' heavily on landing, causing some damage to the undercarriage but luckily no injuries to himself or the instructor. Despite this, Harold was assessed as a gifted pilot and rose through the ranks, being quickly commissioned as a pilot officer by the end of October and awarded his 'wings'.

Plt Off. Harold Jepson was selected to be a flying instructor, but this was far from what he wanted. Having transferred from the Army, he had wanted to fly in a front-line squadron, but the training of student pilots was of the utmost importance to the RAF and those men with the natural flare and ability to instruct were always selected with care.

Having been instructed on twin-engine Oxford aircraft, Harold knew that he would be destined for a posting on multi-engined aircraft, most probably in Bomber Command. However, he was to remain instructing in Tiger Moths and Airspeed Oxfords for nearly eight months until, in June 1942, he unexpectedly received a posting to attend No. 1 Glider Training School. In no time at all he found himself in aircraft that had no propulsion whatsoever, piloting Hotspur gliders that were towed into the air and cast adrift in the clouds. Once again, he was assessed and his natural abilities saw him graded as an excellent glider pilot instructor.

Harold's student pilots were from the first Army Air Corps, which included the Glider Pilot Regiment, Parachute Regiment, and Special Air Service. He

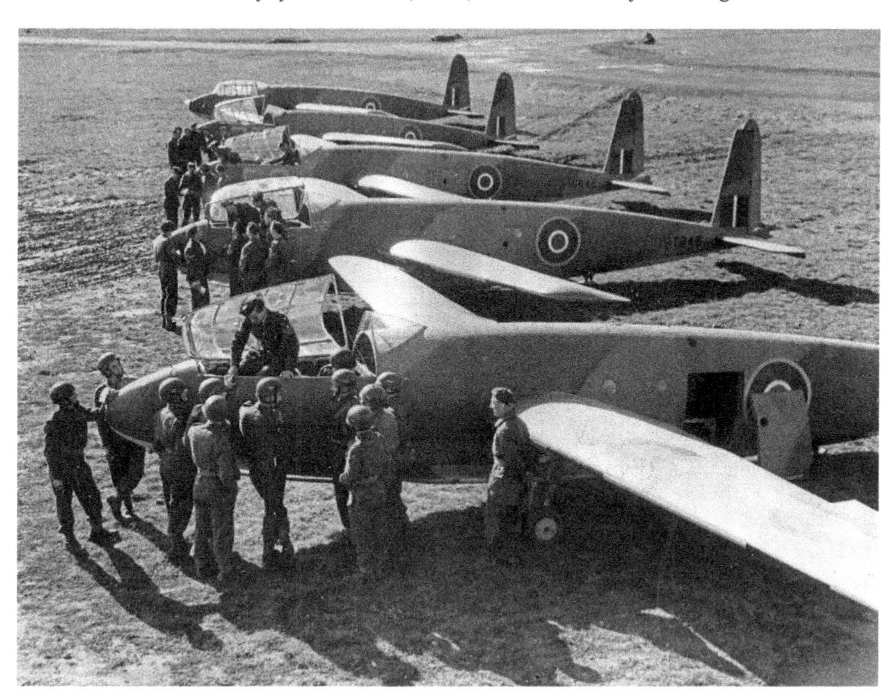

RAF instructors with student pilots under tuition on the Hotspur Gliders. This version of the Hotspur was a high performance glider with a wingspan of 62 feet and capable of gliding silently for long distances, making it ideal for instructional purposes. The later Mark II was designed to be taken into action at low altitude with a steep fast approach, needing little gliding capacity. The wingspan was reduced to 46 feet and the more robust fuselage given two side doors for exit of the troops. No operational tasks were undertaken by the Hotspur as the much improved Horsa glider soon replaced it.

instructed a vast number of students at the glider school, and his log book recorded many names that would later become significant in aviation history. One of those names was S/Sgt Jim Wallwork of the Army's Glider Pilot Regiment, who received instruction from Harold during July 1942 and went on to become the first Allied serviceman to land on French soil on D-Day. After releasing his Horsa glider from the towing aircraft, he piloted it with incredible skill in complete darkness, landing it next to the Caen Bridge, just twenty minutes into D-Day on 6 June 1944. He was flying the first of six Horsas carrying soldiers of 'D' Company, 2nd Battalion Oxfordshire and Buckinghamshire Light Infantry, to capture two key bridges, and was thrown head-first through the Perspex windscreen of his glider as it hit French soil. He later received the Distinguished Flying Medal (DFM) for his part in this daring, and successful, operation.

Among the successes, there were, of course, some tragedies. On 7 September 1942, Harold took student pilot Cpl Thomas Ellidge of the 1st Glider Pilot Regiment on an assessment flight in Hotspur 402. Later that day the student was authorised for his first solo flight and was again taken up in the Hotspur. The Miles Master towing aircraft took to the air with no difficulty, but was later seen to dive into the ground and burst into flames, pulling the glider into a steep dive and crashing it close to the towing aircraft. No reasonable explanation as to why the glider pilot did not release the tow was ever given. The pilot of the aircraft, Plt Off. James Evans, aged twenty-one, was killed, as was Cpl Ellidge, aged twenty.

It was not until March 1943 that Harold eventually left the Glider Training School. He was again posted into an instructional role at a Radio School, flying the Avro Anson on endless training sorties until the end of that year. Eventually, in January 1944, Harold embarked on operational flying. He arrived at his OTU with an exceptional 1,000 hours of flying recorded in his flying log book—an intimidating prospect for the instructors providing the conversion training onto the larger Wellington bombers.

On 4 April, tragedy struck at the base when a sixteen-year-old ATC cadet, Leslie Shearwood, was killed during low-level flying. He was from No. 107 Air Training Corps and was taking advantage of an opportunity to gain some air experience with a willing pilot. Harold would have been used to Air Cadets on station as they regularly undertook week-long summer camps and frequently sought to fly gliders. The pilot, an instructor at the training unit, accidently struck some treetops at Steeple Aston and the aircraft crashed, killing Leslie Shearwood. The inquest into this accident opened at the base on 10 April 1944, the day of Harold's first excursion into enemy-held territory.

Harold piloted a Wellington bomber across to France, over Angers and the Loire Valley, where propaganda leaflets were dropped from a height of 15,000 feet. He returned safely to Little Horwood after a flight of four hours and thirty-five minutes. Raids such as this were known as 'nickelling' operations; by this time, the value of dropping propaganda leaflets had been well established, and the tactic was developed continually during the war by the Political Warfare Executive. These 'nickels', or leaflets, were intended to lower the morale of enemy troops, and help motivate resistance. Enormous quantities of them were produced. The publication *Le Courrier de l'Air*, a French-language miniature newspaper, was also intended to boost morale and was distributed across France. Such miniature magazines often had a camouflaged cover to hide the contents, as the German authorities strictly enforced a ban. A post-war study on the distribution of leaflets by Maj. R. H. Garet suggests that during the war almost 6 billion leaflets were distributed over the western European theatre by aircraft based in the UK.

Converting onto the large four-engine Stirling bombers was Harold's next target. He achieved that at RAF Wratting Common, flying with a regular crew that appeared to be very capable and one which would in all probability remain together operationally. Finally, at the end of June 1944, the operational posting arrived, directing the newly formed crew to RAF North Creake, one of the exclusive aerodromes that operated within the secret No. 100 Group in Norfolk. The emblem of No. 100 Group is the head of Medusa and it carries the motto 'Confound and Destroy'—and confound and destroy they certainly did. Joining No. 199 Squadron at North Creake, Harold would continue flying in the huge and imposing Stirling aircraft, but his duties were to be very specific and challenging.

No. 199 Squadron was providing electronic counter-measures to thwart the German early warning radar systems that were capable of detecting the movements of Allied bombers. It was a battle between the scientists of both countries. While flying on predetermined flight paths, the RAF's No. 100 Group deployed 'Mandrel', a jamming device operated by a member of the crew assigned as the special operator. The navigation section at North Creake devised what was known as the 'racecourse' pattern, in which circuits were flown nearly perpendicular to the enemy coast line. The first circuit was 10 miles long and each subsequent circuit was to take exactly ten minutes; wind adjustments were required to maintain the exact proximity and accuracy of the electronic screen. Two of the squadron's Stirlings, equipped with 'Mandrel', started the operations from opposite ends and this created a high level of jamming. They were followed by multiple pairs of 'Mandrel'-equipped aircraft to disrupt German early warning radar over significant areas.

Additionally, 'Creeping Mandrel' was employed by extending the upward flight and lessening the downward flight of each circuit to create a moving screen. These duties required high levels of navigational and piloting skills, and the Stirling aircraft were stretched to the limits of their capabilities, especially as they needed to fly at their absolute maximum height. The 'Mandrel'-equipped Stirlings were immediately identifiable as they had several aerials protruding down from the floor of the fuselage. These each related to the different types of 'Mandrel' transmitters carried in the aircraft.

Harold commenced his long overdue operational flying in July 1944. The Special Duties squadrons had been a crucial ingredient to the D-Day invasion and they constantly worked among the complex infrastructure of Bomber Command's operations. No. 199 Squadron records reflect the secrecy of their work, stating only, 'Special Mission, Bomber Protection Support by Mandrel Screen'. Harold's flying log book is even more laconic, with entries such as 'OPS' and 'SD' in red ink. Each operation, around five hours in duration and undertaken in the late evenings and early hours, was exacting for the pilots, and the navigators in particular. In September 1944, Harold was required to provide the 'Mandrel' protection while actually flying within the Bomber Command bomber stream. The complex developments of electronic counter-measures had been absorbed into Special Duties squadrons, providing numerous methods of protection. Codenames of 'Carpet' and 'Airborne Cigar' among others were recorded in various squadron record books—they were individual methods of protection that were combined to guard the bombers.

Within this complex structure of RAF counter-measures, Harold would incorporate his duties alongside the special forces of both No. 214 Squadron, dropping the thin metal foil 'Window' strips that created false images, and No. 199 Squadron, jamming the enemy's radar with 'Mandrel'. No. 214 Squadron would cut through the jamming zones and drop additional 'Window' to create the impression that a large bombing force was heading for a likely target area in Germany. The German controllers would muster their fighter forces accordingly, while Bomber Command penetrated the jamming screen at another location to attack a completely different target that was likely to be devoid of fighter protection. This spoof was capable of being applied in reverse, and therefore always kept the enemy in a state of confusion. On 5 January 1945, the impressive and talented Luftwaffe fighter Adolf Galland is quoted as saying:

> Today the night fighter achieves nothing. The reason for this lies in the enemy's jamming operations which completely blot out ground and airborne search equipment. All other reasons are secondary.[7]

In February 1945, the Stirling bombers that had struggled to perform to the high demands of jamming operations were eventually exchanged for the superior Halifax. No. 199 Squadron was the last squadron within Bomber Command to operate in the outdated Stirling aircraft, and the long overdue upgrade was well received. Stirling LJ525 was replaced with a Halifax that also carried the 'Jolly Roger' skull-and-crossbones artwork.

Harold flew a total of forty Special Duties operations with No. 199 Squadron before the war concluded; he was promoted to squadron leader and given command of 'B' Flight. He and his crew had escaped unscathed, and had the satisfaction of knowing that they had protected to the best of their ability the lives of hundreds of air crew personnel who flew on bombing operations into Germany.

The last operation for No. 199 Squadron took place on the night of 2 May 1945, providing 'Mandrel' protection for a raid over Kiel. Intelligence reported that large contingents of motorised troops were converging on the port, where an armada of shipping was assembled. It was feared that these forces were reinforcements for the Wehrmacht in Norway, which was still largely intact at that time. Eighty-nine Halifax aircraft were provided by No. 100 Group to support what was to be the last operation by Bomber Command in the Second World War. Within this contingent of Halifaxes were six from No. 199 Squadron, including RG373 and RG375—two aircraft in which Harold and his crew had flown during the final months of the war. Tragically, while over the target area these two aircraft collided, with terrible consequences. Both

No. 199 Squadron Halifax *Jolly Roger*. The 'Mandrel' aerials can be clearly seen in this image. This was a far superior aircraft to fly for Flight Lieutenant Jepson. It is unknown if he or any of his crew were party to painting the new artwork onto the fuselage. The new Halifax *Jolly Roger* airframe was not unique to Harold's crew and was flown by several pilots. (*Harold Jepson collection*)

aircraft were completely destroyed, crashing at Meimersdorf, just south of Kiel. Thirteen air crew, the majority of whom were on their second tour of duty, lost their lives and now rest in Kiel War Cemetery. They were the last men to be killed during hostile operations for Bomber Command.

On 19 June 1945, the opportunity for ground crews to be flown across Germany on sightseeing sorties was provided at North Creake. Flying low over Germany, Harold was able to identify several of the targets that he had previously flown to in total darkness. For the ground crews it was an opportunity to share with their colleagues the experience of flying and to witness first-hand the utter destruction of the Third Reich, as inflicted by Bomber Command.

A major evaluation took place at the end of hostilities, and Harold Jepson and his crew were engaged in several experimental sorties undertaken to test the seized Luftwaffe radar equipment in Denmark. Following those sorties, RAF North Creake, and indeed No. 100 Group itself, ran down to disbandment. The final entry in the squadron's record book was made on 29 July. The record noted that No. 199 Squadron had been operational for some thirty months and had engaged upon 2,941 sorties of a varied nature within Bomber Command, and that thirty-four aircraft and crews had been lost. The final line reads:

Squadron Leader Jepson leading his men at the march past during the disbandment ceremonies at North Creake. In the distance the squadron's Halifax aircraft have been positioned to face the ceremony.

> The life of 199 Squadron, which though short has contributed in no small measure to the overwhelming success of that splendid organisation Bomber Command which played such a great part in absolute and final victory over Germany.[8]

The King awarded Harold a Mention in Despatches in January 1946 for distinguished service. More surprisingly, in June he was advised that the Air Ministry had awarded him, in order N567/1946, the United States DFC in recognition of joint operations with the USAAF, which had been so significant in the electronic warfare race for air superiority. On 14 April 1945, Harold had flown on operations to Berlin accompanied by several American Liberator aircraft on what proved to be one of the last major aviation incursions into central Germany. The award was conferred by the President of the United States on 14 June 1946, and Harold Jepson is one of only 126 men in the UK forces to receive this award.

9

Harry Orme AFM Glider Towing, SOE Supply Dropping

Harry Orme was destined to be involved as a member of air crew in the first and possibly the most significant engagement on D-Day: the taking of Pegasus Bridge in Normandy. Originally known as the Caen Canal Bridge, it was a vital strategic objective for Operation Overlord, the Allied invasion of France. The attack at Pegasus Bridge is enshrined in history as the first offensive action during the Allied invasion of occupied Europe on that most famous of days, 6 June 1944.

Harry had grown up in a mining family at Hednesford in Staffordshire. He began his service in the RAF as a leading aircraftman in early 1941, and his selection and assessment to serve as air crew eventually saw him posted to the Air Observers School at Penrhos in Caernarvonshire. Harry had hoped to qualify as an observer, a title that was later universally known as navigator; he had excelled in maths and science at grammar school, and these academic skills were deemed desirable for navigators. He had also qualified as a teacher and acted as an air-raid warden before volunteering to join the RAF. Harry was engaged to be married and, at thirty-two years of age, was also much older than the average recruit.

Having been issued with his Observer's and Air Gunner's Flying Log Book, Harry entered his very first account of aerial map reading on 9 July 1941. This humble one-hour-thirty-minute experience in a Bristol Blenheim aircraft was to herald a highly illustrious operational career for Harry. He would later be awarded one of the rarest medals given to members of the RAF during the Second World War. Many of the resident pilots at the Air Observers School in Penrhos were Polish; the names of Sgts Grochowski, Buchowski, and Slomski were frequently entered into Harry's log book. These pilots flew Harry on his regular navigational exercises until his departure to No. 42 OTU at Andover in early 1942. Attached to 'B' Flight and with a regular pilot, John Kruytbosch, Harry continued to fly in Blenheims. Together they engaged in some twenty training sorties, all of which were successful, until on 20 March Kruytbosch applied Blenheim Z6271's brakes too hard on landing. The churned-up ground caused the aircraft to slip off the taxi track, resulting in the collapse of the undercarriage.

Flying with Kruytbosch was a rather eventful experience for Harry. They frequently crewed in Blenheim V5378, and on 21 April that aircraft sustained similar damage with Kruytbosch at the controls. The rather ill-fated team were posted to join No. 13 Squadron, and Harry recorded in his log book that they took an early morning sortie to 'Beat up Guildford' on 17 May. This was a term used to indicate flying low passes over a particular property or area; frequently it would be a place with some association to a member of the crew. It appears that following their escapades over Guildford, Blenheim V6251 returned to Odiham only to taxi into a rather deep unmarked ditch, causing the undercarriage to collapse. Harry again recorded 'Crashed' in his flying log book.

No. 13 Squadron was flying Blenheims operationally, but despite being regarded as an Army Co-Operation Squadron, Harry was not engaged in any of that work. Following the last landing incident he was seconded as the navigator to Gp Capt. Cooper, eventually returning to crew with Kruytbosch in June 1942. Both men subsequently returned to No. 42 OTU the following month. The partnership between Harry and his pilot was finally ended on 16 July, after they had flown together on a training exercise. Fg Off. Kruytbosch subsequently returned to No. 13 Squadron and departed with them for operational duties

Harry Orme wearing his flying uniform consisting of the early 'B' Type flying helmet and the 1940-pattern Sidcot flying suit. His boots are the sheepskin-lined 1939 pattern with canvas upper section. They were always regarded as being very comfortable. (*Harry Orme collection*)

in North Africa. Unbeknown to Harry, during a night operational raid on 14 December 1942, Kruytbosch's Blenheim BA747 struck the roof of a hut on take off, causing the aircraft to crash. All three crew members were killed.

Back in the UK, Harry started to forge another partnership that was to prove lifelong. On 30 July he crewed with Plt Off. John Sizmur, a pre-war pilot from Croydon in Surrey who had arrived at the OTU that month, having been awarded his 'wings' while training in Canada. Once again, Harry flew numerous training sorties until they were posted to join No. 295 Squadron, which had only recently been formed as an Airborne Forces unit at RAF Netheravon. The squadron consisted of three Flights, all equipped with Whitley aircraft, and engaged in training for the various means of transporting troops, including glider towing and experimentation in night-time parachute dropping. In November 1942, Harry made two red-ink night entries to that effect; his flying log book at that time recorded over 250 hours' flying experience. Harry's first navigation over enemy-held territory occurred on the night of 5 December, when No. 295 Squadron dispatched five Whitleys on leaflet dropping operations across France. Plt Off. Sizmur flew their Whitley aircraft to the south coast, crossing at Selsey Bill, and then over the Channel to Paris in a sortie of four hours and thirty-five minutes. Harry's navigation was perfect and the propaganda leaflets were successfully scattered across the French capital, but adverse weather conditions demanded a landing at Thruxton.

The new year required glider-towing exercises to be completely mastered, and towing the Horsa glider was not a simple procedure. When towing a glider the general performance of the tug is impaired, and care needs to be applied—particularly in the take off and initial climb. Attention to the engines in relation to overheating is imperative, and they should not be run prior to take off in an effort to reduce their temperature during the actual take off. The tow rope adopted in Britain tended to be around 350 feet long, but shorter ropes are also documented, and if the tow ropes were overstressed they were known to break. The glider pilots were required to fly slightly above and behind the towing aircraft, with a little slack in the tow rope. Towing sorties at night required the rear gunner of the tug aircraft to illuminate a red lamp, allowing the glider pilot to adjust and maintain that same position while avoiding the turbulent air created by the tug aircraft's propellers. A communication wire was wound within the tow rope to allow direct contact between the two pilots. The training sorties required the glider to cast off from the tow and drop away to perform its independent landing. It was advisable to cast off from the tug with the glider in the high tow position, and there was a centrally located tow release lever in the glider cockpit making it accessible to both pilot and co-pilot at any time. The tug aircraft retained the tow rope, normally releasing it by the universal coupling, to fall to the ground in an identified dropping area. It would be recovered and examined carefully before being used again.

LE COURRIER DE L'AIR

APPORTE PAR LA R.A.F. *LONDRES, 3 DECEMBRE · 194*

Les Nations Unies rendent hommage à la Flotte Française

LES explosions de Toulon ont retenti aux quatre coins du monde. Les Nations Unies, alliées de la France, s'inclinent devant les marins français qui, dans des circonstances tragiques, ont arraché à Hitler la proie sur laquelle il se lançait.

Le sacrifice de la flotte de Toulon enlève à Hitler le dernier vestige de l'espoir qu'il avait de changer en faveur de l'Axe la balances des forces en Méditerranée.

De Coventry à Stalingrad, de Washington à Rio de Janeiro, de Londres à Moscou les Nations Unies rendent hommage à la Marine française, à ses chefs, à ses officiers, à ses hommes.

M. Churchill, dans le discours qu'il a radiodiffusé, déclara à ce sujet:

" Cette flotte, dont la triste fin fut l'œuvre d'une folie fatale, sinon pire, a racheté son honneur par son sacrifice suprême. De la fumée, des flammes et des explosions de Toulon, la France resurgira."

Lord Halifax, ambassadeur de Grande-Bretagne aux Etats-Unis, parlant à Richmond, Virginie, a dit de la Marine française:

" Saluons les braves marins de la Flotte française qui ont préféré la mort plutôt que de voir leurs navires servir contre la liberté française."

" L'épée a jailli de nouveau du fourreau avant d'être engloutie dans l'eau," écrit le *Times:* " les hommes de France étaient mûs par le même esprit que ceux de St. Nazaire et des innombrables patriotes inconnus qui, silencieusement, frappent la soldatesque allemande et la machine allemande depuis l'armistice. 'Ils ont sû mourir' disent les Français; mais ceux de Toulon se sont montrés dignes de vivre — de vivre sous un régime bien meilleur et bien plus résolu que celui de Vichy. Leur acte est le jugement suprême de la collaboration."

Le grand écrivain russe, Ilya Ehrenbourg, rend un hommage vibrant dont voici quelques passages:

" Le 27 novembre 1942 les matelots français ont sabordé le cuirassé *Dunkerque*. En 1940, au mois de mai, dans la ville de Dunkerque, la France fut la victime d'une tragédie sans parallèle. Le 27 novembre le cuirassé *Dunkerque* a remporté une grande victoire sur les Allemands, il est mort à son poste de combat.

" Les nations qui luttent pour la liberté ont entendu le dernier salut du navire qui sombrait. Le 27 novembre 1942 la France tout entière s'est jointe aux Alliés en guerre. Les explosions de Toulon

appliqueront, par de nouvelles victoires, la loi du talion. Les explosions de Toulon seront entendues par les héros de Stalingrad qui anéantissent les bouchers de la France, et dans la fumée de la bataille les défenseurs de Stalingrad crieront: 'Gloire aux marins de Toulon! Vive la liberté!'"

Vichy s'exprime objectivement

Vichy lui-même, pendant les quelques heures qui ont précédé l'achèvement de l'envahissement de la France, reflétait l'atmosphère de dignité qui enveloppait Toulon. Sa radio faisait preuve

DES TROUPES FRANCAISES PARTENT POUR LA TUNISIE

Un contingent des troupes de l'armée française défile sur le quai de la gare de Oran devant une garde d'honneur de soldats américains.

L'Italie reçoit des bombes de 4000 kilos

Pour la onzième fois depuis le début de l'offensive actuelle des Nations Unies en Afrique du Nord et en Méditerranée, une puissante formation de bombardiers britanniques décollait de Grande-Bretagne dans la soirée du 28 novembre pour infliger à l'Italie la plus puissante attaque aérienne qu'aucune de ses cités ait subie dans cette guerre.

Le raid, dont l'objectif était d'une importance telle que le communiqué italien lui-même les qualifia de " ingento " (énormes).

Les Arsenaux royaux, les usines Fiat, les usines d'aviation Caproni et bien d'autres usines de guerre furent attaqués avec un grand degré de précision. Les conditions atmosphériques au-dessus de Turin étaient bonnes et un seul de nos appareils n'a pas

Offensives russes

L'HIVER N'APPORT PAS DE REPIT AUX ALLEMANDS

LE discours de M. Churchill a révélé qu grande opération anglo-américaine en rique du Nord et les offensives russes su front oriental font partie d'un plan qu Premier Ministre britannique avait mis point avec M. Staline, lors de sa visite en Il donne ainsi la preuve concrète que l'initi est passée aux mains des Nations Unies.

Il est fort difficile de pr ce que sera dans l'aveni stratégie russe, qui a déjà d'une fois étonné le monde de juin 1941. Toutefois, cert caractéristiques de la camp actuelle tendent à indiquer l'objectif immédiat du Commandement russe est n'accorder aucun répit aux mées allemandes enfoncées les profondeurs de la Russi elles sont obligées de passer deuxième hiver. Ainsi, au d'engager toutes leurs f disponibles sur le front de S grad, où ils avaient réu surprendre et à mettre en dé les corps d'armée allem les Russes ont déclenché une offensive de grande envergu le secteur central.

Conséquence de ces deux sives, les troupes allem accrochées à Stalingrad da sud et à Rjeff au centre presque encerclées, car les R ont, dans les deux cas, coup lignes ferroviaires vitales. Allemands n'ont pas l'ordre d'une retraite gén Ceci indique peut-être qu'il des réserves disponibles pou contre-offensives sérieuses. peut aussi que le Führer-mandant-en-Chef hésite à d l'ordre d'évacuer de vast fertiles territoires qui font mi tant d'espoirs alimentaires au ventre allemand.

Un développement plus de l'offensive russe à Stali peut mettre en danger les a germano-roumaines opérant le Caucase. Sur le front c une continuation des russes peut mettre en pé armées ennemies basées Smolensk et opérant contre grad.

L'armée russe est assez pour priver les Alleman répit d'hiver dont ils on besoin.

Les Grecs avai

The unusual nose configuration of the Whitley is seen in this impressive image and the oil leaks along the engine covers indicate that this is a well-used aircraft. The landing light inset in the wing is a feature not frequently seen in photographs of the type.

Opposite: Harry retained as a keepsake a copy of a leaflet which had been dropped over Paris. The four-page leaflet was dated 3 December 1942; he had dropped them over France just two days after they were printed. *Le Courrier de L'Air* became a standard information leaflet deployed across France during the Second World War.

During the Second World War a variety of aircraft types were used to tug or tow larger gliders. The Whitley, one of the first heavy night bombers of the RAF, had a characteristic nose-down flying attitude created by the design of the wing. From 1942 onwards, the Whitley was frequently used as a trainer and glider tug.

The Short Stirling was the first of the RAF's four-engine heavy bombers, but it was to be swiftly replaced by the Lancaster and Halifax. However, the Stirling continued to serve in several roles, including tug duties. The Albemarle was designed as a light bomber and was one of very few aircraft to be fitted with a tricycle-style undercarriage. This aircraft was also used for glider tug duties. The C-47, probably the most recognised of all transport aircraft deployed during the war, was adapted from the Douglas DC-3 commercial airliner to carry personnel and cargo and to tow gliders and drop paratroopers. The Halifax heavy bomber, possibly less well-known than the iconic Lancaster but just as important, equipped many squadrons within Bomber Command and became the tug for the largest glider deployed in the Second World War.

The Hamilcar glider was an important contribution to the development of glider towing operations. Flt Lt R. W. H. Carter, piloting a Halifax, made the first flight trials to tow this extraordinarily large glider. This unique combination of aircraft and glider was to be responsible for carrying the heaviest single load of equipment in support of the famous Pegasus Bridge operation, immediately prior to the invasion of France on 6 June 1944.

The Hamilcar crew consisted of a pilot and co-pilot, sitting one behind the other in tandem fashion high above the glider's fuselage. Access to the cockpit from within the fuselage was by way of the cargo bay, or for the pilot and co-pilot, by climbing a ladder to the top of the fuselage and entering via Perspex doors on each side of the cockpit. After reaching the target area, the glider was released from the tow rope and it simply glided to its chosen landing site. As soon as it came to a stop, the crew would exit the cockpit, slide down over the sides of the fuselage and release the valves in the undercarriage struts, which then lowered the fuselage to rest on the ground. The vehicle or tank crew would have started their engine while gliding to the landing site. There was a flexible tube that connected the vehicle's exhaust to a port opening in the side of the glider, so the tank crew would be in a position to drive away in the shortest time possible as an automatic system opened the giant door.

Returning to 1943, Harry Orme and John Sizmur both remained engaged in training, the dangers of which were highlighted during night circuits and landings on 9 January. Harry's crew completed their sorties in Whitley EB311, but Whitley EB300 overshot the landing, causing a stall—during the attempted recovery it flew into the ground, killing the crew of three, one of whom was the nineteen-year-old air gunner Ronald Phillips from Edmonton in Middlesex. Harry frequently engaged in paratroop dropping exercises, which were simply recorded in his flying log book as 'Live Drops'.

On 19 February, an unexpected briefing was called and Harry's crew was ordered to participate in a bombing raid to Distré in France. The target was an electrical substation or transformer, a rather unusual duty for No. 295 Squadron, which had recently taken charge of a few new Halifax bombers that month. The squadron was to send a total of fourteen aircraft on the operation: two Halifaxes and twelve Whitleys. Harry was flying in Whitley KB311, which took off for France at 2105 hours and safely returned at 0220 hours. However, his aircraft had suffered some significant damage from flak—a rather new and potentially deadly experience for the crew. Whitley BD538 and Halifax Z123 were both lost, most likely to flak over the target, and twelve men failed to return to Netheravon. The Whitley had been piloted by Wg Cdr Vaughan; another high-ranking officer, Sqn Ldr Crichton-Miller, an HQ staff officer, was among the crew of the Halifax.

Harry was denied the opportunity of flying in a Halifax until 23 April, one of the problems having been the lack of available flight engineers. All four-engine aircraft needed an engineer in the crew and until they arrived from their Heavy Conversion Training, No. 295 Squadron's crews remained incomplete.

Harry Orme's Flight Engineer at one of his control panels surrounded by dials and switches. The Flight Engineer is responsible for the engines, controlling the air intakes, cooling grills and fuel supplies, he advises the Pilot on managing the crucial fuel supplies.

The larger aircraft was far superior to the old Whitley, and flying in the new type gave a distinct boost to Harry and his crew. The training was incessant; in addition to the odd experiment with long tow ropes or similar matters connected to towing, duties involved shuttle flights to nearby airfields where gliders or crews needed to be collected. During May, Harry had several sorties in Halifax DG390, but on the 16th of that month another crew was tasked with a simple shuttle sortie, transporting a glider crew. A short time into the flight, the Halifax suffered engine failure. It crashed and exploded, killing all the occupants. Two days later, Harry and John performed that same duty in Halifax DK121—the lives of air crews were so often governed by luck. Harry completed the month's activity having recorded forty-five hours of flying time in the new Halifax and having amassed a grand total of 460 hours. He and his crew were evidently ready for more challenging duties; unbeknown to them, the events surrounding the proposed invasion of Sicily would have a direct impact upon their squadron.

Located at the foot of the Italian peninsula, across the Strait of Messina, Sicily is only 2½ miles from the Italian mainland and 90 miles north of the coast of Africa. The invasion of Sicily was conceived at the Casablanca Conference in January 1943. President Roosevelt and Prime Minister Churchill wanted a new operation to meet Stalin's demands to divert Germany's attention from the Eastern Front. Churchill saw this as an opportunity to attack what he described as 'the soft underbelly of Europe'. Operations to invade France would not be ready until mid-1944, so Sicily was therefore chosen as the next

Allied target in what was codenamed Operation Husky. A target date of 10 July was set for the Mediterranean D-Day, an aerial invasion that would engage both British and American paratroops and glider deployments. Gen. Dwight D. Eisenhower was the Supreme Allied Commander for Operation Husky, with British Gen. Sir Harold Alexander commanding the land component, consisting of the US Seventh Army led by Lt Gen. George S. Patton Jr, and the British Eighth Army commanded by Gen. Bernard Montgomery. These leaders—now iconic names in military history—were about to engage in an aerial invasion the likes of which had never before been experienced, and one that would act as a training ground for many of the officers and enlisted men who landed on the beaches of Normandy eleven months later.

No. 295 Squadron played a significant role in the planning for Operation Husky. The Allied landing on Sicily required British Horsa gliders to be delivered to North Africa, and the squadron's Halifax aircraft were the only ones capable of performing that task. Horsa gliders were built by the Airspeed Aviation Company in Portsmouth; the city's well-developed woodworking industry helped to accelerate production, with the first production Horsa taking to the air in September 1941. The design called for the glider to be built in sections at various woodworking factories before assembly at the Airspeed factory. It was then test flown by the RAF. Built largely of wood, the Horsa had a wingspan of 88 feet and a fuselage length of 67 feet. The landing gear could be jettisoned after take off, and shock-absorbing skids provided the means of landing safely. The Horsa went into full production after the invasion of Sicily and became the most prolific glider to be used by British airborne forces in the Second World War.

The RAF codenamed the glider delivery mission to North Africa as Operation Beggar, and the Glider Pilot Regiment came up with an individual operational order—Operation Turkey Buzzard. Regardless of the name, forty Horsa gliders were to be towed from England to North Africa over some 1,350 miles of open sea, and through areas susceptible to interception by enemy aircraft, in particular the Bay of Biscay. In addition, the ever-present dangers of weather fronts created harrowing prospects. It was a groundbreaking proposal; nothing like it had been carried out previously. No. 295 Squadron's specially modified Halifax bombers had a much-increased range and endurance over the standard Halifax, and each glider would have a crew of three pilots to allow them some rest during this marathon non-stop flight.

In May 1943, No. 295 Squadron moved between RAF Netheravon in Wiltshire and RAF Holmsley South in the New Forest area of Hampshire. Harry and his crew flew endurance sorties, towing a glider over ten hours and covering a distance in excess of 1,350 miles. Their Halifax had additional fuel tanks fitted in the bomb bays, while all extraneous weight within the aircraft had been removed. The squadron had ten adapted Halifaxes that were to be used in relays to deliver the gliders and their crews, and the long endurance

The high wing 'Horsa' cantilever glider weighed 7,000 lbs and was constructed from thirty individual sections. The components arrived from the various factories and were assembled by employees of the Ministry of Aircraft Production. (*Ministry of Aircraft Production*)

flights established each individual aircraft's fuel consumption—a vital element. The navigational responsibility sat heavily on Harry's shoulders, but it was only one of many critical duties. The aircraft were risky to fly in the event of a single engine failure—the remaining three engines could not produce sufficient power to allow the pilot to get the aircraft out of trouble, while the extra fuel tanks in the bomb bay increased the risk of fire if the pilot should be forced to make a belly landing. A team of ground crew were dispatched to North Africa in order to receive the Halifax aircraft and undertake the servicing and repairs to ready them for their return flights to England.

The Halifax had towing rigs mounted beneath the rear fuselage and aft of the tail wheel, and the heavy tow rope was connected to the rig and laid out

A dramatic illustration of a Halifax and Horsa glider combination at the point of becoming airborne together.

along the runway. The glider was attached to the towing rope, and on take off the tug pulled forward slowly until the rope became taut; as gently as possible the combination moved forward in unison. At approximately 70 mph the Horsa glider had sufficient lift to make it airborne, while the Halifax required an air speed of 95 to 100 mph to gain the lift required for it to take off and for both aircraft to become airborne. The communication link in the tow rope was vital, and once in the air the glider pilot chose to present his aircraft either above or below the flight line of the Halifax. However, the pilot of the towing aircraft was always in command of the combination while it remained connected. The glider pilot had the capability to jettison the Horsa's undercarriage, a design facility that on long tows reduced the drag effect in the air—this was done on all of the transfers to North Africa. A replacement undercarriage set was carried internally and the glider would land on its central skid as intended by its designers. In the case of the transportation to North Africa, the replacements were attached to allow the glider to take off on the final tow to the destination in Tunisia.

On 31 May, Harry flew to Netheravon to collect his glider for the first deployment of Operation Beggar. He and his crew were briefed to tow the Horsa to the designated aerodrome at Portreath on the Cornish coastline, where the runway ended somewhat abruptly not far from the cliff edge. This was the most southerly airfield from which it was possible to operate in the UK, and was therefore chosen as the departing venue for all aircraft engaged in this long-distance Special Duties operation. Harry landed at the Cornish airfield in the early evening of 2 June; his first tow to North Africa was set for the following morning.

Having been given a detailed briefing, Harry embarked on the very first operation to North Africa with three other tugs. At 0745 hours on 3 June, John Sizmur skilfully edged forward in Halifax EB139 and took up the slack on the tow rope connected to Horsa LG733, crewed by Maj. Astley John Cooper and A/Sgts Denis Hall and Sotirios Antonopoulos. The latter was simply known to all as 'Harry'. The Halifax quickly provided the lift for the glider, but Maj. Cooper kept the glider just airborne while waiting for the Halifax to gently lift off the runway. On reaching the end of the 1,800-yard runway, and having gained a little height, both aircraft dipped below the cliffs—a rather perturbing sight caused by the runway's location, perched high above the sea. The connected aircraft then gently gained additional height and, on an agreed section of headland, the glider jettisoned its undercarriage. The first three hours of the journey was spent flying at around 500 feet in the comforting presence of the three other Halifax combinations and an escort of RAF Beaufighters. But that fighter protection was only temporary, and at the limit of their endurance, the Beaufighters peeled away and returned home, leaving the convoy of Halifaxes to protect themselves and the gliders. The remainder of the journey was conducted at low level across the Bay of Biscay to evade—as much as possible—the Luftwaffe's long-range patrols. Their only defence were the rear gunners, who had the rather unusual sight of the tow

The typical 'tug crew' rear gunner's view from the turret.

rope stretching out from below their turret and terminating at the glider that was either above or below their direct line of sight.

Harry and his crew were progressing steadily until they reached a position estimated to have been 200 miles north-west of Cape Finisterre, Spain. The weather deteriorated and the glider pilots were faced with the physically arduous task of controlling aircraft ideally suited to fly at around 60 mph, but being towed at between 120 and 140 mph in extremely poor conditions. Holding a position above or below the tug was a constant challenge for them. One of the instruments to assist them in this purpose was the cable angle indicator, sometimes known as the 'angle of dangle' indicator. Early versions had a single dial that was able to show the position of the glider relative to the tug, both horizontally and vertically. The indicator was operated by the tow rope via a coupling between the rope and the indicator needle, which was mainly a mechanical connection. However, later forms of the indicator were coupled to an artificial horizon, which to some degree anticipated lateral displacement so that control corrections could be made before the situation became serious. The cable angle indicator was the only device that enabled the tug and glider combination to fly in cloud or at night, but it was far from perfect as any slackening of the tow rope would temporarily give erratic readings.

Glider pilots were advised to monitor the amount of slack in the tow rope, and to ease the glider's control column forward slightly to prevent any snatch effect upon the rope when the tug aircraft took up slack. If the slack was appreciable, the method was to ease the control column until the rope became taut, and then ease back to minimise a snatch that would strain the tow rope. However, these actions required reasonable visibility, and it appears that the glider attached to Harry's aircraft was unable to hold its position in the low cloud and poor conditions—the tow rope snapped under the strain. The glider crew were faced with an emergency ditching into the sea. John Sizmur immediately experienced a lack of drag on his controls and realised that the glider had parted from his Halifax. With the weather deteriorating, visibility dropping, and a very low cloud base, Harry was immediately required to plot the aircraft's exact position—the lives of the glider crew were very much at risk. With 'Harry' Antonopoulos at the controls, the glider safely ditched into the sea having emerged from the clouds only 100 feet above the choppy surface. The crew of three—all uninjured—put on their Mae West lifejackets and climbed into the emergency rubber dinghy. They cast adrift from their glider, which rapidly filled with water but remained semi-submerged due to its wooden construction.

In an excellent piece of navigation under terrible conditions, Harry had accurately calculated the coordinates of the ditched glider. He directed the Halifax back to the location of the incident, where despite bad visibility and low cloud, they sighted the glider and confirmed its exact location. Harry and his crew were forced to return across the Bay of Biscay to Portreath, where they reported the incident. As a result of the precise information given by Harry, the Royal Navy frigate HMS *Teviot* located the glider within ten to twelve hours of its ditching, and the crew were successfully rescued and returned to Londonderry in Northern Ireland. Harry's squadron dispatched an aircraft to collect the survivors, returning them first to Netheravon and thence to Portreath to be passed fit and to engage once more in Operation Beggar.

The exceptional navigation demonstrated by Harry would eventually result in a recommendation for an Air Force Medal (AFM), the same award that would be recommended to glider pilots Hall and Antonopoulos, who we will hear more of shortly. The remaining glider pilot, Maj. Cooper, lost his life on 14 July 1943, during the actual invasion of Sicily. The King had, however, approved the award of the AFC for his actions alongside Hall and Antonopoulos prior to his death. Cooper's (Officer) AFC award was announced along with his crew's (NCO) AFM awards on 11 November 1943.

The events of 3 June 1943 were simply recorded in Harry's flying log book as 'Portreath—Rabat-Sale, Ex Beggar—Glider Lost'. John Sizmur recorded in his log book, 'Exercise Beggar-Tow to Rabat-Sale north-west Africa Glider Lost—Crew picked up after 10 hours by Royal Navy'.

Shortly after the excitements of 3 June, Harry was tasked with another expedition to North Africa. At 0555 hours on 6 June 1943, Halifax EB139 gently

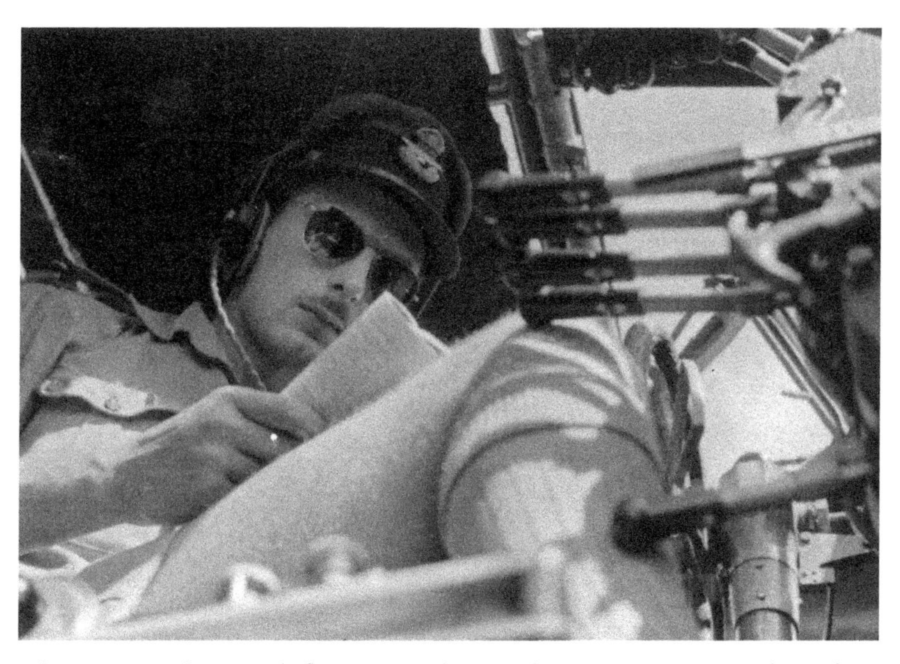

John Sizmur at the controls flying across the Bay of Biscay. He is wearing the uniform appropriate for their destination in North Africa.

took up the slack tow rope connected to a glider and took off from Portreath. This operation proved to be less eventful, and the crew arrived intact at Rabat-Salé after eight hours and fifty-five minutes in the air. The return venture two days later was achieved in seven hours and fifty minutes. Operation Beggar was proving successful, but the supply shuttle of gliders and tugs to Portreath from UK airfields also brought dangers for pilots of No. 295 Squadron. The Australian pilot Frederick Schultz had completed a round trip to and from North Africa and was transporting a Halifax from Holmsley South to Portreath on 11 June, when unexpected fog dramatically reduced visibility. His aircraft struck high ground, killing four members of the crew who perished in the flames.

The following day, Harry and his crew flew to Portreath for their next sortie with a tow to Africa, which was due to embark on the morning of 13 June. The sortie was successful and took nine hours and ten minutes to complete. It was followed by a safe return two days later in a swift seven hours and forty minutes. Harry had had a lucky run, but back at Portreath he was greeted with news that one of the Halifax and glider combinations that had departed on 14 June had failed to arrive and was regarded as missing. The navigator in the Halifax was Frederick Payne, who Harry knew fairly well, and the Horsa crew included Sgts Denis Hall and 'Harry' Antonopoulos. What was more disturbing was the fact that the aircraft had gone missing almost exactly at the same location as the incident on 3 June. It later transpired that two marauding long-range Luftwaffe Condor aircraft had come across the combination and attacked the Halifax. Forced to cast off from their tug, the glider had ditched into the sea. The pilots were aware that they were approximately 140 miles from the Spanish coastline, but remained tied to the floating remains of their glider for two days. The situation became dangerous when the weather turned; they cut themselves adrift and the large sea swells pushed them away from the floating glider. After a further two days, their dinghy was upturned by the rough sea, which resulted in the loss of some vital supplies. Sgt Hall had become seriously ill, and Sgts Antonopoulos and Conway were both suffering from dehydration, exposure, and swollen feet due to them being constantly immersed in water. It was not until day eleven that the ditched glider pilots were sighted by the Spanish fishing boat *Gaviotta*, which responded to the sounds of their survival whistles. They were eventually landed in the port of Vigo, where the British Vice-Consul arranged for the survivors to be treated in hospital before arrangements were made to take them to Gibraltar and then to the UK. Unbeknown to them, their Halifax tug crew had all perished, having been shot down into the sea. The dangers of crossing the Bay of Biscay had been illustrated, and many crews who successfully completed such towing missions counted their blessings. However, more crossings were required.

While Sgts Hall, Antonopoulos, and Conway were stranded at sea, Harry Orme and John Sizmur had been engaged in several internal shuttle flights between Portreath, Hurn, and Holmsley South. On 23 June, Harry's crew took a new Halifax on an endurance run of eight hours to test the fuel consumption in readiness for the trip to Morocco. Later that evening they were to take Halifax DJ989 from Hurn to Holmsley, but after just ten minutes in the air, both port engines failed. John Sizmur made an immediate forced landing, extensively damaging the aircraft, which then burst into flames as the additional fuel tanks exploded. Incredibly, the entire crew escaped with no serious injuries; it had been a masterful demonstration of emergency flying. This action resulted in the award of the AFC to Plt Off. Sizmur after the completion of Operation Beggar.

Terrible news arrived of another Halifax-Horsa combination on 27 June 1943. It had apparently been shot down over the Bay of Biscay with both crews killed. On the 29th of the month, Harry and his rather shaken crew boarded another Halifax that was sitting on the runway connected to yet another glider. Once again, they were to endure the passage to Rabat-Salé in French Morocco. After crossing the Bay of Biscay at the normal low altitude, John Sizmur advised the glider crew they would gain height to 3,000 feet. The sortie was successfully achieved in an amazingly short seven hours. Harry and his crew were relieved from the anticipated return sortie, which was flown by Gp Capt. Cooper DFC from HQ No. 38 Group, who returned them in an Albemarle the following day. Their Halifax was to be used by another crew flying the second leg of the glider transits into Tunisia.

The sorties to Tunisia involved crossing the Atlas Mountains to a temporary airfield at Sousse, which was destined to be one of the main bases for the invasion of Sicily. From here, mostly US-crewed C-47 transports were employed for the short tows and parachute dropping. Flying from these Tunisian air strips was not an easy task as the runways were constructed on soft sand using interlocking steel panels. When a tug aircraft started its engines it immediately generated an impenetrable dust-cloud, and from that moment all visual contact between glider and tug was lost. The glider pilots were required to give their undivided attention to the few feet of tow rope visible just outside the cockpit until they were safely in the air. These were conditions that Harry and his crew would soon experience for themselves, but in the meantime there were yet more towing sorties to complete.

Having risen at an unearthly hour for briefing and breakfast, Harry and his crew departed at 0500 hours on 6 July. They made good headway with a fighter escort, but nearly two hours into the flight, not long after the escort had departed, they encountered very bad weather and were forced to return to base. The next morning a further attempt was made and the weather held; the crew arrived at Rabat-Salé after a slightly extended flight time of eight hours and thirty minutes. The 1st Battalion Glider Pilot Regiment war diary recorded that a total of twenty-seven gliders had been delivered to North Africa since the start of the operation—a remarkable feat of logistics and airmanship.

On 8 July, Harry was transferred across the Atlas Mountains to Sousse for the next stage of Operation Beggar. To safely cross these formidable mountains, with summits reaching 7,000 feet, the gliders needed a further 3,000 feet of altitude to avoid turbulence—it was not unknown for them to lose 1,000 feet in one unpredictable thermal.

The invasion of Sicily was to commence from several airfields in Tunisia on the evening of 9 July, and the Horsas transported to North Africa at great cost to Harry's squadron were about to carry out their vital part in the invasion. Despite travelling to Sousse, Harry and his crew were not deployed on the invasion force; in hindsight, this was most fortunate, as the invasion came at a high cost. Many of the smaller and vastly inferior American Waco gliders, built on site in North Africa, were cast adrift too early, and in addition were mistakenly engaged by Allied anti-aircraft fire—in effect, a massacre of British glider troops took place. The airborne drop of paratroopers was just as unfortunate, with hundreds of men being dropped over great expanses far removed from their designated dropping zones. The fog of war created many Allied casualties both in the air and the sea. The plight of one British glider pilot, Sgt William Bayley, was later described in *The London Gazette* entry for 27 January 1944:

> In July 1943 [he] was the first pilot in a Waco glider detailed for a flight to Sicily [...] faced with very adverse weather. For five hours he was unable to leave his position in the glider and owing to the strength of the wind his hands were soon rubbed raw by the wheel of the glider. Eventually he made an excellent descent into the sea and at once saw to the safety of his passengers. Assured of this, he dived into the interior of the submerged aircraft, salvaging arms and equipment, and afterwards he swam around encouraging the men on the wing of the glider until they were rescued. Throughout this trying experience Sergeant Bayley showed great courage and fortitude, giving no indication of the pain or difficulties he was encountering and, by his cheerful confidence, set a magnificent example to all.

Sgt Bayley was duly awarded the DFM.

High casualty figures created severe discord between the British forces and the American tug pilots, who were accused of casting off their tows early. Harry and his crew spent the rest of July on various duties including extensive repairs to their Halifax, which they had named *Kute Kate*. Harry's log book details that he was detained at 'Ain Oussera' in Algeria for seventeen days.

Unbeknown to Harry, his squadron continued to suffer losses associated with the operation. These included Halifax EB145 on 14 July, while Halifax DK131 was lost when returning to the UK on 19 July, and DG391 in similar

Halifax *Kute Kate* undergoing extensive repairs in Algeria, July 1943.

Kute Kate's engine rebuild on the desert airstrip. The exposed panels reveal the engine controls built along the inner leading edge of the wings.

Harry Orme sitting in the shade on a box with his crew sheltering underneath their Halifax.

circumstances two days later. Having flown in all of these individual aircraft, Harry knew many of the nineteen crew members who perished in the sea and have no known graves.

It was not until 4 August that Harry returned to Britain—John Sizmur piloted Halifax DG388 safely back to the airfield at Hurn in Hampshire. Operation Beggar had been completed. It therefore came as rather a surprise to Harry that it was to be superseded immediately by Operation Elaborate and that he was to continue supplying Horsas to the Mediterranean. No. 1 OADU (Overseas Aircraft Dispatch Unit) was to be formed at RAF Portreath, and Operation Elaborate was to take place between 15 August and 23 September 1943.

Harry returned to Portreath on 16 August to see Halifax DJ994 depart for Salé with its glider under tow. Both aircraft initially disappeared from sight before gently reappearing as they gained height above the viewpoint high up on the cliffs. Sadly, DJ994 would not be seen again—this combination was added to No. 295 Squadron's losses when the aircraft were reported missing. This was the unfortunate prelude to Harry's next Operation Elaborate flight the following morning. Harry's luck held, however, and after ten hours and thirty minutes, he landed safely in Salé. He and his crew were then required to fly several sorties onto the next destination—an airfield at Froha in Algeria—simply noted as 'F strip' in his flying log book. This was the stopover point before the final destination of Sousse in Tunisia.

Halifax rear gunner's turret with the glider tow connection positioned immediately beneath. The tow rope is laid out in the sand ready to take the Horsa into the air for transit to Sousse.

Harry returned to Hurn on 21 August, only to be advised that another Halifax-Horsa combination that had departed on the 18th had been attacked by several Luftwaffe Ju 88 aircraft in the Bay of Biscay. The rear gunner had shot down one of the attackers and the detached glider crew had ditched into the sea, in turn being fired upon by the German aircraft. Incredibly, the badly shot up Halifax escaped the attack and the glider pilots were rescued by HMS *Crane* after being adrift some six hours in their dinghy. Harry was also informed that his crew had two additional 'Elaborates' to fly, both rostered for the following month. The first was accomplished with ease, but the final tow to North Africa was destined to replicate the very first 'Beggar' that he had undertaken back in June.

On 23 September, Harry's crew at Portreath underwent the same predictable routine. Briefings gave little extra information but the weather conditions were always given the utmost attention. The crew were allocated Halifax DG384, another newly converted aircraft. Following the safety checks, Plt Off. Sizmur began taking up the slack and edging towards gaining speed with Horsa glider HS109 in tow. The standard complement of three personnel were in control of the glider, which lifted off and, as usual, deposited its undercarriage to be recovered later that day. The three young glider pilots—from Eastbourne, Cardiff, and Birmingham—took their hourly slots controlling the glider, and constantly stared at the tow rope that almost appeared to be attached to their feet immediately in front of them. Off the coast of Portugal the weather deteriorated to such an extent that low cloud reduced visibility between the two aircraft, and heavy winds and rain induced too much strain on the tow rope, which gave way as the glider drifted off line. The glider, with a significant section of rope still attached, ditched into the sea. On this occasion, despite Harry's immaculate navigation and plotting, the weather conditions proved too bad to gain any sighting of the glider; after reporting the coordinates of the incident John Sizmur returned to base. The bodies of the glider pilots were never recovered. They are commemorated on the Brookwood Memorial in Surrey.

Harry had recorded 185 hours and 20 minutes of operational flying while engaged on Operations Beggar and Elaborate. He had been directly responsible for actions that had saved the lives of three glider pilots, while also knowing what it was like to lose pilots. No. 295 Squadron had carried out the very first operations of this type during the Second World War, creating a significant contribution to military aerial glider deployments that would eventually have a direct impact upon the D-Day invasion of Normandy.

With that in mind, the RAF expanded No. 38 Wing to Group status. This reflected the importance of the work undertaken in the Wing, which would forthwith engage the strength of nine squadrons. No. 298 Squadron was created with crews from other squadrons, and Harry's crew was among the ten crews from No. 295 Squadron that formed 'A' Flight in that new squadron. On 18 October 1943, Harry navigated John Sizmur from Hurn to their new squadron's airfield, Tarrant Rushton near Blandford Forum in Dorset. The airfield was nearing completion, and No. 298 Squadron had been selected to train specifically for the monumental task of towing the giant Hamilcar glider that was capable of carrying a small tank. When the first Hamilcar arrived at Tarrant Rushton, its size created great apprehension among the towing crews. Gp Capt. Cooper DFC, who had flown Harry back from North Africa during Operation Beggar in his Albemarle, was to oversee the training in company with Maj. Alec Dale, who had been awarded a DFC for his role as a glider pilot during the invasion of Sicily.

The Hamilcar, the largest Allied glider as well as the largest wooden aircraft built during the Second World War, was specifically designed to move heavy vehicles during airborne assaults. The first prototype Hamilcar was flown on 27 March 1942, but production did not begin until mid-1943. It was a huge undertaking to construct the glider and utilised woodworking companies like the Birmingham Railway Carriage & Wagon Company, a locomotive and carriage builder founded in Birmingham and located in nearby Smethwick. These companies had problems storing the glider as it was over 20 feet high, spanned 110 feet, and even when empty weighed 18,500 lbs. A payload of 17,500 lbs could be held within the Hamilcar's 1,920-cubic-foot interior. Its wingspan was 6 feet wider than that of the Halifax deployed to tow it. These dimensions explain why Harry was in awe of the Hamilcar when the first one arrived at Tarrant Rushton.

No. 298 Squadron selected a few crews to be specially trained to land in the extremely confined areas associated with the most secret targets planned for D-Day. A high level of responsibility rested on the navigators within those crews and, needless to say, Harry was among those regarded as experienced and competent. The training was under the instruction of Flt Lt Grant, and Harry was to fly frequently with Wg Cdr Duder, the commanding officer of the squadron.

The principle of the new training was for the tug navigator to plan a course for the Hamilcar glider pilot to fly once released from the Halifax. Additional aids were fitted to the Halifax, namely 'Gee' and 'Rebecca', and both of these references appeared in Harry's flying log book with regularity during November and December 1943. Both devices allowed precise navigation, but 'Rebecca' facilitated the ability to home in on a beacon and land in very close proximity to its transmission. On 6 January 1944, two aircraft participated in a Pathfinder competition in which they navigated to a rendezvous point without the use of 'Pundit' or 'Occult' aids. These beacon registrations for airfields or geographical features were standard navigation and location aids used by the RAF at that time. Harry Orme and John Sizmur participated in the competition, taking off at 1840 hours and returning at 2040 hours. Harry noted in his log book entry 'No Bods', signifying a scant crew, but with no indication of having won or otherwise.

A Hamilcar in tow. This giant glider required two securing points on the wings to attach the tow ropes which then connected to the thick hemp rope that in turn attached to the Halifax tug.

On 8 January 1944, Harry experienced the towing and taking to the air of a Hamilcar. It was without doubt a unique experience, and towards the end of the month he was involved in the towing of a fully loaded Hamilcar with Wg Cdr Duder at the controls of the Halifax. Two days later, John Sizmur took a Hamilcar into the darkness for an extended tow during the late evening on a night-time exercise. On 14 January, the wing commander once again made use of Harry's navigation when participating in an exercise involving thirteen aircraft, during which 115 paratroopers were dropped from just 500 feet onto a pre-planned drop zone.

Another exercise in which the giant Hamilcar gliders took part occurred on 20 January, when No. 298 Squadron was involved in paratroop drops with troops of the 1st Canadian Brigade. Later, ten of the squadron's Halifaxes went up with Hamilcars loaded with Mk VII Tetrarch light tanks. The tow ropes were detached at 1,000 feet. One glider, HH961, overshot the airfield and crashed into a group of a Nissen huts; the tank, with its engine running, shot out of the glider's nose doors at a significant speed and cut a swathe through the huts, eventually stopping some 50 yards away. Both the glider and Nissen huts were destroyed, but the tank remained serviceable. Fortunately, despite the extensive damage, there were no casualties.

The build-up to the airborne invasion of France required No. 38 Group to engage in large-scale exercises—among them was Exercise Co-Operation that took place on the afternoon of 6 February. Part I required eleven Halifax aircraft to drop 108 troops of the 3rd Parachute Brigade, 1st Canadian Parachute Battalion, and thirty-three containers on the drop zone at Winterbourne Stoke; Part II detailed two Stirlings to drop forty-eight containers onto two drop zones; Part III involved ten Halifax and three Stirling aircraft towing Horsa gliders for release at Oatlands Hill. Harry was again required to fly with Wg Cdr Duder on this exercise. Tarrant Rushton airfield came alive once the orders were given targets—the eleven Halifaxes carrying the troops were all airborne within less than five minutes, and the Stirlings and Halifaxes, each towing a Horsa glider, got airborne within ten minutes.

Tarrant Rushton was a significant airfield that played an important role in mounting the initial assault on what was going to be the largest airborne invasion force in military history. When Sir Trafford Leigh-Mallory, the Commander-in-Chief of the Allied Expeditionary Air Force, visited Tarrant Rushton on 12 February, he personally addressed the Glider Pilot Regiment and air crew personnel of Nos 298 and 196 Squadrons.

Harry returned to fly within Plt Off. Sizmur's crew, completing further Hamilcar lifts and cross-country tows, but Wg Cdr Duder had first call on Harry as his navigator. Despite this being a rather privileged position, it rather disrupted his work alongside his long-standing friend John Sizmur. On 3 March, a glider exercise was to take place involving a very high cast-

Above and below: Images of a Hamilcar carrying the 17-lb anti-tank gun and its 30-cwt Morris tractor unit are extremely scarce. The gun was pushed to the rear of the glider with the long barrel projecting towards the tail, while the Morris tractor unit was attached to the tow hook creating a length that was barely enough to hold the entire unit. The radiator of the Morris was projecting into the nose cone of the glider and all unnecessary material like doors, windscreen, and side panel were removed to reduce weight. Those modifications made the towing unit resemble seats on a chassis and very little else. The Hamilcar was unique in its capability to carry such loads; the Tetrarch tank and the Bren carrier can be seen being loaded in these images.

off height, with the gliders landing by 'Gee', 'Eureka', and 'Rebecca' aids. Harry was required to brief his glider pilot on the navigational route to follow after their cast-off, a practical examination of the confined landing training previously undertaken by the selected crews. Exercise Sailor involved ten Stirling aircraft towing Horsas, and ten Halifax-Horsa combinations. These gliders were released in a restrictive six-minute period over Welford from 2,000 feet. The landing zone was identified by a combination of map reading, formation flying, 'Eureka', 'Rebecca', and 'Gee' fixes. Seventeen trucks, nineteen trailers, two jeeps, and 100 gallons of petrol were carried, together with 181 troops of the famous American 101st Airborne Division. Exercise Sailor required all of the tow ropes to be dropped at the nominated drop zone, which was marked by smoke. One Stirling released its glider over Tarrant Rushton when one of the engines of the tug aircraft caught fire in the air—both glider and tug managed to land independently and safely.

Harry received a commission and was appointed as a pilot officer in early 1944. As an officer he was required to purchase his own uniform—during his period of home leave in March 1944, he travelled to Wolverhampton where he purchased his officer's tunic, hat, and greatcoat at Horne Brothers. Harry used several clothing coupons to assist with this significant purchase, which amounted to £39 13*s* 1*d*.

Wg Cdr Duder called on Harry for four additional duties, two of which were penetration Special Duties operations to drop supplies in France to members of the resistance. On the night of 14 March, Harry navigated to an isolated location at Nevers, and on 30 March, he navigated the wing commander to Marmande. This was by far the longest night operation flown by Harry, leaving Tarrant Rushton at 2108 hours and returning at 0424 hours.

Plt Off. Sizmur was also to experience Special Duties sorties into France. Harry took him to Limoges for a container drop on 27 April and Le Puy on 30 April. Many of No. 298 Squadron's Special Duties operations into France supplied the British SAS units that were operating in connection with the SOE network and were part of the planning for the invasion by Allied forces in June 1944.

The squadron's strength at this time consisted of forty-seven officers and 300 men of other ranks; 'C' Squadron Glider Pilot Regiment had ten officers and 100 other ranks on station at Tarrant Rushton. Those men were engaged on 21 April 1944 with Exercise Mush, which intended to land the 1st Airlanding Brigade and troops of the 1st Airborne Division in two lifts with sixteen and twelve Halifax-Horsa combinations into Brize Norton and Harwell respectively. The efficiency of Tarrant Rushton is demonstrated by the first lift of sixteen aircraft towing combinations getting airborne in eleven minutes, and the second of twelve combinations in nine minutes.

The efficiency of getting the D-Day airborne forces into the air and over their respective drop zones was imperative to the overall plan—this was no doubt explained to the air crews on 22 April when Gen. Eisenhower, the Supreme Commander Allied Expeditionary Force in Western Europe, addressed them. He had arrived by air, accompanied by Air Chief Marshal Sir Trafford Leigh-Mallory and Air Vice-Marshal Hollinghurst, the man previously chosen by Leigh-Mallory to command No. 38 Group. Hollinghurst proved to be highly effective at dealing with the intricate problems of acquiring the correct aircraft and experienced crews, and also providing the realistic training necessary for the D-Day landings. Another example of that foresight in training took place on 4 May, when Harry was engaged in Exercise Confirmation. The intention was to drop one container from each of the thirty Halifax aircraft onto a nominated drop zone by moonlight, without the assistance of ground aids. The exercise was successful with fifteen aircraft of No. 298 Squadron dropping twelve containers, and fifteen aircraft from No. 644 Squadron dropping thirteen containers. Two nights later, Harry accompanied three other Halifaxes towing gliders loaded with heavy ballast on another moonlit exercise. The ballast replicated the payload that air crews were expected to carry across the Channel into France; it was essential that the weight of any load was distributed evenly. The Horsa glider was not to be flown with a single pilot unless ballast was present in the second pilot's position. Training exercises were designed to simulate as closely as possible the operational conditions expected on D-Day.

The crews were being stretched in their ability to conduct as many training sorties as possible; in the early hours of 13 May a Horsa glider overshot its landing point at Tarrant Rushton and collided with a stationary Halifax. The collision caused the death of the second pilot, Sgt Blackburn, while the first pilot, S/Sgt Ford, survived but was seriously injured. Also that night, another glider overshot and crashed into another Halifax, sustaining damage but no casualties. One of the giant Hamilcars undershot its landing on 24 May, seriously damaging the undercarriage after striking an obstruction. Another incident, in the early hours of 27 May, saw Halifax 'E' of No. 644 Squadron crash after attempting to take off with a Hamilcar. It came down one mile west of Tarrant Rushton, killing three of the Canadian crew—the youngest, nineteen-year-old rear gunner Walderman Wolf from Iroquois Falls, is buried in Brookwood Military Cemetery. The pilots in the towed glider were very fortunate to escape unscathed.

On 30 May Harry took part in his final moonlit training exercise. Just before midnight, thirty-eight Halifaxes from both of Tarrant Rushton's squadrons took off, each with a Horsa in tow. After being released, three gliders failed to land at base: the first crash-landed 5 miles east of Blandford at Moor Crichel and was completely written off; another came down, damaged, at Shapwick; and the third at Spetisbury, south of Blandford.

At 1400 hours on 2 June 1944, RAF Tarrant Rushton received instructions from HQ No. 38 Group that the station was to be sealed until further notice.

Such actions were being undertaken at airfields across the country. The detailed instructions were circulated to all personnel by the station, ref. TR/S.253/7/AIR:

> With effect from 14.00 hours on June 2nd, 1944, the station is sealed. This will mean:
> (i) All officers and airmen must live at the camp.
> (ii) No one will be allowed outside the camp bounds. These extend in all directions up to the first house or village, i.e., personnel may walk in the country around provided they do not go as far as any civilian dwelling.
> (iii) All leave of any kind is stopped.
> (iv) It is absolutely prohibited for any officer or airman to enter into conversation with any civilian or member of other forces who are not confined to this station.
> (v) Civilians who have volunteered to remain 'sealed' in the camp are confined to camp in the same way as service personnel. Those who have not volunteered to be confined to the camp are excluded. All civilian passes are to be withdrawn immediately.
> (vi) All postings out to stations other than operational stations are 'frozen'.
> (vii) Attached personnel may not leave unless they are proceeding to another No. 38 Group station.
> (viii) Anyone who must make a journey outside the station must obtain written permission from the station commanders, CTO, Station Administration Officer or Station Adjutant. The Station Administration Officer to arrange the form these passes take. Anyone authorised to make a journey outside the station must proceed directly to his destination. Under no circumstances is he to make any intermediate stop or depart from the authorised route.
> (1) Routine runs for stores, mail, etc. will be escorted by a reliable senior N.C.O. Civilian contractor or service personnel delivering loads to this station must report to the guard room and will then be escorted. They must not enter into conversation with personnel on this station.
> (2) Any other visitors to the station will be interviewed by the Adjutant or CTO responsible for necessary security measures to prevent them obtaining information they should not have.
> (3) The above regulations are for the purpose of security, the importance of which cannot be over-emphasised. They must be intelligently applied in spirit as well as in the letter. It is hoped these restrictions will not be in force for too long and on all occasions when air crews are not briefed, the sealing will be relaxed.

Tarrant Rushton was at its height of readiness; the aerodrome was filled with tug aircraft and gliders were distributed across its open expanses. The Supreme

Headquarters Allied Expeditionary Force operational memorandum called for special markings on aircraft in order for them to be clearly distinguishable on D-Day. To achieve success, the markings had to be applied on D -1 to ensure that all aircraft would have broad black and white bands painted on them on D-Day, but not before. The amount of distemper required to mark approximately 10,000 aircraft and gliders was 100,000 gallons, or 1,500 tons. There was not enough immediately available in the UK, so the supply of distemper to civilians was immediately stopped. Overtime was worked in pits and factories and by D-Day sufficient stock was ready; the distemper, and 20,000 brushes to apply it, was available across all airfields. At Tarrant Rushton, the D-Day invasion markings of black and white stripes were painted on both the fuselage and wings of all tugs and gliders. These were for instant recognition, proclaiming that the aircraft were 'Allied', and all forces engaged in the invasion were aware of these markings.

During the evening of 4 June, Harry and his crew attended a briefing at which a film and photographs of the forthcoming operational dropping zones were shown. His dropping zone was DZ 'N', Ranville. Together with the 7th, 12th and 13th Parachute Battalions, the mission was to strengthen Maj. Howard's men on the bridge over the River Orne and on the canal. It was also to clear and secure landing zone LZ 'N' for the gliders, and to establish a defensive zone on the southern flank.

The first wave of gliders was to arrive at LZ 'N' at 0330 hours, and Operation Mallard was to arrive at 2100 hours. What was about to take place was in no doubt at Tarrant Rushton; the months of training were about to be tested, but the weather conditions at that time were unfavourable. The airfield remained locked down with no outside communication whatsoever. Eventually the orders filtered down and the squadrons based at Tarrant Rushton would be engaged in the very first offensive action of Operation Overlord.

It was still 5 June when the first element of the airborne operation commenced. The intention was to land 171 troops and capture intact the bridges across the Caen Canal and River Orne, north of Caen. Six Halifax-Horsa combinations were engaged, and to disguise their intention after releasing their gliders they were to drop twelve instantaneous bombs on a factory situated south-east of Caen.

Wg Cdr Duder was leading the six tug aircraft in Halifax LL355, and he delivered the famous glider pilot S/Sgt Jim Wallwork over the drop zone, right against the Orne River and canal bridges. As noted in Chapter 8, Wallwork has the honour of being recognised as the first Allied soldier to set foot in France on D-Day, even though he was thrown through his cockpit window when he planted his glider so accurately on the canal path. All of the aircraft returned to base, and this vital part of the operation was regarded as having been successful.

Duder had always sought to fly with Harry Orme, but Harry was required to navigate the tug pulling a Hamilcar delivering one of the vital heavy anti-tank guns with its 30-cwt Morris tractor unit. In the early hours of 6 June, Operation Tonga, the main glider operation, commenced. Thirty Halifax aircraft were detailed to release Horsa gliders alongside LZ 'N', supporting the initial *coup-de-main* force east of the Caen Canal, and each aircraft was to drop nine containers on the DZ to the south of the landing zone. Four Halifaxes were detailed to tow and release Hamilcar gliders carrying the powerful 17-lb anti-tank guns. This was the only Allied gun capable of dealing with heavy German armoured vehicles, and it would be pulled by a stripped down Morris C8/AT tractor unit, the combination of which only just fitted into the massive glider's hold. Plt Off. John Sizmur was to fly his Halifax, towing Hamilcar 501 with one of these vital guns inside its fuselage. It was not uncommon for gliders to carry a nickname written on the fuselage, and the number allocated to them in relation to the airborne assaults was chalked on the side, hence the term 'chalk numbers'. Hamilcar 501 was additionally identified as the 'Bag of Bagdad'. Harry was navigating and had briefed the glider pilots, S/Sgt Leslie Riding and Sgt Ronald Harris. The take off in Halifax LL148 was text book at 0202 hours. They safely gained height and commenced the Channel crossing, but a rather unusual occurrence took place just before they reached the French coast: a parachute became entangled on the wing of the giant glider. Two minutes after having crossed the coast, the tow rope parted from the Halifax. In the hope that the glider pilot had sufficient height to reach his landing zone, the Halifax peeled away to begin the return to Tarrant Rushton.

Unfortunately, the 'Bag of Bagdad' did not reach the landing zone. It came down in a small orchard near St Vaast-en-Auge and became the subject of an intense German attack. S/Sgt Riding was mortally wounded, but the co-pilot managed to escape and subsequently joined forces with another couple of wayward members of the Canadian Parachute Battalion who were making towards their drop zones. Three of the Airlanding Anti-Tank Battery gunners who were in the glider were killed in the German attack. Restricted within the fuselage of the glider, they would have had no opportunity to see anything and their only escape was via the huge opening of the nose door or one small escape hatch accessible from a wooden ladder that led to a hatchway just behind the cockpit. The majority of strappings and fixings to the gun and its tractor were released during the descent to allow rapid extraction once on the ground.

Operation Mallard was the third and final airborne delivery on D-Day. Tarrant Rushton supplied thirty Halifax aircraft detailed to release Hamilcar gliders over LZ 'N', and two Halifaxes detailed to release Horsa gliders and drop eighteen containers over the same drop zone. One aircraft, Halifax LL407 piloted by Fg Off. Carpenter, was among those that failed to return from this operation. The previous evening Wg Cdr Duder had captained this aircraft. On this occasion they had towed Hamilcar 'Chalk 235' to the drop zone and released the glider successfully, but almost immediately they were struck by flak and set alight. In dire circumstances they ditched into the English Channel and were later rescued by a naval vessel. Meanwhile, Harry had once again been commandeered by Wg Cdr Duder who, for Operation Mallard, sat at the controls of Halifax LL148 'J'. They returned safely, landing shortly before 2200 hours on what must have been a monumentally challenging day.

Lord Trenchard, Marshal of the Royal Air Force, visited the station on 12 June. As the RAF's father-figure, he was greeted with great respect and his interest in the work of No. 38 Group was appreciated. Tarrant Rushton was frequently used by various aircraft seeking refuge after their exploits over Normandy, and was also kept very busy with operational flying, with frequent tasks to drop supplies to SAS units operating behind the Allied beachheads. On 28 June, Maj. Verney, the SAS Brigade Headquarters Staff Officer, lectured air crews of Nos 298 and 644 Squadrons in the station briefing room on the activities of SAS troops in France. This was of great interest, and the crews engaged in these Special Duties were left in no doubt as to the importance of supporting these men. Maj. Verney had himself been a member of the Special Boat Squadron and had escaped and evaded capture in occupied territory. He was held in very high regard by the air crews.

It had been a busy month for the ground crews of the Servicing Wing. Including gliders, a total of approximately 2,100 flying hours had been flown and a considerable amount of experimental work with Hamilcar loads had been done. The Servicing Wing also had to respond to sudden demands; a request for four Spitfire fuselages to be landed in Normandy led to the rapid design of special lashings, and the delivery was made on 4 July. Hamilcar loads, delivering a specialist angle dozer, bulldozer, scraper, and a T9 tank direct into Normandy beachhead, had also been undertaken.

Harry Orme navigated John Sizmur to Blois in France on 7 July 1944, delivering supplies to the SOE network. No. 298 Squadron was becoming heavily engaged in these supply sorties, and Wg Cdr Duder called on Harry to act as his navigator on the night of 11 July. SOE requirements had increased, reflecting their intense activity behind enemy lines. Supplies were dropped in Dijon, the crew returning safely after the three-hour-forty-five-minute sortie. Several similar supply operations were carried out from Tarrant Rushton that same night.

Next page: Harry Orme wrote on the back of his photograph, 'D Day June 6th 1944, line up of tugs and gliders for second trip to Normandy. Take off 19.00 hours leading aircraft in Hamilcar stream.' Harry's Halifax is the first in line on the right row of aircraft. On the far side of the airfield are several Hamilcar gliders that have no D-Day markings, indicating that they were not deployed on Operation Overlord.

Harry Orme AFM, third from the right, and John Sizmur AFC, second from the left, with their crew in front of Halifax LL148 'J'. The D-Day stripes can be seen crudely applied and the crew's entrance hatch is immediately behind the shortest member of the crew. In all probability, Wing Commander Duder is the other person sporting the pilot's wings on his flying uniform.

In the early hours of 22 July, Marmande was the destination for Harry's crew. They were among several aircraft delivering packages to different locations across France that night; one of their fellow aircraft was harried by Luftwaffe night fighters but managed to escape into the clouds. Weather conditions limited the dropping of supplies that night, but Harry's log book indicates that their operation had been successful. Another four aircraft of No. 298 Squadron and two from No. 644 Squadron operated over France on SOE missions on 28 July, dropping supplies for SAS troops. However, only three aircraft managed to return to Tarrant Rushton, the remainder having been diverted by bad weather to Brize Norton. Harry's Halifax 'E' was among those forced to divert, but after breakfast the weather lifted sufficiently to allow them to return to their home base. Having accumulated over 1,000 hours of flying in his log book by this time, Harry was hugely experienced in navigation; he had found the night-time operations over occupied France to be both challenging and rewarding.

RAF Tarrant Rushton was once again sealed, pending operations on 16 August 1944. The towing duties for Operation Market commenced the following day, with the first lift of seven Halifax-Hamilcar combinations by No. 298 Squadron, and six by No. 644 Squadron taking off for landing zones south-west of Arnhem in Holland. Thirteen Halifax-Horsa combinations of No. 298 Squadron and fourteen from No. 644 Squadron were also detailed to release their gliders over the same dropping zone. All gliders were successfully released except two: the tug of one developed port-inner engine failure and returned to base, while the second landed in a field north-east of Andover after its tow rope broke. Its tug also returned safely to base. Harry and John watched these operations from RAF Tarrant Rushton; they were not rostered to take part in the operation to Arnhem as they were regarded as 'screened', having completed their second tour of duty.

Denis Hall, one of the glider pilots Harry had helped save through his navigational skill back in June 1943, was piloting one of the gliders being towed to Arnhem. Despite being hit by ground fire while over Holland, he successfully reached his drop zone but was injured in the fighting at Arnhem and taken prisoner. He was later force-marched from Stalag Luft III prisoner-of-war camp in winter conditions. Very few prisoners were clothed or fed properly, and he suffered from frostbite in his feet. However, Denis survived the war and was finally liberated by Allied troops.

During the Second World War, there were only 214 RAF recipients of the AFM, a medal awarded to NCOs and men for acts of valour, courage, and devotion to duty while not in active service against the enemy. The AFM was awarded to only two Army Air Corps glider pilots during the conflict; their medals were directly connected to Harry Orme's award, which was published a month later.

> AIR 2 / 8983: Sergeant S Antonopoulos 1608391, Royal Air Force Volunteer Reserve, No 295 Squadron, (Tactical Air Force) (Glider Pilot; Sorties 2; flying hours 10) Sergeant Antonopoulos was co-pilot in a glider which broke loose during one of the first glider towing flights from the United Kingdom to North Africa. He showed considerable resource and high courage in assisting his captain to alight on the sea and during the time spent in a dinghy before rescue. He then volunteered for a second towing flight as a pilot of another glider. On this occasion his glider was shot down by enemy aircraft. Sergeant Antonopoulos skilfully alighted on the sea and assisted his crew to escape. Throughout these trying experiences this airman displayed high courage, resource and determination and it was largely due to his untiring efforts that the crew were saved and successfully escaped to resume duty.

> AIR 2 / 8983: Sergeant D A Hall 1779297, Royal Air Force Volunteer Reserve, No 295 Squadron, (Tactical Air Force) (Glider Pilot; Sorties 2; flying hours 10) Sergeant Hall has been employed on 2 occasions as a co-pilot in gliders flying from this country to North Africa. On the first occasion he assisted his pilot in alighting on the sea and taking to the dinghy with

Harry Orme, wearing the distinctive Air Force Medal ribbon alongside the 1939–1945 Campaign Star ribbon. The brass 'VR' Volunteer Reserve letters, previously worn on his uniform lapels, are no longer displayed; in 1943 the Air Ministry ordered members of the RAFVR to remove their brass and cloth 'VR' insignia. This was an order that affected all RAFVR ranks, officers, and NCOs. Harry elected to wear the original 'O' observer's brevet during his service and chose to purchase the more expensive padded silk type. This photograph was taken in a photographic studio in Cannock not far from his home in Hednesford.

> the other members of the crew. On the second occasion, the glider was shot down by enemy action and Sergeant Hall again assisted in alighting on the sea and subsequently taking to the dinghy. He then gave valuable aid to his captain in escaping to Gibraltar. After his first experience, this airman showed exceptional courage in volunteering for further glider flights.[9]

In comparison with other flying medals awarded during the Second World War, the AFM was issued very sparingly, as shown by the significantly low number of recipients across the services. Harry returned to teaching after being demobbed from the RAF in 1946. He often commented that receiving his medal from the King was the greatest moment in his life. He died in 1991, aged eighty-three years.

10

Frank Moore DFC, CdeG, BSc Film Production Unit, Gestapo Hunter

Frank Edward Moore was born in Cape Province, South Africa, in 1914. Throughout his life he was addressed as 'Ted', choosing to drop his first name in everything other than official documentation. He developed an interest in photography and moving film cameras at an early age, a subject that would later become a significant part of his life.

In the early 1930s, Ted emigrated to England in the hope of finding employment in the movie picture industry; he got a job as an apprentice in the camera department at Denham Film Studios in Buckinghamshire. Designed by Jack Okey, who had been responsible for the First National and Paramount studios in Hollywood, the extensive studio complex at Denham had developed in late summer 1935. It was the largest film production facility in England and officially opened in May 1936, boasting seven sound stages, extensive workshops, restaurants, and dressing-rooms fit for Hollywood stars, together with a new Technicolor laboratory. Ted was instrumental in saving a large amount of camera equipment from a fire that broke out one night. With two other men, he instigated the initial rescue of valuable equipment, thereby preventing a disaster. The company rewarded each man with a payment of £15, a considerable sum at that time. Ted's particular strength was in lighting, and he worked on his first film set in 1939. He was recognised as a gifted lighting technician with a promising career ahead of him in a glamorous industry.

With the outbreak of war, Ted volunteered for service and became a projectionist in the Royal Army Service Corps. No doubt his previous employment was recognised—the operation of projection equipment was considered to be a productive use of his abilities. Ted was serving in France as part of the British Expeditionary Force in 1940, and when France was invaded by Germany, he was among the thousands of men facing the prospect of capture and spending the rest of the war as a prisoner. However, he managed to reach the beaches at Dunkirk and was evacuated, although many of his comrades were killed or captured. The evacuation of troops from Dunkirk had been a monumental task. The events following the recovery of some 300,000 troops from France heralded what is now regarded as the Battle of Britain, and the RAF was charged with defending Britain as the last line of defence against Germany. Ted resigned from the Army and volunteered to serve in the RAF, having been accepted for selection as a pilot in training.

Unexpectedly, Ted returned to his mother country, South Africa, to train as a pilot at No. 21 Air School. The Union of South Africa, as it was known in 1939, was still very much a part of the British Empire, but its mixed British and Boer Government meant that entry into the war on the side of the Allies could by no means be guaranteed. A parliamentary vote subsequently took place, and by a very slim margin South Africa joined forces with the Allies. However, it was not until late 1940 that negotiations pushed forward the planning of joint air training facilities within South Africa. Ted undertook his training as a pilot in 1942—during that year 4,240 RAF cadets graduated, of whom 1,529 were pilots, 2,541 were navigators, and 170 were air bombers. He first took to the air on 16 June 1942, proving to be a highly capable student and going solo within eight hours of initial instruction. On 13 March 1943, Ted qualified for his 'wings' and returned to the UK on a packed convoy troopship.

It appears that his qualifications in photography were acknowledged by the RAF, as they posted him to the Crown Film Unit at Pinewood Studios, where he was to be operationally deployed with the RAF's Film Production Unit (FPU). The Germans had developed an efficient means of filming and using combat images for propaganda purposes from an early stage of the war. This led to the subsequent formation of the FPU, which was facilitated within the Crown Film Unit. One of the unit's most important functions was to be the recording of the RAF's activities during the war; some of this material would later be used by the Ministry of Information to make propaganda films. The RAF film production unit recruited staff from all the services and was officially formed from a basic core of very few men in August 1941.

There were logistical problems in equipping the new unit with suitable lightweight cameras and other equipment, but these were overcome and the unit developed and strengthened accordingly. The Operational Unit was the most important section of the FPU, as it recorded the 'sharp end' of the service's offensive from mid-1942 onwards. The cameramen in the unit were normally qualified airmen who could take over other operational duties within an aircraft in emergencies. They were flying with operational crews, but were not officially part of the squadron's strength. The cameramen developed their own special techniques using clockwork cameras, either hand-held or ingeniously mounted, according to which squadron and aircraft type they were flying with.

In 1943, not long after Ted arrived back in the UK, the FPU developed further with defined units engaged in very specific areas of responsibility.

Pinewood Studios was designated No. 1 FPU and was in effect the unit's headquarters. No. 2 FPU, under the command of Sqn Ldr Arthur Taylor at RAF Iver Heath, covered the vast area of the Mediterranean theatre and recorded the Allied landings on Sicily, the Italian mainland, southern France, and Greece. No. 3 FPU, under the command of Wg Cdr T. Connochie, was required to cover activities in the Far East. No. 4 FPU, formed last in April 1944, was commanded by Sqn Ldr Derek Twist to provide photographic sorties for the invasion of northern Europe from D-Day onwards.

Twist was a film editor before the war, his most notable work being Alfred Hitchcock's famous *The 39 Steps* in 1935. Ted had worked with men like this in the film industry, and no doubt this is why he was seconded into the unit commanded by Twist. This unit was also engaged in the filming of rocket attacks on ground targets by Hawker Typhoon aircraft using wing-mounted 35-mm cameras, and in the systematic recording of the results of the Allied bombing offensive. Much newsreel material was created, and two important campaign films were produced using the footage created by No. 4 FPU. Ted's connection with his old studios in Denham was renewed as the Denham laboratories were processing as much as 220,000 feet of military film per week. By day and by night, over 680 operational sorties were flown in the north-west European theatre alone, and the material was used for subsequent military analysis, photographic reconnaissance, or frequently just for newsreel release.

Ted was to fly with several crews in order to film operational sorties for propaganda and raid-analysis purposes. Following briefings and technical training at Pinewood, he was dispatched to No. 137 Wing at RAF Hartford Bridge in Hampshire, where Nos 88 and 342 Squadrons were based and flying operations with their tactical light bombers. In August 1943, No. 88 Squadron had relocated to Hartford Bridge with their sister No. 342 Squadron, as part of No. 137 Wing of No. 2 Group of the 2nd TAF. These squadrons were attacking German communication targets and airfields in their Boston light bombers. No. 342 (Lorraine) Squadron had been formed from Free French personnel, and had arrived at Hartford Bridge on 6 September 1943. The squadron flew dangerous daylight raids, attacking targets selected for their importance to the Allied disruption of Germany's military productivity and efficiency within France. They also flew frequent sorties in the Pas-de-Calais area on Operation Bodyguard, part of the complex diversion plan in connection with the proposed D-Day invasion of Normandy.

In May 1944, the German V-1 flying bomb campaign was almost ready for deployment from launching sites built in the Pas-de-Calais region. These sites, constructed by slave labour, were relatively small and at first sight insignificant, but what was not insignificant was the stockpile of thousands of V-1 rockets that were ready to be sent across the Channel to drop onto London and the southern counties of England. When the launch sites for the V-1 rockets were detected, No. 137 Wing was tasked with destroying them. Hartford Bridge was a busy station, and Ted was readily accepted by the French personnel who were keen to attack German targets within their home country.

Ted began operating with the No. 137 Wing squadrons in late September 1943. He hitch-hiked around on different aircraft with his film equipment and was not allocated to any particular crew. He was a rare phenomenon: a pilot with 'wings' acting as a hitch-hiker within the unit's strength. His duties required tact and diplomacy to integrate successfully within the close-knit crews. The credibility associated with being a pilot helped, no doubt, but it was a unique and difficult role to undertake.

The Boston light bomber became Ted's regular host aircraft. His first filming operation was an important and dangerous daylight low-level mission to attack the transformer and switching station at Chevilly Larue, north-west of Villeneuve-Saint-Georges at Orly, near Paris. Eleven aircraft led by Col. de Rancourt flew to Paris at midday on 3 October. Two Boston bombers were lost, most probably as a result of the extensive light flak defences. However, the operation was otherwise successful; there were tremendous flashes as the

Cameraman Ted Moore sitting on the fuselage of a No. 342 (Lorraine) Squadron Boston light bomber at RAF Hartford Bridge. (*Ted Moore collection*)

bombs hit the transformer, cutting the power supply to many factories. This daring low-level raid fortunately encountered no enemy fighter interceptions, and Ted's pilot, the Frenchman Lt Petit, allowed him to secure extensive film coverage despite the dangers presented by the high-tension cables that were almost impossible to see. Lt Petit had been especially briefed by Col. de Rancourt to fly as steadily as possible, as the cameraman was in the mid-rear turret and they wanted the entire operation over the target captured on film. The film of this raid was later used extensively for propaganda purposes. Many crew members flying in No. 342 Squadron were from the Paris area and had not seen the French capital since 1940, so the raid created great satisfaction throughout the entire squadron. The destruction of the transformer had serious repercussions for the Germans, as it was the terminal for the high-tension cables which distributed power from the dams of the Massif Central. Recognising the transformer's importance, the Germans had installed an anti-splinter shield around the site, but it was ineffective against the precise low-level bombing deployed by the RAF.

A low-level image of the accurate bombing on the transformer and switching station of Chevilly-Laru in the southern suburbs of Paris. This boldly planned daylight raid was a great success, and as can be seen from this image, it was conducted from an exceptionally low height. Ted Moore's filming secured impressive footage which was of great value to the French propaganda department.

Flying in a Boston, Ted filmed various raids during November and December 1943, including the airfields at Bernay-Saint-Martin and Audinghen, and the V-1 rocket sites at Martinvast and Mesnil-Allard, La Glacière, and Ligescourt. These V-1 sites were particularly difficult to locate. The raid to Mesnil-Allard was initially to be conducted at as low a level as possible by the leading aircraft, followed by the remaining ten aircraft bombing from a higher altitude on their accurate results, with Col. de Rancourt naturally leading the operation. The rocket site was destroyed and Ted had successfully captured the raid on film, but it had cost the lives of three separate crews who failed to return. The ferocity of flak protecting the site damaged all but two of the Boston aircraft that made it back to Hartford Bridge.

The prefabricated nature of the V-1 sites meant that they could be quickly restored to operational status or that new sites simply replaced them. The rocket-launching sites were codenamed by the RAF as 'No Balls', and frequent mention of that term is made in briefings and other written records. These sites were a high priority for destruction, and the aircraft from Hartford Bridge returned to them time and time again, as did Bomber Command, which sent large forces to destroy them. In March and April 1944, the targets also included railway marshalling yards, and Ted worked frequently with No. 88 Squadron, flying ten raids with different pilots. Gen. Eisenhower visited Hartford Bridge on 22 April, rousing the squadrons with a call for their greatest effort yet; a sweepstake was running on when the second front would open up with its invasion of France.

On 26 May, Fg Off. Ted Moore attended an investiture at the French Air Force HQ in London. The Free French authorities, authorised by General de Gaulle and approved by the RAF, awarded him the *Croix de Guerre* medal for operations with No. 342 (Lorraine) Squadron. The citation reads:

> As a cameraman of the Film Production Unit, this officer has completed a number of operational missions with the 'Lorraine' Group. He has always displayed coolness and courage of a high quality sharing as air gunner, in the defence of the aircraft. On 3 October 1943, during a particularly dangerous sortie to the Paris area, Flying Officer Moore secured a film of the utmost value, which being distributed widely has constituted a fine instrument of propaganda on behalf of France.[10]

The *Croix de Guerre* was highly respected in France, and Ted was one of only three men from the FPU to receive such high recognition from that nation.

Opposite: A No. 342 (Lorraine) Squadron Boston 'B'. Ted frequently operated his camera from the rear Perspex gunner's position, which provided a good viewpoint when the pilot purposely banked around a target.

Ted Moore being fitted with his parachute harness, assisted by a French ground crew officer. He is wearing the 1930-pattern Sidcot flying suit, which was ideal as the large knee pockets held some of his camera equipment. On occasion he would be standing up at the rear gunner's cockpit to record the best film possible. In the distance, the Boston can be seen with the ground crew officer illustrating that position perfectly. The early 1940-pattern crepe rubber galosh boots with the central zip offered him the best footwear. During filming and while flying the chest parachute harness was always worn, but Ted's actual parachute was stored within the fuselage, allowing him greater freedom of movement.

Returning to Hartford Bridge, special training gave indications of what was to be required of No. 342 Squadron for the predicted invasion of France. The pilots were tasked to develop their skills of low-level 'treetop' flying while carrying large cylinders with flared nozzles fitted at the rear end of each tank. The navigators were responsible for discharging the contents of the cylinders at precise locations; once initiated, thick white smoke fell into the slipstream and billowed out behind the low-flying Bostons. The D-Day duties of Nos 88 and 342 Squadrons became blatantly obvious—laying a smokescreen across the invasion site to protect the Allied forces. The vulnerability of the aircraft and crews on such an operation was apparent to all. The squadron's aircraft were painted with black and white stripes running around the rear of the fuselage and wings to identify them to the invasion forces. Amid growing speculation, on 5 June 1944, the squadron was finally confined to Hartford Bridge with a lockdown, and all personnel were forbidden to leave the base or communicate with the outside. The armourers loaded the huge smoke containers into the Bostons and everybody waited. Orders were finally posted for a 0200 hours briefing on the morning of 6 June.

At 0130 hours the crews congregated for the D-Day briefing. Ted knew he would be flying with Sqn Ldr Pushman of No. 88 Squadron, a pilot with whom he had flown previously. Two large maps on the wall clearly related to two separate locations in Normandy, and the indicators illustrated two completely different courses to be flown. D-Day was on—the mission was about to commence in earnest, and Nos 88 and 342 Squadrons were to play a crucial role in this momentous day.

Two smokescreens were to be laid between the Allied fleet and the German coastal defences. The capital ships were to be protected along the coastline from the mouth of the Orne to Bayeux, and No. 88 Squadron was to provide that screen. No. 312 Squadron would provide a similar screen for the American fleet, to be laid from the St Marcouf islands to Barfleur Point. Both smokescreens were to be provided by pairs of Boston aircraft dispatched at ten-minute intervals, these combined sorties were designed to offer the best possible protection at very low level across the sea. The commanding officer provided instructions to the crews, reminding them that the smoke to be deployed was a poisonous substance and that it was completely unavoidable for some of it to be sucked into the rear turret position. Ted was instructed to keep his oxygen mask on at all times, despite it not normally being required at such a low level, and that when smoke was deployed, the oxygen level in the mask was to be increased to its full capacity.

The aircraft were due to commence the screen at 0500 hours, the first wave of aircraft departed in pairs at around 0400, followed by other pairs departing at ten-minute intervals. The first smoke was put down just as daylight was breaking. The scene was amazing: the air crews were in the middle of intense gunfire exchanges between the heavy coastal defences and the Allied fleets, huge plumes of water were being thrown up by the heavy shells crashing into the sea, and anti-aircraft flak was being directed into the sky. When an opportunity arose to see through the smoke and debris of war, hundreds of assorted ships stretched as far as the eye could see. Ted filmed the events between the shore batteries and the landing craft off the invasion beaches of Normandy. The smoke drifted away as it reached the surface of the sea due to fairly strong winds pushing along the surface of the water. After four hours and twenty-five minutes, Ted's Boston BZ326 landed safely back at Hartford Bridge. He had filmed the incredible collection of thousands of vessels embarking on the Allied invasion; furthermore, on returning to Hampshire, he had witnessed the amazing sight of powerful sea tugs towing parts of the Mulberry Harbours to be built at Arromanches.

The smoke containers were replaced by the ground crew, and the aircraft was made ready to depart in anticipation of additional orders. One aircraft from No. 342 Squadron failed to return, having crashed into the sea, and another from No. 88 Squadron, flown by WO Boyle, also never returned. Flt Lt Smith reached Hartford Bridge flying his damaged Boston, but his aircraft had been hit by flak, causing serious handling problems and the landing gear had not come down correctly. The Boston slewed onto the ground with its collapsed undercarriage and careered along the runway. The pilot and rear gunner escaped from the ensuing fire, but the fire tender staff were unable to save the life of the navigator, twenty-two-year-old Flt Sgt Edward Allan, who suffered a terrible fate within the aircraft. His remains were later transported to Scotland, where he was buried by his parents and his younger brother in Cathcart Cemetery, Glasgow. A courageous man stationed at Hartford Bridge had risked his life in attempting to rescue Edward from the inferno, receiving burns and later collapsing from smoke inhalation. This unknown individual had displayed the utmost bravery. The pilot and rear gunner from the crashed aircraft both suffered shock, and the pilot also sustained suspected internal injuries. It was a sad end to the day for No. 88 Squadron. No further smoke-laying sorties were required, and the crews stood down accordingly.

After D-Day, Nos 88 and 342 Squadrons were tasked with day and night sorties in the so-called interdiction campaign to isolate the invasion area from German reinforcements until the Allied breakout from the Normandy bridgehead was completed. Ted filmed the decisive daylight operation to attack the German 21st Panzer Division, south-east of the Orne estuary on 13 June, and a similar sortie to Condé-sur-Vire the following day.

Orders were received for Ted to depart No. 137 Wing for No. 138 Wing, which was engaged in fighter and ground attack roles within the 2nd TAF.

Cameraman Ted Moore wearing full flying gear at RAF Hartford Bridge. The aircraft's unique artwork identifies it as being Boston Z 2234 'H' of No. 88 Squadron.

He was to fly in a Mosquito allocated to him and his regular pilot, Vic Hester. Mosquito DZ383 was unique in that it was not attached to any of the squadrons within the Wing. It carried a white question mark on the fuselage and always stood apart from the other aircraft.

Despite its wooden construction, the Mosquito epitomised strength and endurance. It was easily repaired and excelled at low level. Ted would frequently sit alongside the pilot on an improvised navigator's seat; in front of this position was a kneeling cushion positioned above the access into the Perspex nose. Mainly from here, Ted operated his camera equipment and dropped precise bomb loads on specific targets. He viewed the ground through a large, optically flat aiming windscreen while laying in a forward position. He undertook many Special Duties, including several famous daytime low-level raids against various SS and Gestapo headquarters. The first target for Ted to film from a Mosquito was the château at Maulny, which housed a saboteur training school for elite German troops. Ted's flying log book records him taking off at 1955 hours on 2 August 1944, accompanied by nine Polish crews led by Sqn Ldr Rayski. Ted's pilot for this particular raid was Sqn Ldr 'Micky' Bell-Syer, who always flew with a lucky charm—a silver Cartier inscribed plaque—that had been given to him by his wife. It was fixed in his cockpit and he always touched it for good luck. Micky and Ted were to attack the château at Maulny and then film the operation with the movie camera equipment. This was the first of a number of specific pinpoint targets that Ted would film in his role as cameraman to the 2nd TAF.

On 18 August 1944, the Gestapo barracks at Égletons, 50 miles south-east of Limoges, were attacked by fourteen Mosquitos of No. 613 Squadron following a resistance intelligence report that the building was occupied by the secret police. At 1600 hours Ted took off with Flt Lt Hester piloting their distinctive question-marked Mosquito in a raid led by Air Vice-Marshal Basil Embry. The target was specific and required precision bombing; it was successfully identified and attacked between 1802 and 1818 hours, with bombing heights down to just 50 feet. At least twenty hits were scored on the building, and the front and rear walls were completely demolished. The target became enveloped in smoke, into which the attacking Mosquitos poured their combined firepower. Ted's pilot was able to circle the area after their own attack had been completed in order to obtain some good photographic results. Just one Mosquito was lost in the attack, which post-raid analysis regarded as having been highly successful.

The various squadrons of No. 138 Wing were engaged in progressive actions on a daily basis, and the 2nd TAF was tasked with moving bases as the front pushed forward into Germany. On 17 September, No. 613 Squadron was given the important task of bombing German barracks in Arnhem, an engagement directly connected with the Allied airborne landings there. Eight

Ted Moore's photograph of the SS barracks at Egleton, taken from Mosquito DZ383. The old school building has received bomb blast damage that has shattered windows and blown the shuttering from their frames.

Egleton school building seen from sufficient height to appreciate its size. The extensive smoke illustrates the accuracy of the bomb strikes inflicted by the Mosquitos.

Mosquitos were to be deployed, and Ted was requested to film the raid and then follow up with filming the actual airborne invasion.

However, with the camera equipment installed and the four individual bombs loaded onto Mosquito BZ326, Vic Hester was required to take off immediately for another operation of the utmost importance—an individual sortie to bomb an isolated telephone exchange. It had been established that the German telephone network, which would be used to report the airborne invasion, was routed through one particular exchange and it was therefore necessary to destroy it immediately. The exchange was situated in a disused military barracks at Arnhem, and Ted calculated that it could be destroyed and that they could then film the invasion as originally ordered.

Taking off immediately, and with no opposition, the target was located. It was a small target to destroy and they anticipated needing to fly several approaches. Ted was once again positioned in the Perspex nose of the Mosquito and charged with the responsibility of dropping the bombs. The initial approach was too low to make the best use of the terrain, and as he peered ahead, Ted caught a terrifying sight: over twenty German Tiger tanks, crewed with black-uniformed troops, were eyeing up the exceptionally low-flying Mosquito. Ted dropped the first bomb as the tanks opened fire, but the Mosquito was hit and Vic Hester suffered several wounds in his left leg. In the knowledge that their target was of the utmost importance, Ted and Vic knew that they would need to re-engage with the tanks to ensure that the telephone exchange would be blown up. Ted bandaged his pilot's left leg as best he could and then returned to the Mosquito's nose cone to drop the remaining three bombs. This final attack was made using a more tactical approach in an attempt to avoid the tanks. The bombs were dropped and they immediately left the area to fly to the paratrooper dropping zones in Arnhem. Ted filmed the drop and also the unexpected German armoured strength. Vic Hester managed to fly the Mosquito back to base at Lasham where he received medical treatment, and Ted took the urgently needed film of Arnhem to the photographic unit where it was developed and immediately flown to Field Marshal Montgomery for his personal inspection. No. 613 Squadron's operations record books provide details of the above attacks: 'Arnhem barracks F/L Hester made a low-level attack for the benefit of his camera (F/O Moore) and received a .303 bullet in the leg.' Sadly, Vic Hester's injuries meant that he was no longer fit to fly.

Ted Moore found himself attached to another low-level Mosquito squadron within No. 140 Wing of the 2nd TAF. This Wing was under the command of AVM Embry. Despite his rank and status, AVM Embry had sought permission from the highest authorities to fly with his men, but since his escape from France in 1940, the Germans had circulated his description and placed a price on his head. Unique restrictions were imposed on him as he was in possession

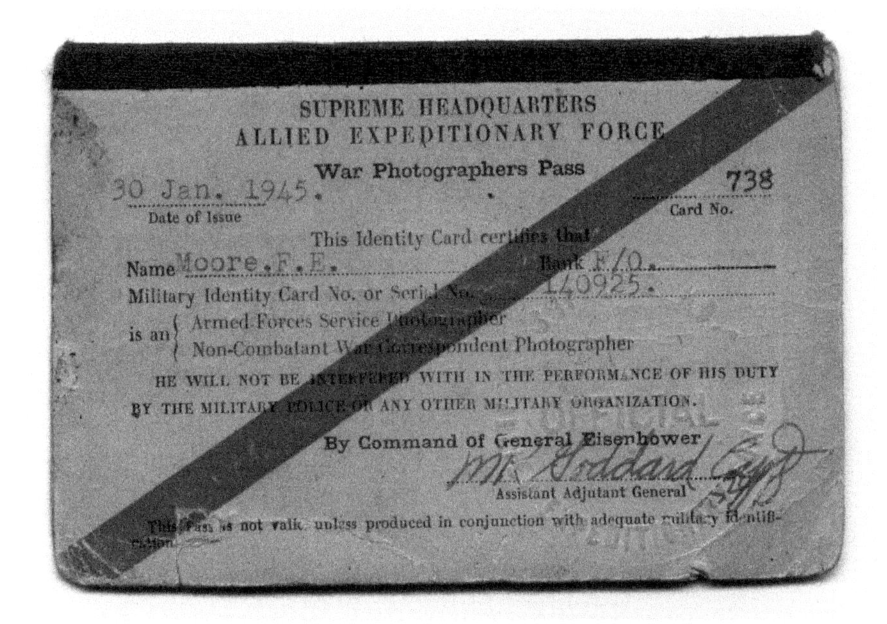

SUPREME HEADQUARTERS
ALLIED EXPEDITIONARY FORCE
War Photographers Pass

30 Jan. 1945. — Date of Issue

738 — Card No.

This Identity Card certifies that

Name Moore. F. E. Rank F/O.

Military Identity Card No. or Serial No. 140925.

is an { Armed Forces Service Photographer
Non-Combatant War Correspondent Photographer

HE WILL NOT BE INTERFERED WITH IN THE PERFORMANCE OF HIS DUTY BY THE MILITARY POLICE OR ANY OTHER MILITARY ORGANIZATION.

By Command of General Eisenhower

Assistant Adjutant General

This Pass is not valid unless produced in conjunction with adequate military identification.

Flying Officer Moore's Allied Expeditionary Force War Photographers Pass, authorised by General Eisenhower.

of information of the utmost importance. When engaged in any operational flying, AVM Embry became 'Wg Cdr Smith' and was issued with genuine identity discs and the uniform of a pilot named Smith of that same rank.

No. 140 Wing consisted of No. 464 Squadron RAAF, No. 487 Squadron RNZAF, and No. 21 Squadron RAF. These squadrons were engaged in spectacular raids that were frequently filmed with movie and still camera footage. Mosquito DZ414, a regular FPU aircraft, was identified by a single 'O' on its fuselage, and Ted became the regular cameraman in the aircraft with his pilot, Flt Lt Kenneth Greenwood. Among the most important operations filmed by Ted were two raids upon Gestapo headquarters, which are now carved into the history of the RAF and are unquestionably linked with the iconic Mosquito aircraft.

Briefings were extensive for raids against these important targets, with detailed scale models being constructed for the crews to study. The first such raid for Ted was an attack on the Gestapo headquarters, located in the heart of Copenhagen. The Shellhus (Shell House) was, and still is, situated on Kampmannsgade, 500 yards west of the impressive town hall in the Danish capital, surrounded by roads on three sides. The six-storey building, camouflaged with green and brown paint, was used by the Gestapo as their information and intelligence centre, and high-value suspects were detained there for extensive interrogation and torture. They kept their most important prisoners on the top floor of the Shellhus (others they detained in Copenhagen's Vestre Prison), knowing that this would prevent the building from being attacked by the RAF.

The Shellhus was frequently occupied by men like Dr Karl Hoffman, the country's Gestapo chief in Denmark. SS-Sturmbannführer Hoffmann arrived in Copenhagen in September 1943 to investigate resistance and accelerate the persecution of Danish Jews. Another senior Nazi working in the Shellhus since January 1944 was Otto Bovensiepen, a subordinate within the Reich Security Office whose specific task was to crack down on resistance-led sabotage. The Gestapo had recently been very successful in intercepting and arresting several key members from the Danish underground movement. At the time of the operation, information from Maj. Lippman of Danish Military Intelligence indicated that an estimated twenty-six captured members of the resistance were in the building. The Gestapo had similar buildings in Aarhus and Odense.

On the morning of 21 March 1945, a special force of Mosquitos from No. 140 Wing took off from RAF Fersfield in Norfolk to participate in Operation Carthage; Ted was responsible for filming the attack. The Mosquitos took off in three waves of six, together with two Mosquitos of the FPU, one of which included Ted and his pilot Ken Greenwood. After flying across the North Sea for over two hours at a low level, the Mosquitos made landfall exactly as

The 'Shellhus' or 'Shell Headquarters' building in its pre-war splendour.

planned and the city of Copenhagen soon came into view. Mustangs of Fighter Command escorted the Mosquitos on both outward and return journeys; during the attack they were detailed to silence flak positions in the vicinity. The three waves of attack formed as planned, but tragedy struck. Ken Greenwood and Ted Moore were flying on the port wing of Wg Cdr Kleboe's Mosquito when it struck a high lighting pole on the railway approach to the target building. Ken was forced to make a violent manoeuvre, climbing to port and swinging immediately back to starboard in order to level out, by which time he was on the Shellhus. Wg Cdr Kleboe's Mosquito had swung to port, climbed slightly and then dived towards the ground. He could no longer control his damaged aircraft and it crashed into the grounds of the Jeanne d'Arc school, bursting into flames. The crash scene was only a few seconds' flying time from the Gestapo HQ and directly on the flight path of the following aircraft. Subsequently the crash site at the school was mistaken for the target, and bombs were dropped on the site, inflicting heavy casualties in the school as the children were being ushered into the cellars. These terrible circumstances led to eighty-six children and ten nuns losing their lives. Some were to be drowned in the cellars as a result of the firefighting measures deployed at the scene of devastation.

Pilots had great difficulty in establishing the correct target within split seconds. The Shellhus was well alight, and some prisoners were escaping amid the confusion as events unfolded. Several were forced to jump from the fourth floor, a decision that ultimately caused their deaths. However, many other agents and detained resistance operatives were able to escape. One SOE agent, Poul Borking, who had been parachuted into Denmark and was later captured by the Gestapo, was being interrogated at the time of the attack but successfully escaped from the building. Another man, Mogens Ludolf Fog, a Danish physician, politician, and resistance fighter who had helped to set up *Frit Danmark*, the illegal non-partisan resistance newspaper, escaped along with Prof. Poul Brandt Rehberg, who became a valuable witness in post-war criminal trials. The entire raid lasted only four to five minutes and had cost many lives, but the immediate reaction from the Danish underground was one of praise for the airmen who had risked their lives. Many Gestapo officers and collaborators were killed in the operation. There are several conflicting calculations relating to the death toll, but it is believed that the figures rest between fifty and 150 individuals. Eighteen of the twenty-six men held in the cells within the Shellhus are thought to have escaped from the building. Despite the tragedy involving the loss of life at the school, this raid was considered to have been a success by the Danish resistance movement, which sent the following message:

> Sincere admiration your wholehearted co-operation Shellhus bombing ... Main building totally destroyed.... Regrettable accident wholly understood by everyone here.... Congratulations and thanks to RAF.

The Shellhus Gestapo HQ building in Copenhagen was left burning after the RAF raid. The roof has almost been completely destroyed and the internal floors were alight. The east and west wings had also been destroyed.

The view from an adjacent building. This image was taken at a time when the east and west wings were burning. One individual can be seen running past the corner of the building.

Listed below are the Mosquito serial numbers and crews of No. 140 Wing involved in the attack at the Shellhus Gestapo headquarters in Copenhagen:

No. 487 Squadron
RS570—Gp Capt. R. N. Bateson/Sqn Ldr Ted Sismore
PZ402—Wg Cdr F. M. Denton/Fg Off. A. J. Coe
This aircraft returned damaged as a result of flak; the starboard flap was shot away and the hydraulics became faulty. However, Wg Cdr Denton managed a controlled belly landing on the airfield.
PZ462—Flt Lt R. J. Dempsey/ Flt Sgt E. J. Paige
This aircraft was hit by flak and was flown back to base on a single engine.
PZ339—Sqn Ldr W. P. Kemp/Flt Lt R. Peel
SZ985—Fg Off. G. L. Peet/Fg Off. L. A. Graham
NT123—Flt Lt D. V. Pattison/ Flt Sgt F. Pygram
Unable to return to base, this aircraft was flown towards neutral territory, but unfortunately ditched near the island of Hven and the crew drowned.
DZ414 Flt Lt K. Greenwood/Fg Off. Moore, Film Production Unit

No. 464 Squadron
PZ353—Flt Lt W. K. Shrimpton, RAAF (Pilot)/Fg Off. P. R. Lake, RAAF
PZ463—Flt Lt C. B. Thompson/Sgt H. D. Carter
PZ309—Flt Lt A. J. Smith, RAAF/Flt Sgt H. L. Green, RAAF
SZ999—Fg Off. H. G. Dawson, RAAF/Fg Off. P. T. Murray
This crew were killed as a result of crashing after the raid.
RS609—Fg Off. J. H. Palmer, RAAF/2Lt H. H. Becker, RNorAF
This crew were killed as a result of crashing after the raid.
SZ968—Wg Cdr Iredale, RAAF/Fg Off. Standish

No. 21 Squadron
SZ977—Wg Cdr P. A. Kleboe/Fg Off. K. Hall
This aircraft struck a tall lighting mast and was seen to crash within a few seconds' flying time of the target.
PZ306—Sqn Ldr A. F. Carlisle/Flt Lt N. J. Ingram
LR388—Sqn Ldr A. C. Henderson/Flt Lt W. A. Moore
HR162—Flt Lt M. Hetherington/Fg Off. J. K. Bell
DZ383—Fg Off. Kirkpatrick/Sgt R. Hearne
This aircraft was Ted's previous Mosquito with the white question mark painted on the fuselage. It had suffered some flak damage but managed to return to Rackheath in Norfolk. The camera film was urgently removed and Sgt Hearne was taken immediately to develop its eagerly anticipated contents.
PZ222—AVM Embry (alias Smith)/Sqn Ldr Clapham

Ted Moore and Ken Greenwood undertook over twenty operational sorties while attached to No. 140 Wing and their partnership was highly successful. One last operation was required of them: the final Gestapo HQ attack at Odense. History has elevated Odense to be the exemplification of the daring and dangerous Mosquito operations against Gestapo HQs during the Second World War. The flying log book of Flt Lt Moore demonstrates the dramatic role that the FPU played in these historic operations.

Odense was to be the third attack on targets in Danish cities in less than six months. The target, a former school building requisitioned by the Gestapo in 1943 and used for the interrogation and torture of suspects, was small and situated on the island of Fyn. Only six Mosquitos from the Wing would take part. Once again, the resistance movement had made a direct request that Odense be bombed; the Danish resistance having suffered significantly, and many of its operatives were detained in Odense. The old agricultural school was known to the locals as 'Torture Castle'; its many rooms provided the Gestapo with ample cells within which to confine their prisoners.

The tone of the German occupation of Denmark changed in 1943. While there had been some resistance to the Germans during the first years of the occupation, acts of sabotage became more prevalent as the resistance movement gathered strength. Rather than yield to new German demands for military courts to try saboteurs, the Danish Government resigned on 28 August 1943. Martial law was declared and German authorities arrested Danish civilians, Jews and non-Jews alike, and Danish military personnel. The Germans took direct control over the Danish military and police with the objective of completely eradicating resistance in Denmark. In 1944 some 1,500 Danish police officers were sent to Buchenwald concentration camp—they were regarded as a potential threat, having previously displayed loyalty to their government.

In early April 1945, the Germans surrounded their Gestapo HQ at Odense with barbed-wire fences and thoroughly disguised the building from enemy aircraft with camouflage netting. They were determined not to be caught by the 'Gestapo hunters' who had struck at other locations in Denmark.

From the airfield at Melsbroek in Belgium, the six Mosquitos from No. 140 Wing took off at 1400 hours on 17 April. They were carrying both fuselage- and wing-mounted 500-lb bombs with short-delay fuses. The Mosquitos were led by Gp Capt. Bob Bateson and the Wing Tactical Navigation leader, Sqn Ldr Ted Sismore, the man who had successfully planned and participated in the Shellhus raid. Among the air crew was AVM Basil Embry, using his alias and wearing his false uniform. On a similar approach to the Copenhagen raid, the Mosquitos crossed the Jutland peninsula and continued onwards to the large island of Fyn. At 1605 hours, the air-raid sirens in Odense began to sound, alerting everyone to the fact that enemy bombers were heading towards the city. Gp Capt. Bateson's navigation was impeccable, but the target was very difficult to find because of the effectiveness of its camouflage. The leading Mosquitos had to circle the area for almost thirty minutes before the target was finally identified—great effort was placed on minimising danger to the public. Three bombing runs had to be made, with the delay-fused bombs being dropped only on the fourth run. The fifth run was made by Ken and Ted, who spent so long over the target area that they tempted fate. However, the movie camera and still images were secured, with some images obtained from the lowest altitudes possible.

One Mosquito suffered as a result of bomb blast—one of its engines was seriously damaged—but it managed to return to an Allied airfield safely. The remainder returned to Melsbroek without incident, as did the fighter escort detailed for their protection.

The work of Flt Lt Moore and his pilot Flt Lt Greenwood was recognised by Air Cdre Atcherley at No. 2 Group HQ. They were both recommended for the award of the DFC:

> Flt/Lt. Kenneth GREENWOOD 67669 RAFVR 487 RNZAF Squadron.
> During his tour of operational duty, Flight Lieutenant Greenwood has executed many sorties during which he has attacked enemy airfields, railways and road transport causing much damage and disruption. He has invariably

A low-level still image of the Gestapo HQ heavily camouflaged, but only one small portion of the building remained intact.

displayed a high degree of courage and determination and has set a fine example to all. In an attack on the Gestapo Headquarters at Odense, Flight Lieutenant Greenwood secured photographs which well proved the success of the operation. His determination on this occasion was characteristic of that which he has shown at all times.

Flt/Lt. Frank Edward MOORE. 140925 RAFVR No. 4 F.P.U.
This cameraman is personally responsible for many outstanding good films of the operations of the 2nd Tactical Air Force. They have been of the greatest training and public relations value. Some of the notable operations which he has accompanied as cameraman have been the low-level attack on the power station at Chevilly Larue (Paris) by the Lorraine Squadron in Bostons, the low-level attacks on Chateau Maulny, the school at Limoges, Chalons, Arnham, 'Clarion', Copenhagen and Odense in Mosquitos and he also accompanied the Mitchell Squadrons on operations during the Rhine crossings. In addition to this Flight Lieutenant Moore with his pilot Flight Lieutenant Greenwood DFC was for a period attached to Fighter Command to photograph the Spitfires dive bombing the V2 sites at The Hague. Flight Lieutenant Moore has shown himself to be a most efficient and gallant cameraman and has rendered valuable service to 2nd T.A.F.[11]

Only nine DFCs were awarded to FPU personnel during the Second World War, and the previous award of the *Croix de Guerre* makes Ted's medal combination for a 'cameraman pilot' exceptionally rare,if not unique.

In early post-war Denmark, a ceremony was held in Aarhus during which Air Chief Marshal Sir William Sholto Douglas, Commander-in-Chief, British Air Forces of Occupation, presented a payment of 470,000 kroner, which equates to an estimated £20,000 at that time, to the Crown Prince of Denmark. Prince Olaf had been escorted back to Oslo by No. 140 Wing Mosquitos, which shadowed his journey in HMS *Apollo* on 13 May 1945. This monetary gift presented by the Air Chief Marshal was to aid those Danes injured during the raids on Gestapo premises at Aarhus, Copenhagen, and Odense. The money had been raised by squadron personnel of No. 140 Wing, and from collections during two impressive RAF flypasts that had taken place in June and July over Copenhagen. Among those at the presentation ceremony were many of the surviving crews who had taken part in the three pinpoint raids on Denmark. On 17 May 1945, personal letters of appreciation and a set of cuff-links were presented to the crews engaged on the famous raids. The cuff-links were chosen to represent the links between the two countries. Sadly, by this time the 'hitch-hiking' cameraman Ted Moore had departed back to Pinewood Studios in England and his pilot Ken Greenwood likewise was absent. Many years later, Ken Greenwood was presented with a set of cuff-links during the unveiling of a memorial to the nine airmen who were killed on the Copenhagen Gestapo HQ raid. That memorial remains mounted on the wall of the present Shellhus building; it consists of a bronze cast of a propeller from one of the downed Mosquitos. Below it is a plaque recording the names of the nine crew members who were killed in the attack. A memorial was also erected at the site of the Jeanne d'Arc School in Frederiksberg, fittingly commemorating the brave nuns and schoolchildren who so tragically lost their lives.

Ken Greenwood retired to live in Newton Abbot, Devon, while Ted Moore returned to his roots in the film industry, working for Rank Organisation film producers as a lighting technician and cameraman. During the 1950s he was employed on many pictures, including the early James Bond productions, and won a BAFTA award for his work on *From Russia with Love*. The six Bond films with which he was involved were all exceptionally successful. He was recognised as one of the industry's finest widescreen cinematographers, and in 1966 he was awarded an Oscar for his talent. His last major work was made in 1980, and he suffered a stroke shortly afterwards and died at the age of seventy-two.

Ted helped create nearly fifty major films in his lifetime, but his remarkable footage of operational raids conducted during the Second World War must be recognised as the most important. They are invaluable to the history of the RAF and can still be viewed by the public at the Imperial War Museum in London—a fitting testimony to his extraordinary life.

The memorial at the school in Frederiksberk depicting a nun and two young pupils by the Danish sculptor Max Andersen. This photograph was taken on the eighth anniversary of the accident.

11

Norman Kerr DFC, AFC, AE Siren Disruption and Pathfinder Operations

The impressive awards bestowed upon Norman Kerr reflect on his seven years of service in the RAF. The young Glaswegian enlisted into the RAFVR in March 1938 with a personal ambition to learn to fly. He had no idea that he would become one of only 217 men to be awarded the DFC and AFC medal combination during the Second World War. The addition of the Air Efficiency Award (AE) made Norman's impressive combination of medals extremely rare.

Norman was seventeen years old when the RAF gave him the service number 741637; this would remain his unique identity number until he received a commission. Officers were recognised with an 'Officer's number', which again was uniquely allocated. When the possibility of another war with Germany became clear, the RAF increased the capacity of its air crew training programme, and this eager young Scot was swept up with thousands of others into the RAF's slick selection and training process. After flying training, aged only nineteen, Norman wore the silk and boldly padded pilot's 'wings' on his flight sergeant's tunic. It was now July 1940 and he was trained and authorised to pilot one of the RAF's Wellington bombers into war.

The Battle of Britain was being waged over the southern counties and the threat of invasion by Germany hung over the country. Norman was posted to the airfield at Stradishall in Suffolk, where No. 214 Squadron was based and operational. The squadron, flying Wellington bombers, was engaged in offensive operations to thwart the potential invasion of Britain by attacking the French ports in which the enemy's invasion supplies and materials were beginning to accumulate. They also took the initiative in bombing major targets in central Germany, but Norman would not be given that opportunity yet. In 1940, young and newly qualified pilots were eased into operational duties by acting as 'second pilot' for the first few operations. This was a practice that proved to be a luxury, as it was soon recognised that the OTUs fully prepared young pilots and no such 'mothering' was required.

Norman was 'mothered' by Sqn Ldr Denys Finlay Balsdon, the 'A' Flight commander who accompanied him on the raids to Göttingen and Eschwege in late July, and then to Gelsenkirchen on 1 August 1940. An international hockey player, Denys Balsdon was a very popular character; he had joined the service in 1933, and Norman was sad to see him leave No. 214 Squadron to take command of No. 97 Squadron. On 18 December 1941, while returning from a daylight attack on the German battleship *Gneisenau* in the port of Brest, Denys Balsdon's aircraft, which had been damaged by anti-aircraft fire over the target, crashed on landing at Coningsby and the whole crew were killed.

Norman continued flying on No. 214 Squadron while being shadowed by Plt Off. Alec Cranswick DSO DFC, another popular member of 'A' Flight. They undertook ten operations during August and September 1940, among which were two sorties to the Black and Harz Forests in Germany where they dropped devices designed to ignite once they had landed among the woodland areas. The idea was to start large swathes of fire that would decimate crops and the supply of wood available to German industry. The devices were known as 'Razzles' and needed to be transported wet before being dropped from the aircraft. Once they dried out, the Razzles would spontaneously combust. However, these raids were judged to be unsuccessful and were therefore discontinued by the RAF. Plt Off. Cranswick, who later flew with the Pathfinder Group, was regarded as a magnificent pilot. He sadly lost his life flying with No. 35 Squadron in 1944.

Eventually it was decided that the young Norman Kerr was capable of commanding his own crew, flying Wellington R3233 on his first unsupervised operation to bomb Brussels on 17 September 1940. He commanded a crew composed entirely of sergeants, and R3233 was to become his regular aircraft. Norman flew it on frequent operations, including against the significant targets of Cologne and Hamburg among several others in October. He was given the opportunity to fly to Berlin in November 1940—three of the eight operations he flew to major German targets that month were to the capital. The Air Ministry was keen to demonstrate that the fight was being taken to Berlin, and the RAF utilised several war artists to illustrate the success of their missions. One such artist was Capt. Bryan de Grineau, who was required to personally debrief bomber crews who had flown to attack the city. As a result of the information passed to the artist, he created an illustration that was approved for publication in the national newspapers.

During 1940, many of the raids to bomb major targets were conducted by small numbers of aircraft. For instance, on Norman's first raid to Berlin in November that year, No. 214 Squadron dispatched only three Wellingtons as part of the total strength of just eighty-one aircraft engaged by Bomber Command on targets across Germany, Belgium, France, and Holland. By

The impressive group of medals awarded to Norman Kerr: the Distinguished Flying Cross, the Air Force Cross, the Second World War Campaign Stars and Medals, the MID Oak Leaf, and the Air Efficiency Award.

comparison, Bomber Command would later mount operations with several hundred aircraft, and eventually the famous 1,000-bomber raids. Norman was to experience the growth of Bomber Command for himself, and in the new year, No. 214 Squadron had the honour of becoming an 'adopted' squadron.

The Federated Malay States War Fund had been inaugurated in 1940 with an initial gift of £55,000, secured by *The Malay Mail* newspaper. That money was given for the purchase of aircraft for the RAF, and the British Malayan Federation gave sufficient money to finance the entire squadron. The name 'Federated Malay States' was forthwith incorporated into the squadron's official title. The FMS funds at that time had secured £200,000 specifically for the purchase of Wellington bombers, and several of the squadron's aircraft had artwork relating to the Malay States painted on their fuselages, while the names of some aircraft were specifically requested by the donating officials. It should be noted that later, in early 1941, the Ministry of Aircraft Production advised that a Spitfire squadron could officially be named for £100,000, but to have a heavy bomber squadron named the required contribution was increased to £500,000.

Norman had quickly amassed thirty-three completed operational sorties with No. 214 Squadron and had notably survived four sorties to Berlin in 1940, despite Bomber Command experiencing terrible losses of aircraft and air crews. He was to be posted to an OTU, which was regarded as 'resting' from operations. Norman had applied for a commission and underwent a

A war artist's illustration of the RAF attacks by Wellington Bombers on Berlin in November 1940. (*Associated Press Photograph*)

formal interview with the commanding officer, which would normally involve a few testing technical questions and scrutiny of his service record—which was exemplary. As a newly commissioned pilot officer, Norman departed to No. 20 OTU at Lossiemouth in Scotland.

Instructing pupil pilots who required experience flying the Vickers Wellington was challenging for Norman, and he accumulated many additional hours in the air. Navigational and bombing exercises were flown across the rugged countryside and out across the North Sea, and as with all wartime training in the air, fatal accidents inevitably occurred. Within a short time of arriving, Norman experienced the loss of two crews at Lossiemouth. On 4 February 1941, Wellington R1005 was being flown by Plt Off. Clausen from New Zealand when it experienced trouble on its return after a night cross-country training sortie. As the Wellington was about to land it was ordered to make a pass as the runway was blocked. The aircraft avoided any collision but then plunged out of control into the sea, a short distance away from the aerodrome. There were only two survivors from the crew of six. That same day, another Wellington, R1367, flown by another New Zealander, Sgt Walker, crashed while circling the airfield, killing four of the crew members. The losses at this unit were relatively high—as their Wellington aircraft were mainly old airframes and the ground crews were faced with constant challenges in keeping them airworthy. Several crews were lost in unexplained circumstances while flying over the sea and have no known graves.

Norman's posting as an instructor at the unit was extended, and he was rewarded with a Mention in Despatches on 1 January 1943 in acknowledgement of the fact that, as Chief Instructor, he was engaged in running an efficient pool of flying instructors. Later in 1943, he was recommended for the AFC award for his extended duty and commitment while engaged as an instructor. He had accumulated over 900 hours of flying experience and during the first six months of 1943 had instructed for no fewer than 154 hours. The AFC was subsequently awarded on 2 June 1943 with the following announcement:

> During the past two years this flying instructor has been employed in converting pupils to Wellington aircraft. His standard of flying instruction is consistently high and he commands the respect both of the pupils and of the instructors who come under his command.[12]

A large and imposing house had been let to the RAF at Lossiemouth for the duration of the war, primarily for resting air crews—a kind gesture by the lady occupant who had chosen to live elsewhere. The house was located a few miles up the coast in a small village called Hopeman and provided a beautifully peaceful residence with a good library and excellent food. Norman was an acting flight lieutenant on the instructing staff and developed a strong friendship with Fg Off. John Alcock, one of the navigational officers. These two men made the best use of the facilities at Hopeman, but both aspired to return to operational flying. Postings eventually came for them both to convert onto the versatile and impressive De Havilland Mosquito. Their hope was to form a crew together as navigator and pilot in this aircraft, which had a strong reputation among the men for being exceptionally fast, agile, and exciting to fly.

In January 1944, Fg Offs Alcock and Kerr both arrived at No. 1655 Mosquito Training Unit; rarely could two more experienced men have reported for training duty—one of whom wore the ribbon of the AFC and the MID bronze oak leaf emblem. Flying the Mosquito exceeded Norman's expectations, his years of flying Wellington bombers were suddenly forgotten in the excitement of flying the incredibly fast Mosquito. Within just four weeks, Norman and his best friend were arriving at RAF Upwood in Huntingdonshire, having been posted operational into No. 139 (Jamaica) Squadron.

No. 139 Squadron's title originated from the financial support provided by Jamaica to purchase Mosquito aircraft, but for the crews who flew within the squadron, the connection with Jamaica provided an additional benefit. A tot of rum was kindly provided to the returning crews by the dedicated Caribbean country, which provided ongoing support to the squadron throughout the war. The squadron subsequently became part of the RAF's important No. 8 Group; its motto 'We Destroy at Will' was highly appropriate, as the Mosquito was indeed a potent and formidable aircraft.

In 1942 the Air Ministry had requested the formation of No. 8 Pathfinder Force (PFF) Group to address the urgent need to improve the accuracy of bombing by marking the target before the arrival of the main force. The PFF was built around volunteers who accepted that it entailed flying additional operations: a tour of duty with the PFF required a projected forty-five sorties to be completed, fifteen more than with mainstream squadrons. An active policy of recruiting the very best air crew personnel into No. 8 Group also existed. Its navigators in particular were well above average ability, and 'dead reckoning' was a specific skill that any PFF navigator possessed. The navigator kept a meticulous log of the pilot's instrument readings, which indicated the aircraft's direction and airspeed; by using forecast wind speeds provided at every briefing by the meteorologists, he could then calculate the aircraft's position. However, the weather forecasts were frequently incorrect, and unexpected winds could send an aircraft miles off course and affect its speed over the ground. In order to check where they actually were, the navigator had to spot a landmark, normally a coastal, river, or road feature of some nature, to fix their position accurately. Then he could calculate the actual wind speed and start the dead reckoning process again. Together with the blind-bombing equipment that came into use by Bomber Command as the war lengthened, this practice of dead reckoning demanded exceptional skill from PFF crews.

Air Vice-Marshal Don Bennett commanded the Pathfinders for the entire duration of the war. No. 1409 Flight, part of No. 521 Squadron flying Mosquitos, was created as a Special Duties Flight under Bennett's command. They were undertaking long-range weather reconnaissance PAMPA flights (Photorecce and Meteorological Photography Aircraft), which were dispatched at short notice to specific targets deep within enemy territory in order to establish the exact weather conditions just before a raid. The unarmed Mosquito aircraft utilised their amazing speed to enable these important operations within No. 8 Group to be undertaken.

Navigational devices based on the transmission of radio signals such as 'H2S' and 'Gee' were naturally trialled by squadrons within the Group. These devices all subsequently improved navigation and target identification within Bomber Command. Bennett's Group also developed a system of coloured flares that were attached to parachutes and dropped, showing different combinations of colours for each night suspended in the air. These were capable of being deployed to control main force bombers, keeping the stream together or turning them on a given point. In addition, the markings could be deployed to drop spoof flares to intimate fabricated Bomber Command operations.

A report to the British War Cabinet, CAB 66/28/22, provides evidence of the additional role undertaken by the Mosquito crews of No. 139 Squadron, commanded by Don Bennett:

> The RAF are now mounting numerous small raids throughout occupied Europe to keep the air defences on a state of constant alert. Sometimes these were mounted as diversions to large-scale raids by the main Bomber Command force. On other occasions single aircraft were despatched simply to set off the air-raid sirens and disturb the sleep of the residents and munitions workers. Berlin was a particular target for this purpose.

The fast and agile Mosquito was ideally suited to these operations, which were soon identified as Siren raids. They were to become highly effective at keeping the Luftwaffe guessing as to the intentions or numbers of aircraft that engaged in these operations. The sounding of air-raid sirens created disruption night after night in districts where manufacturing was prevalent; the cessation of night working in factories and the disturbance to the sleep of those who were to start work the following day all assisted in disrupting war productivity across Germany. One trick was to set off the sirens within an hour or so of the 'all clear' having been sounded, which simply intensified the effect. Additionally, these sorties required the enemy to mount night fighter defences that consumed their fuel and expended other materials, adding to the frustration experienced by the Luftwaffe.

The damage inflicted by one 4,000-lb bomb or smaller bomb loads dropped by the Mosquitos might be regarded as insignificant, but Siren raids most certainly contributed to the overall campaign conducted by the RAF. The Mosquito's speed usually enabled it to evade enemy fighters, and the free-ranging aspects of these types of operations were enjoyed by the crews who undertook them. Sorties to Berlin and back in a Mosquito could be achieved in about three hours and forty-five minutes, whereas the same return trip for Bomber Command's Lancasters or its other heavy bombers would take at least eight hours.

Norman had now been promoted to the rank of Flight Lieutenant and, in company with his navigator, was keen to begin operations with No. 139 Squadron. They were to commence their service on the squadron with four consecutive raids on Berlin during the first few weeks of February 1944.

On 5 February, they were among six Mosquitos that took their bombs to Berlin. One Mosquito that departed ahead of them aroused the defences of Hanover, and the flak and searchlight defences over that city created an effective landmark for Norman and the remaining Mosquitos, who diverted past Hanover and swept into Berlin. Norman's first Mosquito expedition into Berlin was far removed from his early 1940 experiences in the lumbering Wellington bombers. He landed his Mosquito back at RAF Upwood, having been in the air for just under four hours.

The second raid on Berlin, on the 10th, was longer—five hours in the air. No. 139 Squadron contributed twelve Mosquitos, supporting a combined operation to the German capital of twenty-one Mosquitos from various squadrons. The extended length of this operation indicates the additional time spent over Berlin. The next raid took place on the 15th and again lasted five hours in the air, supporting Bomber Command's force of 891 aircraft. No. 139 Squadron committed nine Mosquitos, some carrying flares and target indicators to be dropped approximately 70 miles north-west of Berlin, others taking off from Upwood at fifteen-minute intervals, tasked with fire watching and bombing the central configurations of fires started by the main force.

Norman's last contribution to the battle for Berlin was on the 19th, in a diversionary attack on the city while Bomber Command's main force attacked Leipzig. Ten Mosquitos left Upwood with instructions to depart from the bombers on the indication of a route-marker flare. The Mosquitos left the bombers heading for Leipzig and headed for Berlin, dropping spoof fighter flares and 'Window' to create the impression of a protected main force, which of course they were not. Fighter flares were likely to indicate to the Luftwaffe that Allied night fighters were deployed and utilising the illuminated flares to assist in protecting the bomber force.

In response to the increasingly destructive Allied bombing campaign, Germany had strengthened its defences and counter-measures; in particular, the flak and anti-aircraft defences around its major cities were increased. German architect Friedrich Tamms designed new, extraordinarily strong bunkers for the Reich Ministry for Armaments and War Production. They were built by the Reich's civil engineering organisation headed by Fritz Todt, who used hundreds of forced labourers from all over Europe to build enormous concrete fortresses, each one holding four heavy guns. Known as 'Flak Towers', they were manned by expert gunners, and each pair of towers was additionally provided with the smaller and most effective four-barrelled 2-cm light flak guns. They were also always accompanied by a further tower that provided radar and control equipment to make the heavy guns particularly effective. These huge complex structures acted as civil defence headquarters and air-raid shelters for many thousands of city dwellers; their size and solidity was such that even direct hits by Allied bombers could only inflict superficial damage. Sixteen such structures were eventually completed: three pairs in both Berlin and Vienna, and two pairs in Hamburg.

Wg Cdr Womersley DSO, DFC, commanding officer of No. 139 Squadron, flew with Norman and eleven other crews to bomb Frankfurt on 22 February 1944. One aircraft badly damaged its undercarriage during the take off from Upwood and was immediately directed to the emergency landing ground at Woodbridge.

RAF Woodbridge had been opened on 15 November 1943, and was situated just east of Ipswich. It was no more than one massive runway encompassing a width of three normal runways and extending in length for some 3,000 yards. From the air it looked nothing more than a huge slab of concrete, but to the air crews nursing home damaged aircraft and potentially injured colleagues, it represented sanctuary and hopes of survival. Aircraft that were unable to land in a conventional way, or those that crash-landed, were attended to immediately by the emergency ground crews at Woodbridge.

Aircraft using RAF Woodbridge often landed heavily and many suffered undercarriage collapses as a result. The width of the runway was such that other aircraft were still able to land despite the presence of a crashed bomber—the crashed aircraft were simply bulldozed off the runway as it was imperative to keep the runways clear. At night, the runway was illuminated by three sets of lights, creating three individual runways, with the most southerly runway prioritised as always available for any emergency. Pilots like Norman required no communication or authority to use it, which in effect made it a non-regulated emergency facility.

In late February 1944, No. 139 Squadron received four newly modified Mosquitos with extended bomb doors and reinforcements, which allowed the aircraft to carry the 4,000-lb 'cookie' bomb. The fact that the Mosquito could carry such a huge bomb load relative to its size was breathtaking. The Mosquito B Mk XVI could fly at altitudes of up to 40,000 feet thanks to its pressurised cockpit, and could also carry the 4,000-lb bomb in the enlarged bomb bay. With additional wing fuel tanks, the Mosquito could take one of these mighty bombs to Berlin and still evade the defending night fighter force.

The briefings at Upwood were frequently very detailed and intense, as the duties for No. 139 Squadron were vital to the success of other raids by Bomber Command. Timing was of the utmost importance and the navigators' work therefore required finite accuracy. During the afternoon of 25 February, Norman, who had recently been promoted to the rank of Acting Squadron Leader, and the nine remaining crews received briefing details of a spoof raid to Schweinfurt while the main force of nearly 600 bombers was to attack Augsburg. Norman was to drop spoof aerial route markers, a sequence of flares dropped on parachutes that were used to guide the fictitious main bombing force along its predetermined route. These decoy route markers could be seen clearly in good weather conditions and would therefore draw enemy night fighters towards them and away from the actual bomber stream. It was the first time that the squadron would deploy 4,000-lb 'cookies', two of which were destined for Saarbrücken or Mannheim, depending on the level of success achieved with the deception. Mannheim turned out to be the target, and all the Mosquitos returned safely some four hours after leaving Upwood.

These special modifications required the aircraft to carry additional fuel, and two moulded papier-mâché tanks were fitted under each wing. These held an additional 50 gallons of fuel, and once that had been consumed the tanks were simply dropped off, usually while the aircraft was still flying over Holland and heading towards Germany. The bomber version of the Mosquito was unarmed and relied on its speed to escape from conflict, but the fighter version was fitted with four 20-mm cannons and four .303 machine guns in the nose of the aircraft—the absence of the Perspex nose cone made the type instantly recognisable.

On 3 March 1944, Norman was given the opportunity of carrying one of the 4,000-lb bombs to Düsseldorf. Just two Mosquitos departed from Upwood that night; their brief was to sight an aiming point, illuminated by a Mosquito from No. 109 Squadron, and drop the 'cookie' directly on the accurately marked target. The red target indicators were easily identified. When Norman dropped the huge bomb the sudden loss of 4,000 lbs of weight sent the wooden Mosquito skywards with significant force, but immediately

A Mosquito aircraft fitted with the extended bomb doors that allowed the 'Cookie' bomb to be held in the bomb bay. Additional fuel tanks are being carried under the wings.

the aircraft regained its remarkable agility and he headed for home.

The following night, Norman was required to take Mosquito ML941 on a solo raid carrying another 'cookie' to Duisburg. The crew climbed the small ladder to enter the side fuselage door that accessed the cockpit, where Norman had the benefit of steel protection below his pilot's seat. His parachute was fitted into the well of the seat. Sitting immediately alongside him was his navigator, who also had access into the Perspex nose cone where he controlled the dropping of bombs or flares from the aircraft's bomb bay. Taking off at 0210 hours, they gained height and proceeded over the English Channel towards Germany where they located a pinpoint navigation fix on the Rhine and commenced their timed run to Duisburg. The enemy flak defences were intense, and their bomb was dropped in the centre of the concentrated gun flash area. This was a classic nuisance raid, with one aircraft creating air-raid alarms, evacuations, and anti-aircraft flak deployments. Norman returned to Upwood at 0505 hours, eager to complete the debriefing and get some rest.

Also that March, Norman took his aircraft on dedicated Mosquito-strength operations to Cologne (twice), Kassel, and Munich, in support of Bomber Command operations. A similar operation on 24 March supporting a preliminary light raid, itself a prelude to a heavy attack by Lancaster and Halifax bombers, resulted in Norman being unable to continue into Germany. The siphoning of the fuel from the wing tanks failed and he dropped his bomb onto Borkum, the westernmost of the East Frisian islands. It was to be a short-lived disappointment, however, as Norman successfully flew to Berlin the following night and, on the 31st, completed the month with an operation to Kassel.

Several Mosquitos were fitted with a system that was identified both in written records and in flying log books as 'Y'. It referred to the 'H2S' radar navigation equipment developed in 1943, which was regarded as astonishingly advanced and was kept top secret for as long as possible. This accounts for the use of the simple 'Y' written in the squadron records. The device had a rotating parabolic dish that mapped the ground beneath the aircraft even through cloud. An image created on a small screen in the aircraft differentiated between dark areas for sea, bright areas for land, and very bright for built-up areas. For those reasons, it worked well on coastal targets or on those with broad rivers. The 'H2S' sets were installed in Pathfinder aircraft to assist in the accurate marking of targets with coloured flares, but the disadvantage of the device was that the sets transmitted a signal. The Germans would eventually identify those aircraft by electronic counter-measures, and within months enemy fighters had an airborne device for homing in on RAF bombers using 'H2S'. It was an example of the 'cat and mouse' trade between Luftwaffe and RAF scientists during the war, but 'H2S' had a spectacular effect on bombing accuracy and No. 139 Squadron most certainly used the equipment to their advantage.

British scientists kept working to give the RAF a technological advantage, and in 1944 they produced an advanced 'Gee' navigation system. This was also known as 'G-H' and had been the early, almost primary, electronic navigation aid developed in the war. The upgraded system allowed RAF bombers to send radio pulses to two ground stations in Britain, which then transmitted them back to the aircraft. By measuring the time interval between the outgoing and returning pulses, the navigator could instruct the pilot towards the target and determine the precise point for an accurate release of the bomb load. But the system was not perfect: it could be used by only a limited number of aircraft at any one time and had a limiting range of around 300 miles.

John Alcock, sitting next to Norman, utilised 'H2S' in Mosquito DZ632 during their operation to bomb Berlin on 9 May 1944. It proved to be a successful sortie, taking four hours and thirty minutes to complete. The following night, Norman accompanied eleven Mosquitos on a 'H2S'-led operation to attack Mannheim and Ludwigshafen. They were carrying a 'cookie', while other Mosquitos were engaged on other duties. Mosquito KB161, flown by Fg Off. Lewis and navigated by Fg Off. Woollard DFM, was tasked with dropping marker flares. The raid progressed well, but an unexpected event developed as Mosquito KB161 returned home. A marker flare had caught in the aircraft's bomb bay, having failed to fall away, and the flare's barometric fuse ignited as the aircraft descended, causing a fire to break out in the bomb bay. It soon became apparent to the crew that they would need to bail out immediately by parachute. The escape hatch situated on the floor of the cockpit area was opened and Fg Off. Woollard attempted to escape, but was forced back by the slipstream. However, with the assistance of his pilot he managed to fall free from the Mosquito and operate his parachute, which ultimately saved his life. The Mosquito crashed near Cambridge, but with the twenty-three-year-old pilot still inside the cockpit. Unable to escape, he had faced the reality of the tragic situation as the aircraft plummeted into the ground.

Sub-Lt Benjamin Vlielander-Hein had originally been a naval officer but had qualified as a navigator in the Royal Netherlands Naval Air Service. He found himself posted to No. 139 Squadron and was involved in one of their more unusual Special Duties. The squadron briefing on 12 May 1944 was called to organise an operation that was to take place in the early hours of the following day. This was to be a special operation on the Kiel Canal, known at that time as the Kaiser Wilhelm Canal, a long, wide, and deep canal in Schleswig-Holstein, linking the North Sea at Brunsbüttel to the Baltic Sea. During the war it was a direct route for large iron-ore cargo vessels from Sweden. The detailed briefing explained that the objective was to precision drop sea mines into the canal, but as it was a relatively small target area, it required dropping from an exceptionally low altitude to ensure that the mines did not drift away from the target. Personnel from No. 139 Squadron were advised that they were to provide flare illumination of the canal and create a spoof raid on Brunsbüttel, while another Mosquito squadron would plant the shipping mines by parachute into the deep canal. A specifically chosen section of the canal was to receive the mines, and the squadron would fire green Very lights to mark the route to the target area. Wg Cdr Womersley was to lead the squadron, which took off at 0200 hours.

The spoof crews consisted of three Mosquitos that diverted to Brunsbüttel at the head of the canal to drop two 4,000-lb 'cookies', while nine other Mosquitos dropped ninety-four white flares over the canal between 0347 and 0355 hours. The illumination allowed the mines to be dropped precisely at the point identified in the operational briefing. All the aircraft returned safely, including Norman's Mosquito LR475, which he landed at 0520 hours. The debriefing provided strong evidence that the raid had been very successful, and post-raid reconnaissance confirmed that shipping was prevented from entering the canal for several days.

For the remainder of May 1944, Norman returned to the routine of conducting raids to Berlin, Düsseldorf, Duisburg, Ludwigshafen on two occasions, and Hanover. They were all successful, with his navigator providing exceptional accuracy. On 15 May, Wg Cdr Womersley advised Norman that he had recommended him for the award of the DFC. Norman had achieved an impressive 290 hours and thirty minutes of operational flying, and his achievements while flying in No. 139 Squadron were recognised in the following recommendation:

> This Officer has now completed sixty-three sorties against the enemy. He carried out a first tour of operations consisting of thirty-three sorties in Wellington aircraft in 1940 and has now completed thirty sorties towards his second tour in Mosquito aircraft with this Squadron. His first tour of operations involved many deep penetrations of enemy territory and included four attacks on Berlin. While with this Squadron he has been employed in many varied roles such as taking part in spoof attacks, dropping spoof route markers and fighter flares, etc. The majority of his sorties however have been completed in the role of anti-morale raider and have been carried out against many of the enemy's most heavily defended targets. For his long list of successful sorties and the courage and devotion to duty shown by this Officer I recommend the award of the DFC.[13]

Air Vice-Marshal Bennett, commander of No. 8 (PFF) Group, strongly endorsed the recommendation and the award was later published in *The London Gazette*. However, Norman's elation in adding the DFC to his AFC medal ribbon was tinged with regret—his navigator, who had played an important role in their successful record, had not also been recommended for an award. That situation would eventually be addressed four months later when John Alcock was recommended for the DFC.

In June 1944 Norman flew eight capital raids—raids on large cities or significant enemy targets—which included Berlin on three occasions and Cologne twice. He usually carried one 'cookie' to these targets, but the Germans were deploying far greater numbers of dummy ground markers in their attempts to draw attacking aircraft away from the primary target areas. However, these efforts made no impression on the Mosquito operations, which were all completed successfully. By this time, No. 8 Group was deploying greater numbers of Mosquito-strength operations to the many primary targets attacked by mainstream Bomber Command squadrons.

In the summer of 1944, Norman was rapidly approaching the completion of his second operational tour of duty—a rare achievement. No. 139 Squadron had been diverted to attacking Hitler's oil refineries, and on 4 July Norman joined the strength of twenty-four Mosquitos that accurately bombed Scholven near Gelsenkirchen. The next day he received orders to return to Scholven—it would prove to be one of his most troublesome operations.

The squadron records indicate that thirty-four Mosquitos were briefed for this operation, and Norman's squadron was to supply six aircraft. Twenty-eight Mosquitos were hauling 'cookies' in their bomb bays—one for each aircraft—and other aircraft carried marker flares and the standard load of six 500-lb bombs. The pilots hauling 'cookies' always took advantage of the entire length of runway, as it provided a little reassurance should any engine fault cause an aborted take off. The longer run was also necessary as the aircraft could only manage a gentle climb because of the weight of the heavy 'cookie'. Carrying the 4,000-lb bomb always entailed additional risk as it was immediately armed after loading by the ground crews, whereas smaller bombs could be armed from the cockpit when required. Norman was to fly in Mosquito MM127, an aircraft he had previously flown operationally. He lifted off the runway at Upwood to commence his seventy-fifth operational sortie at 0015 hours on 6 July.

Mosquito MM131, flown by Flt Lt Armin, experienced an engine failure that forced him to return to Upwood within an hour of his departure, but the remaining aircraft reached the target safely. Once there, they came up against heavier flak defences than anticipated, with over fifty searchlights operating in three defined

Opposite: Mosquitos were dropping their 4,000-lb 'Cookies' with regularity. The picture illustrates a bright glowing target indicator with the tracks of searchlights creating smears across the picture. The main road running across the picture is the Charlottenburg, which continues through the Tiergarten district of Berlin, and the River Spree is clearly identified. This Mosquito bombing raid photograph was released for publication by the Air Ministry in 1944.

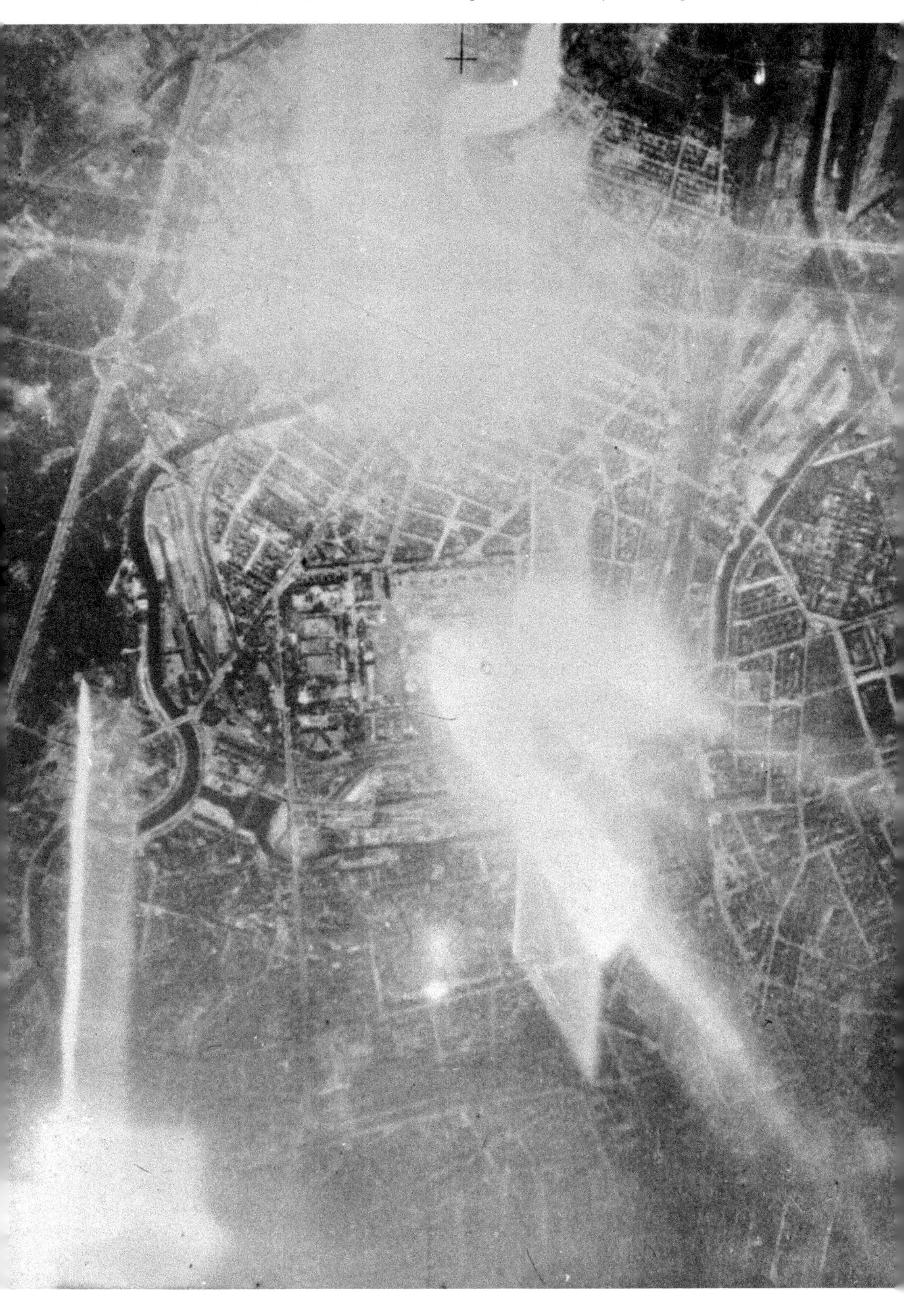

A 4,000-lb 'Cookie' bomb being loaded into a Mosquito by the ground crew. This official photograph, released by the aircraft manufacturers De Haviland in June 1944, illustrates the enormous size of the bomb in comparison to the aircraft's bomb bay.

cones. The marking Mosquitos deployed their flares and the raid progressed well. The Germans deployed a dummy target indicator fire some 6 miles north of the actual target, but all the attacking aircraft ignored it, and at 0137 hours a large explosion lit up the entire area making it visible for many miles. The flak, however, had been tremendous, and Norman suffered the loss of his starboard engine. Faced with the prospect of returning on just one engine, he knew that an unlucky encounter with an enemy night fighter would prove catastrophic. But expert navigation by John Alcock got them back home via the most direct route; with a great sense of relief, they landed MM127 back at Upwood at 0246 hours. The ground crews had a lot of repair work to do—fortunately, Norman and John were not required on the following night's operations.

John had made friends with the Dutch navigator Benjamin Vlielander-Hein, probably as a result of them both attending the squadron navigators' dedicated briefings. In all probability, John discussed with Benjamin his experiences of the previous night, and little did the Dutchman realise that a similar but more significant situation would arise on his next flight with his RNZAF pilot, Flt Lt Robins. They departed from Upwood shortly before midnight, making for Berlin, but as they crossed France their Mosquito MM146 was struck by flak. This was another crew that would simply be recorded as 'failed to return' on the operational records. Naturally it made John realise how lucky

The loading of a 'Cookie' into a Mosquito's bomb bay. The three 'arming tags' are in place on the front end of the bomb. These tags were removed with their attached pins once the enormous bomb had been loaded into the aircraft.

he and Norman had been in surviving their own encounters with flak. It later transpired that the crew of MM146 had managed to reach neutral Sweden and were interned in accordance with international regulations. They were eventually released and managed to return to the UK.

After another successful Berlin raid on 10 July, Norman knew that he had flown enough hours to be considered 'tour expired'. This was confirmed when he was told his next briefing would be the last of his tour. The brief on 14 July was to attack Hanover in Mosquito DK324. That aircraft carried the identification letter 'R' on its fuselage and had been John and Norman's favoured aircraft during their fifty-one Mosquito operations with the squadron. This final operation was an 'anti-morale' sortie and proved to be an uneventful.

Tour-expired for the second time, Norman Kerr left Upwood in early August 1944. He was posted to an instructing position at No. 1655 Mosquito Training Unit at nearby RAF Warboys. John Alcock was to remain at No. 139 Squadron, receiving his DFC later that month. Sadly, before they parted company, Norman and John witnessed a traumatic crash at Upwood on 7 August. At 0100 hours, Mosquito KB202 was returning from a sortie to Germany when fog caused several aircraft to be diverted to other airfields; however, Flt Lt John Kenny and his navigator Martin Levin had started their landing before the airfield was completely enveloped in fog. They were a highly experienced crew, but the conditions caused them to overshoot the runway and crash into an end-of-terrace property used for air crew accommodation. Two men from No. 156 Squadron, also based at the station, had recently entered the house, having themselves been engaged on operations in their Lancaster that night. Flt Sgts Allan Rookes and David Winlow were killed in the crash, as were the crew in the Mosquito which had burst into flames.

The Mosquito units of No. 8 Group had performed exceptionally well in their various duties. During 1944 alone, No. 139 Squadron flew 2,443 operational sorties, and only twenty-two Mosquitos were lost during operations undertaken from the airfield at Upwood. These were remarkable achievements for a small unarmed twin-engine bomber made of wood. Emphasising that point, the Bomber Command Review published in 1945 stated the following:

> The value of the Mosquito attacks as a supplement to the attacks by heavy aircraft is unquestioned, and their contribution to the success of the combined bomber offensive was both significant and praiseworthy.

On 1 March 1945, Norman was given the Air Efficiency award. This decoration had been instituted in 1942 for long and meritorious service in the RAuxAF and the RAF Volunteer Reserve. He was then posted to carry out Mosquito ferrying duties, delivering the aircraft to various locations, until his retirement from the RAF on 19 October 1945.

12

Michael Gardiner AFC, DFM Avro York Transport

Michael Gregory Gardiner was born at Chertsey in Surrey on 2 December 1920. His father, also Michael G. Gardiner, had served in the last of the South African wars and in the First World War, reputedly in the Battle of the Somme. Michael Snr was a person of some character who later became a staunch member of the Communist Party, which no doubt drew him to the attention of the authorities and was of some concern to his son, who was at the time serving in the RAF.

Between 1931 and 1936, Michael was sent to various Catholic boarding schools in Sussex. The strict regimes he experienced had a profound effect and led him to reject religion for the remainder of his life. Michael's first employment was as an office boy at Gerald & Son of London Road, Norwich, where he worked during the latter half of 1936. In May 1937, aged sixteen, he joined the RAF as a boy entrant. The Geneva Disarmament Conference had just failed and Germany was expanding its military forces faster than had ever been expected. Michael signed up for nine years.

Michael was trained as a wireless operator and immediately posted to the electrical and wireless school at Cranwell. Between 1937 and 1938, he was admitted to the hospital at Cranwell for three extended periods, apparently suffering from scarlet fever—a serious condition that could have potentially affected his ability to continue in the service. However, his recovery was complete and uncomplicated. In November 1938 the Electrical and Wireless School Apprentice Wing became No. 1 Electrical and Wireless School, and Michael was later promoted to Aircraftman 1st Class, having qualified as a wireless operator on 10 February 1939.

AC1 Gardiner was posted to No. 75 (Bomber) Squadron at RAF Honington. This squadron had been designated as a Group pool squadron, an early concept of what later became the OTU, where crews received their final training. Michael flew his first trip with the squadron on 13 February 1939, a short thirty-five-minute sortie with his pilot Sgt Jones in Harrow bomber

K6994. Several other short sorties followed in what constituted the assessment process prior to becoming a qualified member of air crew. On 22 April 1939, Michael remustered as a wireless operator 'under training', clearly having passed selection for the role of air crew.

When war was declared against Germany on 3 September 1939, No. 75 Squadron was already in process of relocating their Wellington bombers to various locations. On 1 September, Michael had flown with a crew delivering one aircraft to Newmarket Heath and he was involved in the delivery of another three days later to Harwell. This distribution concept was meant to limit losses of aircraft through enemy bombing, but it proved to be a rather impulsive decision that created other logistical problems with aircraft distributed across multiple locations.

Michael's training with his squadron concluded on 19 November when he became a fully qualified air crew wireless operator. His flying log book at that time records 191 hours and 20 minutes of daylight flying, and 69 hours and 15 minutes of night flying. This was an extensive period of training when compared to that of the many hundreds of volunteers who were to follow Michael into service as RAFVR wireless operator air gunners. Their training was consolidated and refined in order to be completed in the shortest time possible.

Harrow aircraft, serial K6994—the first aircraft in which Michael gained initial air experience and the one in which he subsequently flew on many occasions. (*Michael Gardiner collection*)

Later that month, Michael underwent air gunnery training with 'A' Flight, No. 215 Squadron at RAF Jurby on the Isle of Man. Qualification with basic air gunnery came easily to him, and he returned directly to No. 75 Squadron where he continued flying on various cross-country and dummy bombing runs in the squadron's Wellington bombers. The squadron was performing formation flying on a frequent basis, as it was believed at that time that bombers in tight formation created good defensive capabilities. This perception was later proved to be flawed when the RAF suffered heavy losses of air crews to Germany's fighter pilots. On 10 April 1940, Michael's crew were undertaking a formation cross-country sortie when two Wellingtons struck each other in mid-air—the risks associated with flying in tight formation were high, even without enemy fighters.

No. 75 Squadron amalgamated with No. 148 Squadron and jointly formed what was to be become No. 15 OTU. As summer approached, the Battle of Britain was about to play out over southern England, and no doubt Michael was becoming a little frustrated at the time spent in training. He was now a temporary sergeant, wearing the stripes on his tunic and feeling ready for whatever lay ahead of him. The first opportunity to fly operationally came on 23 July 1940. The crew, captained by Flt Lt Searl, were to fly over occupied Europe, dropping propaganda leaflets on northern France and then bombs over the Luftwaffe airfield at Brest. This night-time operation, lasting four hours and twenty-five minutes, provided Michael with his first taste of flying over enemy-occupied Europe.

On 10 August, Michael was posted from No. 15 OTU at Harwell to No. 99 Squadron at Newmarket. His flying log book by this stage recorded an impressive total of over 700 hours' flying time. Newmarket Heath racecourse was taken over by the Wellingtons of No. 99 Squadron from nearby RAF Mildenhall, and the grandstand was used for the station staff and accommodation. Twelve of the squadron's aircraft had attacked the German fleet off Heligoland in December 1939, and six bombers had been destroyed by enemy fighters. This action influenced Bomber Command's decision to favour night attacks rather than daylight attacks, and also forced a re-evaluation of the defensive qualities of tight bomber formations. Michael joined the operational strength of No. 99 Squadron, but he appears to have been a surplus member of crew as he flew to three targets with different crews during August 1940.

Eventually Michael became the regular wireless operator air gunner to Sgt Herriot's crew, and they consistently favoured Wellington bomber R3222. Taking the war to Germany during the Battle of Britain was exceptionally fulfilling for the crews of Bomber Command, but the threat of an invasion of the UK was a very real prospect. Each and every raid undertaken was important, and Michael was engaged in experimental operations in which fire bombs were dropped into the Black Forest area of Germany in an effort to deplete its extensive stock of natural timber. These proved to be ineffective, but raids on French ports to bomb Germany's invasion barges were effective, and good results were recorded in his flying log book, which he completed with excellent detail.

At the close of 1940, Michael had flown a grand total of 924 hours and 20 minutes. Within that figure, 174 hours and 10 minutes had been operational flying, attacking thirty targets with No. 99 Squadron. Bomber Command's campaign to take the fight to Germany and occupied France in 1940 is well illustrated by Michael's list of targets attacked:

Bombing storage plant at Kolleda—16 August
Bombing transformer station at Frankfurt—27 August
Bombing airframe factory at Berlin—30 August
Incendiary raid on the Black Forest—2 September
Bombing railway yards at Hamm—4 September
Bombing barges lying at Emden—8 September
Bombing barges and docks at Antwerp—13 September
Bombing barges and docks at Calais—15 September
Bombing gas works at Berlin—23 September
Bombing invasion port at Le Havre—28 September
Bombing oil refinery in the Ruhr—1 October
Bombing the 'Scharnhorst' at Kiel—13 October
Bombing the 'Scharnhorst' at Kiel—15 October
Bombing Krupp's armament works at Essen—20 October
Bombing synthetic oil refinery at Leuna in the Rhur Valley—26 October
Primary target Berlin not located, bombed AA Batteries—29 October
Bombed Potsdam railway station in Berlin—1 November
Berlin abandoned operation; force-landed at Stradishall—6 November
Bombed railway marshalling yards at Munich—8 November
Bombed oil refinery at Gelsenkirchen—13 November
Bombed docks at Hamburg—15 November
Bombed hydrogenation plant at Buer in the Ruhr—17 November
Bombed docks at Kiel—19 November
Bombed docks at Duisburg—22 November
Bombed railway yards at Mannheim—28 November
Bombing arsenal at Turin, Italy—4 December
Bombed U-boat base at Lorient, NW France—8 December
Bombed Aachen—10 December
Bombed docks at Bremen—13 December
Mannheim bombs jettisoned; engine failure—23 December

VEMBER 1940

Time carried forward :— 557·55 279·

Date	Hour	Aircraft Type and No.	Pilot	Duty	Remarks (including results of bombing, gunnery, exercises, etc.)	Flying Times Day	Flying Times Night
40	18·05	WELLINGTON R 3199	SGT. SUMNER	WAR OPERATIONS 18	BOMBED POTSDAM RAILWAY STATION IN BERLIN. INTENSE A.A. OPPOSITION.		7·5c
40	2030	R 3222	SGT. SUMNER	WAR OPERATIONS	ABANDONED OWING TO WEATHER CONDITIONS		·10
40	1730	R 3222	SGT. SUMNER	WAR OPERATIONS 19	TO BOMB TARGET IN BERLIN - 'ICED UP' AND W/T TRANS. BURNT OUT BY STATIC OVER HOLLAND - FORCED LANDED AT STRADISHALL		3·25
0	1230	R 3222	SGT. SUMNER	X. COUNTRY	RETURN FROM STRADISHALL	·15	
0	1030	R 3222	SGT. SUMNER	AIR TEST	W/T + ELECTRICAL — O.K.	·15	
0	17·30	R 3222	SGT. SUMNER	WAR OPERATIONS 20	BOMBED MARSHALLING YARDS IN MUNICH OPERATION VERY SUCESSFUL		8·05
40	17·15	R 3222	SGT. SUMNER	WAR OPERATIONS 21	BOMBED OIL REFINERY AT GELSENKIRCHEN		5·05
40	11·30	R 3222	SGT. SUMNER	AIR TEST	W/T + ELECTRICAL — O.K.	·20	
40	17·00	R 3222	SGT. SUMNER	WAR OPERATIONS 22	BOMBED DOCKS AREA AT HAMBURG		5·50
40	17·00	R 3222	SGT. SUMNER	WAR OPERATIONS 23	BOMBED HYDROGENATION PLANT AT BUER IN THE RUHR AREA		5·00
40	1000	R 3222	SGT SUMNER	AIR TEST	W/T + ELECTRICAL — O.K.		
40	0130	R 3222	SGT SUMNER	WAR OPERATIONS 24	BOMBED DOCKS AT KEIL		6·3c
40	0230	R 3222	SGT SUMNER	WAR OPERATIONS 25	BOMBED DOCKS AT DUISBERG		4·05
40	1015	R 3222	SGT SUMNER	LOW FLYING	THETFORD WOODS	·50	
40	1730	R 3222	SGT SUMNER	WAR OPERATIONS 26	BOMBED RAILWAY MARSHALLING YARDS AT MANNHEIM		5·5
					TOTAL TIME	559·35	331·4

Flying log book entries for November, illustrating the exceptional run of operations undertaken in the crew's Wellington, serial no. R3222. This aircraft was destined to be lost while operating with No. 99 Squadron.

This period of operational duty would, in normal circumstances, constitute a full tour of duty in Bomber Command; however, for Michael it was seen as proof of his credentials. He was duly posted onto what was considered to be one of the best squadrons within the RAF, No. 7 Squadron.

Stationed at RAF Oakington in Cambridgeshire, No. 7 Squadron was equipped with the four-engine Short Stirling, which had considerably more power and a far better range than any other aircraft at that time. The massive 14,000-lb bomb payload put the aircraft in a class of its own, being double that of any other bomber. It was huge when compared to the Wellington, and at the time its superior payload gave the RAF an advantage.

On 14 February 1941, Michael took to the air in the squadron's Stirling N3641. Wg Cdr Harris undertook an air test in that particular aircraft, which was later photographed on the runway apron.

Stirling N3641 displaying the No. 7 Squadron code letters 'MG'. Michael Gardiner became a member of 'A' Flight No. 7 Squadron, and he returned to operational duties in the new aircraft. Expectations were high for the new Stirling and Michael flew in this particular aircraft on 14 February 1941.

Michael was temporarily promoted to Flight Sergeant, and operations commenced in March. The term 'Special Duties' had had no bearing thus far in his service, but his experience, which continued to grow in both training hours in the sky and operations over occupied Europe, was to prepare him for such duties later on. Once again, Michael endorsed his flying log book with a highly creditable record of operations. The destinations quoted in the log book illustrate the high priority given to Germany's capital ships and naval establishments at this time:

Bombed docks at Ostend—21 March
Bombed docks and town of Kiel—7 April
Bombed docks and town of Kiel—25 April
Bombed docks at Brest, 'Scharnhorst'—28 April
Bombed area of Berlin—30 April
Bombed area of Mannheim—5 May
Intercepted and engaged for 15 minutes by enemy Ju 88 sustaining damage which forced a return—8 May
Proceed to Berlin but bombed Hamburg on return—10 May
Daylight search of Atlantic area for German Navy—27 May
Bomb the Ruhr valley—30 May
Bombed Berlin—2 June
Bombed 'Prinz Eugene' [*sic*] lying at Brest—7 June
Daylight bombed convoy at Dunkirk: Rear Gunner shot down one of three

attacking Me 109s. Aircraft seriously damaged—9 June
Bombed synthetic rubber plant at Marl—12 June
Bomb 'Scharnhorst' at Brest—18 June
Target at Kiel—20 June
Bombed docks at Kiel—23 June
Bombed docks and yard at Kiel—26 June

The German battleship *Scharnhorst* had escaped unscathed despite the RAF's attempts to destroy it while under repair at the docks in Brest. Indeed, it had been a target that Michael had attacked several times. Repairs to the battleship were completed in July, and the German High Command decided to move her to La Pallice, the industrial harbour at La Rochelle. This port was considered by the RAF to be less protected than Brest, and the decision was therefore made to attack the *Scharnhorst* at her new berth at the earliest opportunity.

RAF reconnaissance spotted the battleship early in the afternoon of 23 July 1941, and it was considered that sufficient time was available to mount one attack before darkness; a small formation of six Stirling bombers took off just before 1800 hours. The following report was made relating to Michael's aircraft in No. 7 Squadron's records:

> 3 x 2000 armoured piercing bombs. One hit observed astern of vessel, other two bombs hung up. Attacked by Me's individually from up sun both shot down by rear gunner and seen to hit the sea by rear and mid upper gunners.[14]

The rear gunner was Sgt Bernard Capel, and his exceptional skill in the rear turret was recognised with the award of the DFM; the bomb aimer, Fg Off. George Walker, was rewarded with the DFC for his remarkable accuracy in hitting the *Scharnhorst*. Several weeks later, on 23 August, the following was published in *The Times* newspaper:

> Two Airmen who in daylight attacked the German Battlecruiser 'Scharnhorst' at La Pallice last month secured a direct hit on the ship with a heavy bomb though hampered by intense A.A. fire, are honoured in the latest list of RAF awards. After their successful attack on the 'Scharnhorst', states the official record, they fought off six enemy fighters. By cool accurate fire Sgt Capel shot down the first two whereupon the remainder flew away.

It is not clear what damage was inflicted upon the *Scharnhorst*, but it is thought that the single hit by Gardiner's crew was sufficient to force the battleship to remain at her berth. The following day, a large raid on the vessel was undertaken by the RAF, and the damage it caused has been well documented.

At noon on 24 July, several squadrons of RAF bombers attacked the *Scharnhorst* from altitudes of between 10,000 and 12,000 feet. Five bombs hit her starboard side simultaneously and in a nearly straight line. Two bombs were of the 500-lb high-explosive type, the others being 1,000-lb semi-armour-piercing-type bombs. Sufficient damage was caused to the battleship for the raid to be regarded as a complete success. It was hoped that, for the time-being at least, this important heavy cruiser would be unable to re-enter the Atlantic and attack the vital convoys that were supplying Great Britain.

Normality returned for Michael with another raid to Berlin in August. However, on the 14th a raid to Hanover resulted in a serious crash-landing for the crew. Having found their primary target Magdeburg entirely covered by cloud, they diverted to bomb Hannover. The raid was successful, but upon their landing back at RAF Oakington, the complex undercarriage of the Stirling completely collapsed. The huge weight of the aircraft crashed onto the runway, and only the remarkable skill of Michael's pilot, Fg Off. Witt DFC, DFM, prevented a tragedy. No one was seriously injured, but the Stirling was completely written off.

On 22 August, *The London Gazette* confirmed the award of the DFM to Michael Gardiner. His total of fifty-three operational sorties was far in excess

A Stirling being made ready for another raid deep into Germany—a maximum fuel load of 2,254 gallons would be required to ensure a safe return for the crew. The ground crew are filling one of the wing fuel tanks. The fuel management between the various tanks was the responsibility of the flight engineer.

of a normal tour of duty. When the recommendation finally arrived on the desk of the commanding officer of No. 3 Group, he endorsed it with the following comments:

> This wireless operator has carried out a greater number of operations than any other member of an air crew in this group. His extensive number of sorties have all been undertaken in either Wellington or Stirling aircraft and his only respite from active operations has been for a period of just under three months.[15]

Michael was rested from operational bombing duties and was later posted to No. 1425 (Communication) Flight, flying with Consolidated Liberators—special conversions of the B-24 Liberator bomber—on shuttle services to the Mediterranean area. The duties involved carrying passengers and freight outbound and ferrying crews back to the UK, as aircraft were frequently flown into that theatre of operation and left there for further transit to other destinations.

In October 1941, the Flight was redesignated as No. 511 Squadron, and Michael was to serve in this squadron for a significant period of time. He would meet with many VIP passengers, one of whom was Winston Churchill, who during one such sortie invited Michael for a game of cards. One of Michael's regular pilots with the squadron was Fg Off. Sach, known as 'Baggy' to his friends and crew. Michael and 'Baggy' were to serve together over several years on Special Duties sorties, carrying some of the most important political and military individuals during the Second World War. On 4 August 1942, they transported Lt Gen. HRH The Duke of Gloucester and his aide-de-camp from Khartoum to Gibraltar, and the following day from Gibraltar to RAF Polebrook in Northamptonshire. Michael obtained the Duke's signature, which he pasted into his flying log book. Later, in September 1942, General de Gaulle, the leader of the Free French, his aide-de-camp, Wg Cdr Dias DFC, and Dias's assistant, Flt Lt Burnell, joined Michael and his crew on a flight from Bathurst (now Banjul) in West Africa to the UK in September 1942.

However, it was the significant conference in Casablanca in January 1943 that saw Michael and his crew surrounded by a plethora of high-ranking individuals, who were engaged in the highest level of negotiations for the invasion of occupied Europe. The conference had been kept secret until 24 January, but Michael had transported nine individuals, including Mr Patrick Kinna, Churchill's private secretary, to Casablanca on the 13th in an operation identified as 'Op Static'. During the ensuing days, while serving on that operation, several short sorties with various high-profile personnel were flown to Turkey, Morocco, and Egypt.

On 30 January, Winston Churchill, Maj. Randolph Churchill, Cdr

Time carried forward :—	788.15	574.35
Remarks (including results of bombing, gunnery, exercises, etc.)	Flying Times Day	Night
CAIRO TO KHARTOUM (WADI SEIDNA).	5.15	
KHARTOUM - GIBRALTAR.		
PASSENGERS:- LT.GEN. H.R.H. THE DUKE OF GLOUCESTER.		
2 AIDE DE CAMPS AND A BATMAN	3.00	11.15
GIBRALTAR TO POLEBROOK (U.K.) PASS. AS ABOVE	8.10	

H.R.H. THE DUKE OF GLOUCESTER.
KHARTOUM TO GIB. GIB TO U.K.
4-5/8/42 FLT. SACH AND CREW.
IN A LIBERATOR.
Henry.

Michael Gardiner's log book with the signature of HRH the Duke of Gloucester.

Consolidated Liberator *St Helen*, the aircraft that carried a significant number of dignitaries attending war conferences and strategy meetings within the Allied-held territories. The aircraft is clearly displaying camouflaged paintwork and the front side windows have been purposely blanked out. The crew, left to right, are Squadron Leader Sach, Flight Lieutenant Halcro, Sergeant Thomas, Flying Officer Price, and Flying Officer Gardiner.

Thompson, and Gen. Brooke, together with Churchill's Metropolitan Police personal bodyguard and his private secretary, were transported from Adana in Turkey to Nicosia in Cyprus.

In June 1943, Michael Gardiner was awarded the King's Commendation for Valuable Service in the Air. He had flown over 900 hours of Special Duties with No. 1425 Flight/No. 511 Squadron, carrying some of the most important personnel involved in the conflict. This award entitled him to sew a small bronze-coloured oak leaf onto his flying tunic, a simple, understated item but instantly recognisable as a high reward for his flying service.

Michael was rested from the responsibilities of these duties, only to be hospitalised with jaundice in 1944. Upon his return to fitness he was attached to a relatively dull Air Delivery Unit, but when he was posted to a Heavy Conversion Unit his fortunes changed and he was engaged in training crews to operate Liberators and the larger Avro Yorks. He was promoted to the rank of Flight Lieutenant and subsequently returned to fly operationally with Avro York aircraft, performing duties within a VIP Communication Flight. He was once again flying with his friend 'Baggy' Sach on familiar duties and routes. The bond between these two men was extremely strong, and it is clear that strings were pulled within the service to facilitate their continued partnership.

No. 1359 Flight, initially administered by No. 511 Squadron, became absorbed into the famous No. 24 (Communication) Squadron, with the whole unit then concentrating on VIP and Special Duties flights. Michael remained with this unit and flew many hours with 'Baggy'. Some of the more notable sorties he undertook included flying Field Marshal Montgomery, and Winston Churchill once again, whom he took to Paris to receive the *Médaille Militaire*, a unique honour for a foreign citizen.

Field Marshal Montgomery's tour of Australia and New Zealand was undertaken in Avro York MW101 during the summer months of 1947. This particular aircraft had been built to VIP standards for use by Chiefs of Staff and cabinet ministers, and Michael and 'Baggy' were part of its regular crew on that tour.

Avro York MW101 continued to serve until June 1955, when it was sold to the British Aluminium Company as scrap. Only four Avro Yorks were ever built to VIP standards—MW100, MW101, MW102, and MW107—and Michael flew in all except MW107. That aircraft had been dispatched to South Africa for General Smuts, a man with the unique claim of having been the only individual to sign peace treaties after both world wars against Germany.

Michael parted company with 'Baggy' Sach and No. 24 Squadron at the close of the September 1947, only to return when the squadron saw a flurry of activity in readiness for the great Berlin airlift, Operation Carter Paterson, a title that was swiftly changed to the simpler Operation Plainfare.

The Berlin airlift was a massive undertaking to feed some 2 million people

JANUARY 1943. (CONT).

Time carried forward 907.35 704.45

Date	Hour	Aircraft Type and No.	Pilot	Duty	Remarks (including results of bombing, gunnery, exercises, etc.)	Flying Times Day	Flying Times Night
29.1.43	0600	LIBERATOR.I. A.M.911	S/LDR. SACH.	COMMUNICATIONS	CAIRO TO ADANA (TURKEY). PASSENGERS:- GEN. SIR HAROLD ALEXANDER, AIR MARSHAL DRUMMOND, GEN. SIR H. MAITLAND-WILSON AND STAFFS.	3.10	
30-1-43	1430	A.M.911	S/LDR. SACH	COMMUNICATIONS	ADANA TO NICOSIA (CYPRUS). PASSENGERS:- RT. HON. WINSTON CHURCHILL, MAJOR RANDOLPH CHURCHILL, COMMANDER THOMPSON, INSPECTOR THOMPSON, MR KINNA, GENERAL SIR A. BROOKE.	1.10	

W/C O.C. 511 SQDN.

S/LDR. O.C 511 SQDN. 'B' FLIGHT.

JAN. 1943	DAY	NIGHT
TOTAL FLYING FOR MONTH	12.20	16.10
TOTAL FLYING WITH UNIT	258.20	245.05
GRAND TOTAL	911.55	704.45

TOTAL HOURS 1,616.40

TOTAL TIME 911.55 704.45

Michael Gardiner's log book recording one of Winston Churchill's transit journeys.

An Avro York displaying the Union Jack, placed above the cockpit by the crew to indicate the presence of the Prime Minister or a passenger of similar status.

This appears to be an official photograph with Flight Lieutenant Gardiner and 'Baggy' Sach standing either side of Field Marshal Montgomery in front of their Avro York. The crew boasts a wealth of flying experience. The crew member on the far right, the navigator, is wearing the Pathfinder badge on his tunic lapel pocket, and Michael Gardiner, third from the right, has the 'Signaller's' brevet on his tunic.

in the Western sectors of Berlin. It had been preceded by a long period of increased tension between the Russians and the Western Allies, the Russians having made a concerted effort to remove these 2 million people from West Berlin and West Germany. They used a range of tactics that included blocking the transportation of basic supplies into West Berlin and intimidating West German civilians. At midnight on 23 June 1948, the Russians cut electrical power to the Western sectors of Berlin. The following day they severed all road and barge traffic to and from the city, simultaneously stopping all supplies from the Soviet sector. From 24 June, the Western sectors of Berlin were effectively under siege and their inhabitants would have to be supplied with everything by air. The only route remaining open to the Allies were the three previously agreed air corridors leading from the Western sectors of Germany to the Western-controlled areas of Berlin. Each corridor was twenty statute miles wide, extending vertically from ground level to 10,000 feet. The original airlift requirement from Wunstorf was for 161 Dakota sorties per day, lifting 440 tons, in addition to the existing scheduled RAF Dakota services into Berlin.

Two Avro York aircraft and several C47 Dakota aircraft engaged in the Berlin airlift. Michael Gardiner's aircraft is seen starting up the engines while the other Avro York aircraft is ahead and about to depart. The intensity of flights engaged in the airlift was exceptional and unrelenting.

On 2 July, just two days after the signing of the joint operational order to commence Operation Plainfare, the first large Avro Yorks flew into Wunstorf. Additional airfields were once again brought up to operational standards and the massive logistical undertaking began. The various Allied aircraft were allocated the most appropriate airfield in order to maximise efficiency, and the turnaround times were impressive. The three air corridors were operated at fixed heights, with aircraft arriving at Gatow in Berlin every three to five minutes. Thousands of German civilians were required to provide the labour force needed to move such quantities of material. On 17 December 1948, a cargo of canned meat that arrived at Gatow was acknowledged as the 100,000th ton of provisions brought in by Operation Plainfare. However, it was not just food that was flown in: coal, petrol, clothing, medical supplies, and all basic requirements that were needed to sustain such a huge number of people had to arrive by air.

The beginning of 1949 saw the tonnage flown into Berlin surpass all previous records, and the Russians began to realise that the Allies had created a masterpiece of logistical supply into the Western-controlled sectors of Berlin. They tried to thwart the supply of materials in numerous ways, including jamming the Allied radio frequencies. The combined monthly tonnage and flights, however, continued to grow until, in April 1949, some 26,026 flights were undertaken, delivering 235,363 tons of supplies in a single month.

The vast majority of goods were transported in sacks, but an average sack only lasted for three journeys. The daily losses due to wear and tear were 17,000 sacks, equating to a replacement programme of over 500,000 sacks a month. The Central Office of Information estimated that that this alone represented a monthly cost of £50,000.

The airlift continued until 1 August 1949, and from then a gradual rundown began, culminating in the withdrawal of all aircraft by 1 October. Throughout the airlift, the RAF alone had transported nearly 400,000 tons into Berlin. Such a record demanded a high level of competence and skill, not to mention dedication. Michael and his crew flew two duty periods covering an extensive fifty-two sorties into Berlin, which entailed flying some 130 hours between 6 September and 27 September 1948, and from 22 February to 11 March 1949. Among the 101 fatalities recorded during the airlift, forty British and thirty-one American servicemen lost their lives in accidents resulting from hazardous weather conditions or mechanical failures. The remainder were civilians who perished on the ground, often from aircraft crashing into their homes.

When No. 24 Squadron returned to normal duties, Michael resumed his work escorting VIPs, including Field Marshal Sir William Slim on his tour of the Middle East and Far East, followed by another tour to South Africa. In June 1950, Michael's accumulation of over 4,000 hours' flying time, with 2,865 hours engaged in flying with Transport Command, was recognised with the award of the AFC. The recommendation made reference to the fact that Michael was a signaller and technician of outstanding merit.

Michael later received a technical commission and was posted overseas for several years. Promoted to the rank of Squadron Leader, he served within the Directorate General of Signals. As the Cold War continued to escalate, creating a rapid development in radio intelligence, counter-intelligence, and interpretation, he was most gainfully employed. The final period of service for Michael involved 'War Duties', planning for nuclear activations over the UK and Europe—a chilling task that he was happy to leave behind. Sqn Ldr Gardiner AFC, DFM, recipient of the King's Commendation for Valuable Service in the Air, finally retired from the RAF on 2 December 1975, his fifty-fifth birthday.

On 22 March 1993, after an enjoyable day visiting one of his old service friends, Michael settled down in an easy chair and passed away peacefully. He was seventy-two years old. On 30 March, the RAF paid its last farewell to Michael Gardiner when two Red Arrows undertook a low flypast at his funeral service in Saffron Walden parish church.

13

Frederick Flint BEM
Air Dispatcher

During the Second World War, many men serving as ground crew harboured the desire to fly as members of an air crew. Many who applied were rejected on quite fickle medical grounds, and simply returned to their former roles or posted to a ground role in one of the overseas theatres of operation. Roles undertaken on the ground were diverse and absolutely critical to the functioning of aircraft. They made up the support structure of the RAF, and the vast majority of personnel who thronged the aerodromes of Bomber, Fighter, and Coastal Commands were ground staff.

Frederick Walter Flint was a qualified flight mechanic and engine fitter. He held the rank of Leading Aircraftman, and despite being a highly respected flight mechanic with significant experience, he knew that his chances of promotion were slim. Frederick was married, had a son, and was older than most of those who served alongside him—the majority of whom were eighteen to twenty years of age—and his colleagues addressed him as 'Pop Flint'. In early 1941, Frederick quite unexpectedly received a posting to the Far East and was given a period of leave prior to his embarkation notice, which required him to report to the docks at Liverpool on 31 July 1941.

All Allied convoys departing from the UK were given an identification code. Frederick's convoy was WS.10 and consisted of nineteen steamers, one of which was RMS *Windsor Castle*, upon which Frederick was provided with a bunk for his passage first to South Africa and ultimately to India. The convoy was to be escorted by a combination of destroyers and armed merchant cruisers during the entire passage. The German U-boat threat was significant in the Atlantic, and all passengers were expected to take their turn in providing a round-the-clock U-boat watch. With so many men on board, it was not an arduous task, and was regarded more as a positive use of their time. One of the service personnel Frederick was bunked with was Horace Welham, who came from a similar service background. They became close friends and spent a great deal of time together during the sea passage and later serving together operationally on the same squadron in India and Burma.

On Wednesday 6 August 1941, Frederick awoke to see the convoy shrouded in fog; it lingered for most of the day, but he did catch a glimpse of a convoy steamer fairly close to the starboard rear quarter of the *Windsor Castle*, which was positioned to the rear of the convoy. Just before 2200 hours, Frederick was about to bunk down when the ship lurched violently, and the noise of metal gouging and scraping reverberated through the ship. Having been briefed on the significant U-boat threat, his first thoughts were that the ship had been struck by a torpedo. The ship shook once more, and then the noise faded away. Without any formal instructions, he and his colleagues picked up their lifebelts and made for the prearranged safety stations. It was a chaotic situation—some men went to the wrong stations, while others were still making their way towards their correct positions. The safety sergeant eventually called the roll at Frederick's location and the groups of men were moved onto the lifeboat deck. That deck had been badly damaged, but not by enemy action or a sea mine—the *Windsor Castle* had been struck by another ship in the convoy. An entire row of lifeboats had been torn away from the starboard side, but the hull was sound, and eventually the men were returned to their bunks.

The steamer *Warwick Castle* had been the cause of the collision, and had suffered serious damage to her bow which understandably impeded her ability to cut through the water efficiently. Following Royal Navy protocol, the convoy steamed ahead, leaving the damaged *Windsor Castle* and *Warwick Castle* on their own to make speed as best possible—they were 'sitting ducks', completely vulnerable to German submarines.

In daylight, the extensive damage was obvious to see. Near the end of 'C' deck there was a massive impact point in the ship's hull just above the waterline. There was another just below the level of that deck, and an extensive V-shaped indentation in 'D' deck. A Walrus aircraft that had taken off from one of the convoy's cruisers appeared in the sky and circled the *Windsor Castle*, signalling for quite some time. The aircraft returned a few hours later and a cruiser came towards them, also signalling. For those on board, this whole episode was a spectacle they had not expected to witness, but most importantly, they were no longer isolated; the *Windsor Castle* was being provided with some protection. The Walrus was able to land on the sea and was taken on board the ship by crane. The convoy had reduced speed and it was hoped that the two ships would be able to rejoin it, but the *Warwick Castle* was very badly damaged and her bow was taking in water. It was therefore decided that she should make for Halifax, Nova Scotia, with an escort detached from the convoy.

Another frightening experience took place shortly after the collision when depth charges were deployed by the cruiser after a sighting of a submarine periscope by the U-boat watch. Frederick and his fellow passengers were only too aware of their vulnerability. The ship's speed was increased in an effort to make towards the convoy, which, once sighted, brought them some comfort. Africa was reached in early September, followed by India, their final destination, without any further incident. It was with some relief that Frederick disembarked after his long journey. He and Horace were both posted to No. 31 Squadron, stationed at Lahore in the Punjab, where they were billeted in a tent with two other men. Servicing the dilapidated Vickers Valentia aircraft at Lahore was a challenge for the ground crews, as these old aircraft had been in use since the 1920s. To make matters worse, the squadron's mechanics were required to work in awful conditions.

In December 1941, Japan declared war against the Allies, attacking Pearl Harbor in Hawaii at 0755 hours on 7 December. No. 31 Squadron was by then engaged in transporting wounded men back to India, and Frederick and Horace were immediately dispatched to Akyab on the coast of Burma. The Japanese capture of many airfields in their successful invasion of Burma practically cut off substantial numbers of troops and civilians, and No. 31 Squadron was unexpectedly thrust into supplying as much food and as many materials as possible from the air.

No. 31 Squadron was the only transport squadron in India, but it had fortunately received three new Dakotas that were ideal for what was expected of them. The Dakota was constructed with a reinforced floor that was strong enough to carry exceptionally heavy loads. It was used in most major aerial battles during the Second World War, towing gliders and dropping parachutists, and in Burma it proved vital in dropping supplies and recovering stretchered patients from the front lines.

At the temporary airstrip in Akyab, the physical conditions were poor in the extreme. The Japanese advance and subsequent fall of Rangoon saw No. 31 Squadron eventually retreat back to Lahore. Regular flights carrying supplies and reinforcements to the front, and returning with seemingly endless wounded servicemen, became the daily routine for the squadron. Seconded to air crew, Frederick was required to engage in daily dispatching duties, dropping supplies, and then stewarding the loading of stretcher cases and the walking wounded for the journey back to Lahore. Like many ground crew in such circumstances, he received no training for his new role and the dangers that went with it. It created mighty personal challenges that needed to be overcome, not the least of which was air sickness; it was not a gentle transition, sitting at an open doorway of an aircraft and looking down over endless miles of forest hundreds of feet below. In many cases, he sat there performing the same duty with no restraints, pushing the loads out with both feet. Worse would follow when flying through the turbulent weather conditions that were frequently encountered above the forest terrain.

Some remote jungle airstrips were used by No. 31 Squadron to facilitate the delivery of supplies to the furthest reaches of occupied territory, where isolated Allied Chindit forces were operating. Fort Hertz in the north of Burma was one of the airstrips used to supply these gallant soldiers, and any Dakota that landed there needed to be camouflaged immediately to avoid detection by the constant Japanese reconnaissance flights.

Supply dropping to the Chindit Campaign, one of the largest Allied Special Forces operations of the conflict, was a highly dangerous duty for Frederick. The Chindits (the 77th Indian Infantry Brigade), led by Maj.-Gen. Orde Wingate DSO, operated deep behind Japanese lines in the remote jungles of northern Burma for many months, relying on air drops for their supplies—a responsibility that sat primarily with No. 31 Squadron. The units on the ground frequently had an RAF trained operative who was able to select the drop zones and communicate with the aircraft by radio. Food supplies, such as rice sacks, would be dropped at treetop height, but arms, weapons, and other supplies were dropped at around 600 feet with parachutes to ensure their safe landing.

The word 'Chindit' will always have a special resonance in military history; every Chindit endured what is generally accepted as the toughest sustained Allied combat experience of the Second World War. The Chindit expeditions behind Japanese lines in occupied Burma during 1943 and 1944 transformed the morale of British forces after the crushing defeats of 1942. However, the men effectively suffered slow starvation and were constantly exposed to diseases such as dysentery, malaria, and typhus. In the isolation and tropical humidity, any wound or sickness potentially meant death. Combined with these physical challenges, living and fighting under the jungle canopy, with the ever-present threat of ambush or encountering the enemy unexpectedly, caused intense mental strain. These courageous men relied entirely on the supplies dropped by the Dakotas, and ultimately on men like Frederick, who became skilled in deploying the food and equipment needed for them to survive. Those who could no longer continue through the intense jungle were often left behind with virtually no hope of survival. Some severely wounded men requested a lethal dose of morphia to ensure that they would not be captured alive and tortured by the Japanese.

Although 'just' a ground crew engine fitter, Frederick was accumulating many flying hours, frequently starting operations in the early hours with an estimated duration of around three hours, followed by another operation mid-morning with similar hours in the air prior to standing down. It was a gruelling schedule. The mountainous terrain of Burma was always capable of claiming the lives of tired air crews. Any crew member crashing or otherwise landing in such territory was under no illusion of the fate likely to befall him—most probably decapitation, as the Japanese traditionally provided their officers with swords to remove aviator's heads in a respectful death. The danger from the Japanese fighters was, of course, always present; Dakota FD793 was shot down while engaged in a supply drop over Tiddim on 28 November 1943, killing the crew of five, captained by WO Robert Richards. Frederick flew with several pilots, including Sqn Ldr Honeyman and Harold Levin, who was known to all as 'King Levin'. Another pilot was WO 'Lummie' Lord, who went on to win the VC over Arnhem while flying a Dakota.

Frederick's status as ground crew meant that he was not issued with an official flying log book, but he did keep some records of hours flown, despite any papers or books being frequently attacked and consumed by white ants. Living in such basic conditions, it was almost impossible to prevent these ants from damaging everything, including clothes, which he tried to preserve inside his suitcase. His personal notes detail the flying duties he undertook in Dakotas FL537 and FD788, as well as aircraft operated by the Chinese National Aviation Corporation (CNAC), which employed various private individuals to fly delivery sorties on a contract basis.

Horace Welham advised the author that Frederick was part of the crew that made the very first flight to Kunming in China, a trip that was known as 'The Hump', as these sorties were carried out at a great height in order to pass over the Patkai Mountains. They were made without the help of any oxygen or warm clothing. If the weather was inclement, which it frequently was, the Dakota would be flown on instrument readings and it would be necessary to reach some 16,000 feet to ensure a safe clearance. The only special measures known to have been provided for British or Commonwealth crews was the provision of a single Vickers machine gun, mounted at one of the emergency windows, and Frederick had received barely any instruction in its use. The duration of an average flight over 'The Hump' would be two days, and the added complication of very sparse fuel supplies in Kunming meant that the aircraft of No. 31 Squadron were forced to carry their own fuel to ensure a safe return journey. These supply sorties over the Patkai Mountains were essential in providing the Chinese forces with the supplies and weapons needed to fight the Japanese.

The unique danger of flying over the jungles of Burma is clearly illustrated by the loss of Dakota FL576. On 24 May 1944, Sgt David Bell and his crew of four from No. 31 Squadron were delivering supplies to a drop zone near the Irrawaddy River. It was their last sortie of the day, but they failed to return; it later transpired that they had crashed several miles north-east of Imphal. The wreckage was found many months later by an Allied patrol who buried the remains of three crew members at the remote crash site, but no trace could be found of the other two crewmen. All of the crew are now commemorated on the Singapore Memorial to those who have no known grave.

In July 1944, No. 31 Squadron moved to the newly constructed Basal station in India for a rest from front-line duties. Unfortunately, during the transition from operational status, Dakota FZ585, flown by twenty-two-year-old Flt Sgt Storrie, went missing on what the squadron records quote as a 'Special Duties Sortie' to the Imphal Plain. This aircraft was never found and its crew of four are also commemorated on the Singapore Memorial. The loss of this crew provided a sobering backdrop to the notification received by the squadron that LAC Frederick Flint was to be officially recognised for his exceptional duty in the air. On 6 August, Sqn Ldr Honeyman AFC, who was acting as the commanding officer of the squadron, addressed a parade of the entire contingent of men. He announced:

> On behalf of His Majesty the King I have great pleasure in presenting Leading Aircraftman Flint with the British Empire Medal. I feel this award is an honour, reflecting on the Squadron as a whole, and in particular those members of ground crew who flew as members of supply dropping crews at the period covered by the citation.[16]

The citation read:

> This airman in addition to his normal maintenance duties has carried out 250 hours' flying as a member of a supply dropping crew operating over Northern Burma. His work has been arduous and at times hazardous. His keenness and devotion to duty has been marked.

Frederick was one of 1,750 men in the RAF to be awarded the BEM in the period between 1940 and 1947. He was repatriated to the UK via Bombay, where he posted a letter to Horace Welham explaining how he had been selected for the award out of twenty men. These men, like him, had served in the air on Special Duties dropping supplies as a dispatcher to the Chindits over the last two and a half years. He was later to receive a reply from Horace, reminding him that he had been the first to fly 'The Hump' over the Patkai Mountains into China, and was without doubt worthy of recognition. Their friendship had been forged by their service together in India and Burma and they would remain in contact with each other. In August 1945, Horace invited Frederick and his family to his wedding, and they met again two years later, when Horace travelled down to Frederick's home in Hatfield to see his friend, who had returned home from hospital suffering from cancer. Frederick Flint died a few hours after Horace's visit, having spent time reminiscing about their experiences over Burma.

Post-war recognition of the dangers associated with supply missions over 'The Hump' saw the US mint a special Chinese medal that was awarded to all USAAF crews who had participated. However, no such recognition exists for British or Commonwealth personnel who were likewise engaged on those perilous Special Duties operations. They received the Burma Star campaign medal, recognising service in the Burma Campaign from 11 December 1941 until victory was secured over Japan on 2 September 1945.

Appendix A
Flying Log Books

Members of the fighting services engaged in flying duties were required to keep a personal record of flights undertaken, and flying log books were issued to all pilots and air crew personnel who flew as part of the RAF or the Commonwealth air forces during the Second World War. The aspiring young aviators who were handed the simply bound, card-covered books regarded as the property of His Majesty's Government, accepted the need to keep an accurate and detailed record of their progression during training and operational flying.

Proficiency assessments were required to be completed annually, and the commanding officers or their deputies were tasked with inspecting and signing these books on a monthly basis. When these log books were compiled they were of the utmost importance to the individual as they provided evidence of their qualifications and accumulated hours of operational flying, and in the case of Bomber Command, the number of operational raids. The requirement for regular inspection and endorsement meant that the books were handled frequently; the card covering soon became exposed on the corners and the spines became worn—signs that the owner had been in service for some time. The books usually had the owner's name and service number written on the page edges so that he could quickly locate his particular book in a large stack after assessment or monthly inspection.

Pilots' flying log books were larger than the observers' and air gunners' flying log books, as more detail needed to be recorded in theirs. As you would expect within military service, the books were identified by unique reference numbers: Form 414 for pilots and Form 1767 for observers. There were other differences in the basic formats of these flying log books; those in South Africa were issued with a covering of red for observers and green for pilots, which made them instantly recognisable, whereas those in India were issued with a cream-coloured cloth covering, and it was not uncommon to see any type of log book covered in leather binding to help preserve it. Those men who flew longer periods of service frequently bound additional log books together. The individual's promotion through the ranks was laid out in the front pages, with many having lines drawn through the lower ranks as they progressed towards a commission and officer status.

Flying log books were not required to be carried in the air. The log books of the unfortunate men who failed to return from operations and were thus regarded as missing in action were dispatched to an Air Ministry central depository. If any of these men survived, evaded capture, and returned to their squadron, their log book would be restored to them. Any log book returned from the depository was instantly recognisable by a small registration sticker applied to the outside cover, carrying the depository's unique registration number. In cases where pilots or air crew were confirmed as killed in action, or lost their lives during training accidents, their flying log books were frequently sent to their next of kin with a small printed slip normally included.

The vast majority of flying log books were recovered by the Air Ministry on completion of the recipient's service and subsequently placed into storage as official documents. The accumulation of log books was substantial, so their storage became a problem. The Air Ministry later let it be known that they could be returned to the individuals that had compiled them, but by 1959, in spite of announcements in the press, the vast majority remained unclaimed. Placed on shelving, they stretched for some 6,500 feet in length. Additional flying log books from the Admiralty and War Office added to the concerns of the Air Ministry, and the problem was placed before the Paper Committee, which subsequently recommended the destruction of the stored log books with the exception of a few selected specimens. This decision resulted in further press announcements, and additionally the BBC broadcast that log books not claimed by 15 September 1960 would be destroyed. However, less than 100 feet of shelving was reclaimed as a result of this publicity, and the Air Ministry therefore still faced a significant storage problem. Following the deadline, the decision of the committee was put into effect. Flying log books perceived to be historically important were selected for retention—including those of foreign nationals flying with the RAF, those of pilots with exceptional experience, and those of members from distinguished squadrons—but this selection was restricted to no more than a 20-foot run of space.

The nation lost thousands upon thousands of flying log books when those irreplaceable historical documents were simply destroyed. Sadly, these documents have been denied to the generations that followed those brave men. Those log books that were claimed or retained by the men who served in the air during the Second World War now represent valuable time capsules of operational duty, without misinterpretation or distortion of fact: the Bomber Command crews who penned green ink entries recording daylight operations, and red ink entries for night operations; the Coastal Command crews who wrote of endless hours spent hunting the German U-boats that threatened to cut off food supplies to the UK; and the Fighter Command pilots who endorsed their successes against the Luftwaffe with symbols or words during the Battle of Britain.

For this reason alone, those surviving flying log books are rightly treasured as rare possessions. This book has been composed around the entries made within them, written by young men who would never have expected their simple log books to be regarded as symbols of valour and commitment for future generations.

Appendix B
Pilot and Air Crew Campaign Medals

British campaign medals for service in the Second World War were governed by rules determined by the Monarch on the advice of the British Government. In June 1946, the Committee on the Grant of Honours, Decorations and Medals produced a document, Command Paper 6833, that determined the grant of such decorations during the period between 1939 and 1945. The Battle of Britain clasp to the 1939–1945 Star originated from the Air Ministry memorandum submitted by Sir Arthur Street and Air Vice-Marshal Harris on 11 July 1944.

The following eight campaign stars were issued; the qualification period for each is shown in brackets:

1939–1945 Star (3 September 1939–2 September 1945)
Atlantic Star (3 September 1939–8 May 1945)
Air Crew Europe Star (3 September 1939–4 June 1944)
Africa Star (10 June 1940–12 May 1943)
Pacific Star (8 December 1941–15 August 1945)
Burma Star (11 December 1941–2 September 1945)
Italy Star (11 June 1943–8 May 1945)
France and Germany Star (6 June 1944–8 May 1945)

All the above are six-pointed medals struck in bronze, with the cypher of King George VI in the centre. The title of each star appears around the cypher, and a different ribbon denotes each separate medal. The colours of the ribbons have symbolic significance and are believed to have been influenced personally by the King.

The criteria for the award of medals to those who had fought in the Second World War were finalised in 1948, and in accordance, the medals were issued unnamed. Additionally, it was decided that no more than five stars could be awarded to one person. Regulations relating to the award of the Pacific,

Burma, Atlantic, Air Crew Europe, and France and Germany stars prevented this from happening. Those who did qualify for more were awarded a clasp with the title of one of the stars for which they qualified. This clasp was then attached to the ribbon of one of the other stars, as laid out in the regulations. A recipient might qualify for both the Pacific and Burma stars, but was only ever awarded one of these—the first campaign medal that the recipient became entitled to. He would then receive a clasp or bar with the title of the second star earned, which was worn on the ribbon of the first entitled medal issued. If an individual qualified for a combination of two or three campaign stars—Atlantic, Air Crew Europe, and France and Germany, for example—the first entitled star was automatically awarded, and the recipient would then receive a clasp with the title of the second star to which he was entitled, which would be worn on the ribbon of the first. A third star or clasp in this instance could not be awarded. However, the 1939–1945 Star, Africa Star, and Italy Star could be awarded regardless of qualifications for all other stars.

1939–1945 Star

The medal was awarded to personnel who had completed six months' service in specified operational commands overseas between 3 September 1939 and 8 May 1945 (2 September 1945 in the Far East), although the minimum period was reduced in certain cases when, at certain specified times, just one day's service was required. RAF air crew qualified with two months' service in an operational unit, including at least one operational sortie. Non-air crew personnel had to complete six months' service in the vicinity of an operational army command, except that service at Dunkirk or in Norway, for example, also counted. However, RAF ground crew who serviced and maintained the aircraft that fought in the Battle of Britain did not qualify. Its ribbon is of equal stripes of dark blue (symbolising the Royal and Merchant navies), red (Army), and light blue (Royal Air Force).

Battle of Britain Clasp

A clasp or bar was awarded to Fighter Command air crew who saw action during the Battle of Britain (10 July 1940–31 October 1940). It is denoted by a gilt rosette when the ribbon of the 1939–1945 Star is worn alone, but a bar inscribed 'Battle of Britain' is affixed to the ribbon when the medal is worn. Only air crew of sixty-one named squadrons and of the Fighter Interception Unit were eligible for the addition to the star.

Air Crew Europe Star

The ribbon is a wide central stripe of light blue (symbolising the sky) flanked by narrow stripes of yellow (enemy searchlights) and at the outer edges by black (night flying). The Air Crew Europe Star was earned almost exclusively by RAF and Commonwealth air crew personnel and could be awarded only after qualification for the 1939–1945 Star. It was given for sixty additional days' service in an RAF unit engaged in operational flying over Europe from bases in the UK with at least one operational sortie undertaken. After 5 June 1944, operational flying over Europe qualified air crew for the France and Germany Star.

Defence Medal

This medal was awarded to all service personnel for three years' service at home, one year's service in a non-operational area (e.g. India) or six months' service overseas in territories subjected to air attack or otherwise closely threatened. It was generally issued in cupro-nickel, but the Canadian medals were struck in silver. The ribbon has two broad stripes of green (this green and pleasant land) each with a thin strip of black (the blackout) down its centre with a wide orange stripe (fire-bombing) between the two green stripes.

War Medal 1939–1945

All full-time personnel of the armed forces wherever they had served received this decoration, provided they had served for at least twenty-eight days between 3 September 1939 and 2 September 1945. Civilian war correspondents and ferry pilots who flew in operational areas also qualified. The Canadian version was again struck in silver, while the remainder were issued in cupro-nickel. The ribbon has a narrow red stripe in the centre with a narrow white stripe on either side, flanked by a blue stripe, with a red stripe on each end. This ribbon supports the MID oak leaf, if awarded.

The Bomber Command Clasp

HM The Queen approved the design for the new award of the Bomber Command clasp in 2012. This retrospective award is to be worn on the ribbon of the 1939–1945 Star and follows the previous design of the Battle of Britain clasp. Royal approval, given sixty-seven years after the war, followed the independent medal review consultation conducted by Sir John Holmes concerning Bomber Command personnel who had been engaged in a highly significant Second World War campaign and yet had received no recognition, unlike other such campaigns. In 2013, this unsatisfactory situation was finally addressed by the retrospective issue of the Bomber Command clasp. Sadly, many entitled recipients had died without knowing that this late post-war recognition was to be given. The scale of the achievement of these brave men was expressed by Winston Churchill in 1945, when he wrote to Arthur Harris, Air Officer Commander-in-Chief, Bomber Command:

> All your operations were planned with great care and skill. They were executed in the face of desperate opposition and appalling hazards; they made a decisive contribution to Germany's final defeat. The conduct of the operations demonstrated the fiery gallant spirit which animated your air crews, and the high sense of duty of all ranks under your command. I believe that the massive achievements of Bomber Command will long be remembered as an example of duty nobly done.

Despite Winston Churchill's support, the immediate post-war Labour Government, headed by Clement Attlee, disapproved of personal recognition for Arthur Harris and the men under his command. In the months after the war, there had been some concern expressed in government circles about the amount of destruction and civilian casualties caused by Bomber Command. Harris stalwartly defended Bomber Command's actions, and became the first British commander-in-chief not to be made a peer after declining that recognition due to the government's refusal to create a separate campaign medal for his air crews. Angered by criticism of Bomber Command's wartime actions, Harris moved to South Africa in 1948, where he remained until 1953. Returning home, he was induced to accept a baronetcy by Churchill and became the 1st Baronet of Chipping Wycombe until his death on 5 April 1984.

Twenty-nine years after the death of Sir Arthur Harris, the surviving men who had served as air crew under his command finally received their Bomber Command clasp to add to their 1939–1945 Star. It was granted to those who had served for at least sixty days, or completed a tour of operations on a Bomber Command operational unit, and had flown at least one operational sortie on a Bomber Command operational unit between 3 September 1939 and 8 May 1945.

Endnotes

1. *The London Gazette* 17 November 1944, p. 5281, joint citation 121460 Whittle and 128679 Shanahan.
2. Article from the Canadian *Star Phoenix* newspaper, published by John Hardwick 1944.
3. *The London Gazette* 31 January 1946, p. 750, citation 1888304 Watson.
4. *The London Gazette* 22 August 1941, p. 4864, citation 43463 Webb; *The London Gazette* 16 January 1945, p. 413, citation 43463 Webb.
5. 'Enemy Defences Reports: Mediterranean Allied Photographic Wing Report 46', Kiel University.
6. 'The Illusionist', an article in *Flight*, 6 December 1945, pp. 610-11.
7. Dr Alfred Price, 'Confound and Destroy' in *RAF: The Official Magazine* No. 7, pp. 66-72.
8. National Archives AIR 27/1172/27-50, Operational Records No. 199 Squadron Forms 540.
9. National Archives Periodical Awards Operational Command Summary of Recommendations.
10. National Archives—Offer Notified by French Air Force Headquarters AFL3 *Croix de Guerre*; Air Ministry File A725299/42, National Archives AIR2/9645/9646/9647.
11. Air Ministry File A804208/45; *London Gazette* 14 September 1945, p. 4579, citation 140925 Moore; *London Gazette* 22 June 1945, p. 3727, citation 67669 Greenwood.
12. *The London Gazette* 2 June 1943, p. 2452, citation 115342 Kerr.
13. *The London Gazette* 15 August 1944, p. 3772, citation 115342 Kerr.
14. National Archives Operational Records No. 7 Squadron Forms 540.
15. *The London Gazette* 22 August 1941, p. 4864, citation 551542 Gardiner; *The London Gazette* 2 June 1943, p. 2474, citation 50222 Gardiner; *The London Gazette* 8 June 1950, p. 2805, citation 50222 Gardiner.
16. National Archives AIR 27/352/7-18, Operational Records No. 31 Squadron Forms 540.

Bibliography

Allison, L. and H. Hayward, *They Shall Not Grow Old* (Commonwealth Air Training Plan Museum, 1996)

Bowman, M., *De Havilland Mosquito* (Crowood, 2005)

Carter, N. and C., *The Distinguished Flying Cross and How It Was Won, 1918–1995* (Savannah, 1998)

Chorley, W. R., *Royal Air Force Bomber Command Losses* (Midland Counties, 1996)

Clark, F., *Agents by Moonlight* (Tempus, 1999)

Clarke, R. W., *British Aircraft Armament* (PSL, 1993)

Clutton-Brock, O., *Footprints on the Sands of Time* (Grubb Street, 2003)

Gibson, E. and G. Kingsley Ward, *Courage Remembered* (HMSO, 1989)

Halley, J. J., *The Squadrons of the Royal Air Force & Commonwealth, 1918–1988* (Air Britain, 1988)

Maton, M., *Honour Those Mentioned in Despatches* (Token Publishing, 2010)

Maton, M., *Honour the Air Forces* (Token Publishing, 2009)

Merrick, K., *Flights of the Forgotten* (Arms and Armour, 1989)

Middlebrook, M. and C. Everitt, *The Bomber Command War Diaries* (Viking, 1987)

Peters, M., *Glider Pilots in Sicily* (Pen and Sword, 2012)

Rawlings, J., *Coastal Support and Special Squadrons of the RAF* (Jane's, 1982)

Richards, D., *The Royal Air Force 1939–1945* Vols I, II, III (HMSO, 1953)

Sturtivant, R., J. Hamlin and J. J. Halley, *Royal Air Force Flying Training & Support Units* (Air Britain, 2007)

Tavender, I. T., *The Distinguished Flying Medal Register for the Second World War* (Savannah, 2000)